Peacekeepers, politicians, and warlords

Foundations of Peace

Note to the reader

The United Nations University Press series on the *Foundations of Peace* addresses themes that relate to the evolving agenda of peace and security within and between communities. Traditional or conventional conceptions of security, primarily military and inter-state, have been supplemented, or perhaps even surpassed, by a definition of security which rests upon much broader tenets, including human rights, cultural and communal rights, environmental and resource security, and economic security. To resolve the dialectic between state security and human security it is necessary to envision a wide agenda of international peace and security that embraces these tenets and the potential tensions that exist between them and the inter-state context. International actors, such as the UN and non-governmental organizations, are also increasingly playing a central role in building the foundations of sustainable peace. This series promotes theoretical as well as policy-relevant discussion on these crucial issues.

Peacekeepers, Politicians, and Warlords is the result of collaboration between UNU and Centre for Defence Studies (CDS), Kings College London. The initial field research was carried out by the authors in Liberia, Sierra Leone and Nigeria and the first draft was validated at a workshop organized by UNU (New York) at the UN Secretariat in New York. The UNU/CDS project on the Liberian peace process is a study of "new war" and its consequences, implied by a broader definition of security than traditional inter-state conflict. This study sets out to explain the destructive forces unleashed by a society in transition and conflict and it assesses the complicated response mechanisms needed to restore a workable level of stability to the crisis zone.

Titles currently available:

Peacekeepers, Politicians, and Warlords: The Liberian Peace Process by Abiodun Alao, John Mackinlay, and 'Funmi Olonisakin
Human Rights and Comparative Foreign Policy edited by David P. Forsythe

Peacekeepers, politicians, and warlords: The Liberian peace process

Abiodun Alao, John Mackinlay, and 'Funmi Olonisakin

United Nations
University Press
TOKYO · NEW YORK · PARIS

© The United Nations University, 1999 2000

The views expressed in this publication are those of the authors and
do not necessarily reflect the views of the United Nations University.

United Nations University Press
The United Nations University, 53-70, Jingumae 5-chome,
Shibuya-ku, Tokyo, 150-8925, Japan
Tel: +81-3-3499-2811   Fax: +81-3-3406-7345
E-mail: sales@hq.unu.edu
http://www.unu.edu

United Nations University Office in North America
2 United Nations Plaza, Room DC2-1462-70, New York, NY 10017, USA
Tel: +1-212-963-6387   Fax: +1-212-371-9454
E-mail: unuona@igc.apc.org

United Nations University Press is the publishing division of the United Nations
University.

Cover design by Andrew Corbett

Printed in the United States of America

UNUP-1031
ISBN 92-808-1031-6

Library of Congress Cataloging-in-Publication Data
Peacekeepers, politicians and warlords : the Liberian peace process /
Abiodun Alao, John Mackinlay, and Funmi Olonisakin.
    p.   cm.
  "UNUP-103."
  Includes bibliographical references (p.   ) and index.
  ISBN
  I. Title. II. Mackinlay, John. III. Olonisakin, Funmi.
1. Liberia-History-Civil War, 1989—Peace.
    DT636.5.A426   1999
    966.6203—dc21   99-006832

Contents

List of tables, figures, and maps   vii
List of acronyms   ix
Preface   xi
Acknowledgements   xv

Part I: The Liberian conflict   1

1 Regional peacekeeping after the Cold War   3
2 From peace to chaos: The outbreak of conflict in Liberia   12
3 Regional intervention in Liberia   28

Part II: The Cotonou Agreement   39

4 The Cotonou Agreement and the inherent obstacles to its success   41
5 Why Cotonou failed   52

Part III: The Abuja accords   75

6 Abuja I: Plans for disarmament, demobilization, and reintegration   77
7 Abuja II   90
8 Towards a settlement   102

9	Conclusion: Some lessons from the Liberian experience	115
Postscript		125

Appendices   **127**

1	Details of the Bamako Agreement, November 1990	129
2	Details of the Banjul Agreement, December 1990	130
3	Stipulations of the Lomé Accord, February 1991	131
4	The Cotonou Agreement, July 1993	132
5	The UNOMIL Mandate, September 1993	145
6	The Akosombo Agreement, September 1994	147
7	Accra Clarification of the Akosombo Agreement, December 1994	156
8	Accra Acceptance and Accession Agreement, December 1994	159
9	Abuja Agreement, August 1995	162
10	Final Communiqué of ECOWAS meeting on Liberia, Abuja, August 1996	167

Bibliography	175
About the authors	184
Index	185

Tables, figures, and maps

Tables

5.1	Disarmament statistics, 22 June 1994	61
5.2	ECOMOG strength, June 1994	62
7.1	Troop pledges to ECOMOG, January 1997	93
7.2	ECOMOG troop strength, January 1997	93
7.3	UNOMIL strength, March 1997	94
7.4	Demobilization statistics, January 1997	97
7.5	Revised estimates of faction strength, January 1997	99

Figures

5.1	The link between disarmament and economic restoration	53
5.2	UNOMIL organization	55
5.3	Reporting relationship of UNOMIL and ECOMOG	56
7.1	Trends in disarmament, 22 November–21 December 1996	97

Maps

1	Map of Liberia	13
2	Areas controlled by factions, June 1994	46
3	ECOMOG deployment, June 1994	66
4	UNOMIL deployment, June 1994	67
5	Designated disarmament areas, 1996	85

Acronyms

ACS	American Colonization Society
AFL	Armed Forces of Liberia
ALCOP	All Liberia Coalition Party
CRC-NPFL	Central Revolutionary Council of the NPFL
ECOMOG	ECOWAS Military Observer Group
ECOWAS	Economic Community of West African States
EU	European Union
FAO	Food and Agriculture Organization
FSU	Former Soviet Union
HACO	Humanitarian Assistance Coordination Office
IGNU	Interim Government of National Unity
INPFL	Independent National Patriotic Front of Liberia
LDF	Lofa Defence Force
LNC	Liberian National Conference
LNTG	Liberia National Transitional Government
LPC	Liberian Peace Council
LRRRC	Liberian Refugees Repatriation and Resettlement Commission
MOJA	Movement for Justice in Africa
NATO	North Atlantic Treaty Organization
NDDC	National Disarmament and Demobilization Commission
NDPL	National Democratic Party of Liberia
NGO	non-governmental organization

NPFL	National Patriotic Front of Liberia
NPP	National Patriotic Party
NPRAG	National Patriotic Reconstruction Assembly Government
NRC	National Readjustment Commission
OAS	Organization of American States
OAU	Organization of African Unity
SMC	Standing Mediation Committee (ECOWAS)
SOPs	Standing Operating Procedures
SRSG	Special Representative of the Secretary-General
ULIMO	United Liberation Movement of Liberia for Democracy
ULIMO-J	ULIMO faction under Roosevelt Johnson
ULIMO-K	ULIMO faction under Alhaji Kromah
UNDHA	United Nations Department of Humanitarian Affairs
UNDP	United Nations Development Programme
UNESCO	United Nations Educational, Scientific, and Cultural Organization
UNHCR	United Nations High Commissioner for Refugees
UNICEF	United Nations Children's Fund
UNOMIL	United Nations Observer Mission in Liberia
USAID	United States Agency for International Development
WFP	World Food Programme
WHO	World Health Organization

Preface

When the international community responds to a massive humanitarian emergency, such as the one in Liberia, the operation that results is both complicated and ephemeral. The multifaceted nature of the problems in the crisis area attracts many different responses, ranging from the deployment of thousands of international troops and observers to the brave and well-motivated groups of civilians who act locally. Whether these individual organizations are international, national or local, at each level they play an important part in the overall recovery process. Acting simultaneously but not always in concert with the response operations are the regional and international political leaders. In the best-case scenario, they bring the level of conflict down, step by step, to a relative calm in which the civil and military actors can begin to restore the essential needs of a civil society.

Making a record or an assessment of such a wide canvas of concurrently running events is extremely difficult. In the context of Liberia, the crisis and the international response to it developed in stages. Each stage had its own characteristic form of violence and its own cast of personalities who dominated events, and each stage was punctuated by fresh bouts of extreme violence. These sometimes led to the renewed migration of local populations and the withdrawal of the international relief community and the UN military observers. Their return would bring new personalities and with them a different collective outlook that represented the character of a new response regime. Therefore, looked at as a whole, each chapter of the Liberian peace process had its own idiosyncratic nature.

The records of these previous chapters have in many cases been lost. When military and civil organizations move in a hurry there is no time to think of historical records. In many cases, the papers, minutes, maps, standing procedures, and even the telephone and staff lists that would have been the bread and butter of future research efforts are destroyed. The officials and observers who were key actors in that brief chapter return to their parent organizations. The personalities and essential elements of the episode are dispersed and lost. Trying to reconstruct them and the tensions that lay beneath the superficial chronology in retrospect is difficult. Senior officials will in time publish their individual accounts of what took place, but the environment of these decisions and the cross-culture of personalities that it comprised are hard to re-create. The international response to a complex emergency succeeds or fails collectively and not because of the actions of an individual civil or military element. So far in the 1990s most of these efforts have in some degree failed. Future success requires first of all an accurate appraisal of past failures and, for all the reasons of turbulence and the diversity of actors explained above, this degree of penetrating assessment is hard to achieve in an overview.

To make a definitive assessment of the conflict in Liberia and the international responses would have required more funding and time than we could hope to find for this project. Instead we set ourselves a more modest target: to take two snapshots of the conflict and actors. The first we made in June and July of 1994, visiting the United Nations Secretariat in New York and the Secretariat of the Economic Community of West African States (ECOWAS) in Lagos and travelling to meet many organizations in Monrovia and greater Liberia, as it was then described. Our purpose during these visits was to record as best we could the environment of the Cotonou Agreement and to interview officials while they were still in situ and while the recent past and ongoing events were still fresh in their mind. The second snapshot of Liberia we made in January 1997, when we also visited Nigeria and Côte d'Ivoire. As with the earlier visit, the intention was to capture a stage in the development of the Liberian peace process – the Abuja Accord. From these snapshots of the Cotonou and Abuja accords, we were able to make an assessment of the steps towards peace in Liberia, examining in the process the role of the peacekeepers, the warlords, and the politicians. The focus on the Cotonou and the Abuja accords is deliberate, because they were the two most significant events in the peace process. The agreements that came before the Cotonou accord did not advance the peace efforts in such a significant way. The accords directly after Cotonou did not learn from the preceding mistakes. Finally it was the Abuja peace process that ended the war.

In addition to the wealth of reports and UN documents that are already in the public domain, we gathered up the less enduring records that are usually lost or destroyed when organizations are obliged to move: local newspapers, operational planning documents, staff lists, and all the ephemera of an international response to a massive humanitarian crisis. The problem has been to both distil and provide a context for these documents. To achieve the latter we have explained something of the events preceding the crisis. In the main body of the book we assess the tactical failures of the Cotonou Agreement and the gradual process by which Liberia has achieved a relatively more successful re-centralization of power after a state-wide election in 1997.

This book is not the entire record of the international involvement in the Liberian civil war or of the causes and the course of the war itself. The intention is to emphasize the practical complexities involved in peacekeeping operations, especially when the operation is conceived and executed under a confused perception of the post-Cold War peace-keeping operational tactics.

Acknowledgements

The book relies above all on the primary source information that we managed to collate from a number of interviews in Liberia and also in interested international HQs around the world. In this respect we wish to acknowledge the following individuals who gave their invaluable time and goodwill:

Mrs. Abimbola, Librarian, ECOWAS Secretariat, Nigeria
Lieutenant-Colonel Ajayi, Liaison Officer, ECOWAS Secretariat, Nigeria
Colonel Ade Ajibade, Colonel General Staff, Nigerian Contingent, ECOMOG
Lieutenant-Colonel Mohammed Ashraf, Operations Officer, UNOMIL Liberia
Major Baganda, Liaison Officer, HQ ECOWAS, Nigeria
Major General Ishaya Bakut, former Field Commander, ECOMOG
Mr. Phillip Banks, Liberia National Transitional Government, Liberia
Mr. Lindsay Barret, journalist/writer, Liberia
Mr. Joe Baxter, Chief Electoral Officer, UNOMIL Liberia
Ms. Ruth Ceasar, Ministry of Planning and Economic Affairs, Liberia
Mr. Hugh Cholmondley, Deputy SRSG, UNOMIL Liberia
Major Abayomi Dabiri, ECOMOG HQ, Liberia
Mrs. Ann Davies, Slipway Development Association, Liberia
Mr. St. Jerome Davis, Chief Information Officer, UNOMIL Liberia

xvi ACKNOWLEDGEMENTS

Brigadier Ian Douglas, A&M OUSG, UN New York
Mr. Bill Frank Enoanyi, writer/journalist, Liberia
Mr. Boimah Fahnbulleh, Liberia
Mr. Clifford Flemister, Citizen's Committee for Peace and Democracy, Liberia
Mr. Jacques Fomerand, Director UNU, New York
Major Joe Glasser, Information Officer, US Embassy Liberia
Mr. Trevor Gordon-Somers, Special Representative of the Secretary-General, UNOMIL, Liberia
Ms. Esher Guluma, Programme Coordinator, UNICEF Liberia
Mr. Osman Hassan, Coordinator NPFL area, UNDP Liberia
Major-General John Inienger, Commander ECOMOG, Liberia
Mr. Saa Kanda, Ministry of Planning and Economic Affairs, Liberia
Mr. Biola Lawal, Press Secretary, ECOMOG, Liberia
Mr. Lowell Lynch, USAID, US Embassy Liberia
Colonel Richard Manlove, A&M OUSG, UN New York
Lieutenant-Colonel S. Marengo, Commander TANBAT, UNOMIL Liberia
Ms. Jayne Michuki, Humanitarian Affairs Department UNOMIL, Liberia
Colonel Bill Minnis, Senior Advisor on Demobilisation, UNOMIL Liberia
Colonel Muslim, Chief Observer Gbarnga, UNOMIL Liberia
Ambassador Nyakyi, Special Representative of the Secretary-General, Liberia (1997)
Ms. Jacki O'Connor, Electoral Office, UNOMIL Liberia
Mr. Frank Ofei, Director of Research, HQ ECOWAS, Nigeria
Dr. W. Ofuatey-Kodjo, Professor of Political Science, CUNY, New York
Mr. Okello, Senior Protection Officer, UNHCR, Liberia
Mr. Adebayo Olowoake, African Resource and Development Centre, Nigeria
Major-General Daniel Opande, Chief Military Observer, UNOMIL Liberia (1994)
Lieutenant-Commander Taju Otun, Nigerian Navy, Nigeria
Dr. Jimi Peters, Nigerian Institute for International Affairs
Mr. John Richardson, Senior Liaison Officer, NPFL, Liberia
Professor Amos Sawyer, Centre for Democratic Empowerment, Liberia
Ms. Dorothy Schelart, Director, Good Samaritan Fellowship, Liberia
Dr. Amadu Sesay, Obafemi Awolowo University, Nigeria
Major-General Shamir, Chief Military Observer, UNOMIL Liberia (1997)
Dr. E. H. El Tahir, Chief Humanitarian Affairs Officer, UNOMIL Liberia
Mr. Targema Takema, Nigerian High Commission, Liberia
Mr. Charles Taylor, Commander, NPFL, Liberia

Ms. Rekha Thapa, Deputy Resident Representative, UNDP Liberia
Mr. Carl Tinsman, Resident Representative, UNICEF Liberia
Ambassador William Twaddle, US Ambassador, Liberia
Brigadier Aziz Ul-Haque, Deputy CMO, UNOMIL Liberia
Professor Margaret Vogt, Nigerian Institute for International Affairs
Professor Delvin Walker, Deputy Reintegration Coordinator, UNOMIL, Liberia

PART I
The Liberian conflict

1
Regional peacekeeping after the Cold War

Although the creators of the United Nations had the vision to see beyond the imperatives of the 1939–1945 world war, many of the detailed provisions that were made in the United Nations Charter were never fully realized. In particular, their arrangements for international security were thwarted in a Security Council divided by bi-polar rivalry during the Cold War that followed. In this context the Charter articles in respect of the Military Staff Committee and the obligations to make forces available for collective security on a global scale fell into abeyance. Only the deployment of peacekeeping forces allowed the United Nations to engage in conflict containment. But, to avoid confronting superpower interests, peacekeepers were constrained in their operations. In its initial manifestation, "peacekeeping" had no commonly accepted definition. Referred to here as traditional peacekeeping, it was regarded as an operation involving military personnel, but without enforcement powers, undertaken by the United Nations to help maintain or restore international peace and security in areas of conflict. The principles of traditional peacekeeping included:
- the need for support by the mandating authority, the Security Council;
- the requirement that the operation be deployed only with the consent of the warring parties;
- regulations for command and control of the force;
- multinational composition of the force;
- restrictions that force be used only in self-defence;

- the need for complete impartiality in the performance of the functions of the force.

Peacekeepers would not use force except in self-defence or to resist attempts by forceful means to prevent the UN force from discharging its duties under the Security Council's mandate. Escalating the use of force beyond self-defence was regarded as enforcement. Without sufficiently powerful military forces or the authority to take problem-solving action, except at a very local level, peacekeepers had to rely more on their international status and the moral pressures exerted by the international community.

With only a tiny military staff at the UN Secretariat in New York, the development of peacekeeping doctrine took place nationally among the defence forces that were primarily involved. The overwhelming element of their experience was drawn not from the short or less successful operations (such as in the Congo), which failed to influence their modus operandi, but from the long-standing forces in the desert buffer zones in Suez, Golan, and Cyprus. This relatively unchallenging military activity is now referred to as traditional peacekeeping. In traditional peacekeeping, consent to the peace process and the presence of a UN peace force between opposed armies was sustained at the operational level by state agreement. The absence of civilians and humanitarian relief agencies, the established authority of the United Nations in the separation area, and the relatively accountable nature of the armies involved in the conflict meant that a traditional peacekeeping force on its own could be effective. It relied heavily on consent: a breakdown of consent might reflect a state's change of policy and reconciliation might have to be negotiated at national or international level but very seldom between the military forces at operational level.

After the Cold War, political tension in the Security Council was reduced, allowing the United Nations to become more responsive to conflicts in which US and former Soviet Union interests had previously prevented its effective involvement. As a result, in the 1990s the number of UN forces involved in conflict resolution increased. The nature of conflict had not changed, but the focus of the Security Council had moved to civil wars and inter-communal violence, in many cases to states that had degenerated into anarchy. UN forces were deployed with more intrusive mandates than before. Problems suppressed by the influence of East–West rivalry emerged in regions and states that previously had been comparatively stable. In the post-Cold War era, continuing conflict and humanitarian disasters were less often caused by territorial aggression than by the long-term effects of:

– population increases, which imposed a growing demand for space and resources;

- poverty increases of 40 per cent since 1980 that left 1.4 billion people on the margins of survival, vulnerable to conflict and natural disaster;
- economic imbalance, which faced poor countries with increasing debt and a lack of access to world markets while rich nations continued to maintain and exploit their dominance;
- environmental damage;
- competition for raw materials and vital resources including water;
- collapsing states, particularly artificially created multi-ethnic states, held together by superpower interests during the Cold War, which became vulnerable to demands for recognition of their culturally distinct elements;
- inter-communal violence fuelled by ethnic and cultural self-determination;
- population migration and the displacement of civil communities on a large scale by violence and terror.[1]

The proportion of civilian casualties in war grew and civilians formed by far the greatest number of casualties in this period, either as a direct result of hostilities or as a consequence of disruption and deprivation following a military attack. In the post-Cold War era, civilians increasingly became the primary war objectives and the focus of violence. Rival militias attacked civil communities far more frequently than they attacked each other, measuring their power by their control of local populations; militias threatened and drove out minorities to achieve "ethnic cleansing"; civil populations were deprived of food to attract humanitarian relief, which could be plundered, extorted, and generally added to war resources.

By the 1990s the UN Security Council was in many cases facing emergencies that were essentially not military problems. They were "complex emergencies,"[2] a term that had become part of the international language of the civil aid agencies and defined as: "a humanitarian crisis in a country, region or society where there is a total or considerable breakdown of authority resulting from internal conflict and which requires an international response that goes beyond the mandate of capacity of any single agency and/or the ongoing United Nations country programme." Not all fitted precisely into this definition, which described a trend that included Cambodia, Afghanistan, Somalia, Mozambique, Rwanda, Angola, Liberia, and the Balkan and Caucasus regions.

For the UN forces this was very different from the traditional operations in defined strips of land between stationary armies. In traditional peacekeeping, with few exceptions, the UN forces and peace forces in general assumed a system of sovereign states where for better or for worse a recognized leader and government structure effectively controlled the machinery of state. However, the basis for that assumption was eroding. Complex emergencies often involved states that either had no governments or had contending sources of authority. In the environment of a collapsed state, a host government was likely to have lost control of a considerable part of its territories so that beyond the immediate influence of the capital city the warring factions would supplant its authority. Power had fallen into the hands of warlords, down to street and village level. The factions would proliferate into sub-sub-groups, each with its own agenda for revenge and survival, and, being in a former war zone, weapons were easy to find. The presence of large displaced elements of the population completely altered the operational environment and even challenged conventional wisdom on the use of force. In some cases there were massive population migrations to the urban areas, so that the intervening agencies became midwives to profound social changes. Social structures eroded, husbands parted from wives, children from parents, and disintegration spread pervasively.

Civil emergencies attracted an array of civil organizations, many of which arrived *before* the multinational military forces, whom they might outnumber, and generally their knowledge of the local area was better. In every emergency the military element was sure to have to work alongside at least five major UN agencies dealing with refugees, children, food, health and development, UN civil elements involved with human rights, elections, and the restoration of government structures, and non-governmental organizations (NGOs). There was in effect a network of actors in which the division of tasks would not always be clear cut. Sometimes when an incident took place peace forces would arrive to find agencies and even military monitors from other international organizations already at the scene.

The rules of peacekeeping were also changing. Impartiality, the sine qua non of the traditional buffer zone, was hard to maintain. Relief agencies and peacekeepers could no longer rely on universal recognition of their traditional status as impartial actors. Where starvation, extermination, or removal of a civil community was a military faction's war aim, a relief agency that tried to impede, prevent, or even, by evacuation, facilitate that war aim could not, from the belligerent's view, be impartial. The nature of "consent" had also changed. Complex emergencies were messy affairs and their physical influence could spill over the boundaries of the host state. Displaced populations crossed borders en masse, their sustainment requiring multiple supply routes and making use of regional sea ports and airports and road and rail systems. Faction leaders used neighbouring states as safe havens, as conduits for combat supplies, and as a source of manpower. As a result, regional powers now played a more important role than before. They used their collective geographical encirclement of the crisis zone either to exert strong pressure to support the success of the peace process or to ensure its failure. For the front-line states surrounding a crisis area, acting unilaterally was seldom an effective option – successful action required "consensus" rather than "consent." In the absence of an effective government from which to obtain consent, a strong regional consensus was needed. It might exercise an overwhelming pressure, confronting the lawless and imposing unbearable financial deprivation or irresistible rewards.

During the Cold War, a traditional peacekeeping force would comprise a number of contingents provided from selected countries on the request of the Secretary-General. The contingents would be selected in consultation with the Security Council and with the parties concerned, bearing in mind the need for equitable geographic representation. By tacit agreement, this excluded permanent members of the Security Council from participating in peacekeeping operations, although there were exceptions. As the United Nations became involved in more and more complex emergencies, the character of peacekeeping forces began to alter. The relaxation of East–West tensions in Europe and the withdrawal of the Soviet Union's hegemonic foreign policy influence over the former Warsaw Pact nations allowed more East European armies to participate in peacekeeping operations. Complex emergencies turned out to be more dangerous and challenging and required peacekeeping forces with different characteristics than before. The routine activities of humanitarian response agencies could be interrupted on a day-to-day basis by the predatory activities of local warlords. For this reason the military element of a peacekeeping force had to be more competent than ever before. In addition to its traditional peacekeeping duties, it had to be capable of protecting relief activities and ensuring that the spirit of the mandate was upheld. Not all contributor nations were necessarily capable or even prepared to become involved in operations where a more forceful approach might be needed. In addition, the competence of the UN Secretariat was seriously indicted by the command and coordinating failures in UN forces deployed to Somalia and Bosnia.

These developments led to a division of labour. In some cases where intervention operations were expected to be dangerous or organizationally challenging, the international community would, under the overall authority of a UN Security Council Resolution, subcontract the military requirements into the hands of a coalition force. Examples of these subcontracted operations took place in the 1990 Gulf War, in the US-led intervention in Somalia (Restore Hope), and in the Dayton Implementation Force in Bosnia. In each case these operations had several important common characteristics: the political leadership and determination to intervene had been largely provided by the United States, the most powerful element of the military forces was drawn from the countries of the North Atlantic Treaty Organization (NATO), and the organization, structure, and modus operandi were largely derived from NATO procedures. In terms of this study of West African conflict response mechanisms, the significance of this development was both military and political. Politically speaking, the overwhelming US influence in the launching of these more military operations meant that the UN Security Council's focus of attention began to correspond more closely to US foreign policy interests. Militarily speaking, if a successful international intervention now required the engagement of a nucleus of the world's most powerful armies, the corollary was that any operation that did not comprise substantial elements of this nucleus was destined to experience a significant degree of failure. When the danger of conflict arose and communities were threatened by violence or extermination, the Secretary-General could investigate and observe but, without the commitment of the United States and a substantial military element provided by NATO nations, any intervention, however politically well supported by the wider international community, became extremely vulnerable to the pressures and interference of local warlords.

After the Cold War, the spheres of territorial influence where the major western powers would intervene began to shrink. This left turbulent areas of the world, particularly in Africa and the former Soviet Union (FSU), beyond the interest of the international community. A serious humanitarian crisis or civil conflict might arise but, owing to the influence of the United States over the UN Security Council's priorities for intervention, no properly resourced action could be authorized either by the United Nations or, more significantly, by the coalition of powerful actors that would have to supply the nucleus of military for it to succeed. This meant that in the case of emergencies in Africa and the FSU there was very little prospect of a peace-restoring effort by international forces. In these cases the states at risk and the regional organizations immediately concerned had to look for other options, and in most cases these turned out to be the regional forces. The authors of the United Nations Charter envisaged that regional organizations would have a role to play in the maintenance of international peace and security in these circumstances, and this was reflected in Chapter VIII of the Charter. However, there were few practical provisions either in the Charter or in the organization of the Secretariat concerning how regional structures were to deal with threats to, or breaches of, the peace in the Cold War era. The Charter provided for regional arrangements only under individual or collective security, or where the UN Security Council had authorized a regional organization to use force in dealing with a threat to international peace and security.[3] During the Cold War period, such situations rarely occurred and as a result very little thought was given to the procedural implications of regional actions.

Nevertheless, regional organizations sometimes became involved even though for much of this period the United Nations undertook the primary responsibility for international peace and security. During the Cold War, some regional organizations played a prominent part in dealing with conflicts and breaches of the peace in their respective regions. However, the nature of their involvement often fell outside the conceptual framework already identified for peacekeeping operations undertaken by the United Nations, raising questions about the neutrality and impartiality of the regional actors and peacekeepers.[4] The Organization of American States, for example, assumed primary peacemaking duties in regional conflicts, with a major peacekeeping effort in the Dominican Republic. Questions about the impartiality of the United States, the major power in the region, led eventually to the establishment of the Representative of the Secretary-General in the Dominican Republic. In Chad, the Organization of African Unity, which had by this time developed an important experience in mediating, also undertook a peacekeeping mission involving a regional force drawn from several African armies. Although this force maintained a neutral stance and did not resort to the use of force, it failed to contain the Chadian conflict. This was largely due to its lack of an effective military nucleus of peacekeeping troops that could maintain an authoritative presence in the disputed areas. In addition, the force was operating in physically challenging terrain where logistical support was a factor of military success. In 1976, the Arab League deployed its "Symbolic Arab Security Force" in Lebanon. After Algeria, Morocco, Tunisia, and Egypt declined to provide troops, however, the force could not represent a wider pan-Arab consensus. As a result, it was left largely to the Syrians to deploy their forces in the conflict zone, and Syria could hardly be regarded as impartial to the outcome. Nearly two decades of violence were to follow before Lebanon was able to start rebuilding its shattered state.[5]

None of these regional operations was the result of any systematic cooperation with the United Nations. The UN Charter is unclear about the precise nature of the cooperation that should exist between the United Nations and regional organizations.[6] The lack of detailed analysis of the role that regional organizations could play and what their relationship with the Security Council would be was an indication both of the limited interest in regional arrangements and of a lack of conception of how they could be used. The attempts to deal with conflict at the regional level were not allowed to be expanded and tested in the climate of Cold War rivalry; many were marginalized, only to re-emerge in the post–Cold War era. After the Cold War, the rise of coalition forces deployed under UN authority created opportunities to devise innovative ways in which the United Nations could cooperate with regional structures in the management of conflict and the maintenance of international peace and security. This has prompted a degree of academic research into new ways of coping with the demands placed by the emergence of crises around the world, in part through assigning roles to and cooperating with regional organizations. The UN Secretary-General's "Agenda for Peace" attempted to address the concept of regional arrangements under the Charter and the role expected of regional groupings. It reflects greater regional involvement:

Under the Charter, the Security Council has and will continue to have primary responsibility for maintaining international peace and security but regional action as a matter of decentralisation, delegation and co-operation with UN efforts could not only lighten the burden of the Council, but also contribute to a deeper sense of participation, consensus and democratisation in international affairs.[7]

The first major attempt to execute the kind of cooperation envisioned by Boutros-Ghali in "Agenda for Peace" emerged with the Liberian civil war, albeit not as the result of a carefully orchestrated plan.

In retrospect, the international community has largely ignored the Liberian tragedy. The powerful international forces deployed in the early 1990s to Kuwait, Cambodia, Somalia, and the former Yugoslavia exhausted the rich nations' capacity and willingness to assist. Events in Liberia that were developing during the same period could not threaten their prosperity or security, and media interest was not sufficiently tenacious to prick their public conscience. But, however marginal the events of this West African tragedy must seem, its lessons have a universal significance for future interventions in complex emergencies and for regional conflicts generally. Although the international community, by disregarding the moral issues, can turn its back on Liberia as a commitment, it cannot afford to ignore the lessons of its tragedy. What are these lessons and why are they so important? The purpose of this book is to answer these questions.

The conflict that is the background to this study is seen as a defined chapter in Liberia's recent history. It begins with the bloody coup that removed the Tolbert administration in 1980 and, for the purposes of this survey, ends with the implementation of the Abuja accords. As the narrative unfolded, Liberia emerged as a classic example of a complex emergency, with humanitarian tragedy and disruption reaching the levels experienced in the other scenarios of the 1990s. In chapter 2 we describe how, in an atmosphere of growing violence following the coup of 1980, the organs of the state began to collapse, until a decade later the state's monopoly of power and violence had devolved irretrievably into the hands of warlords and tribal leaders. The warring factions themselves then proliferated, dividing into smaller hostile parties brutally struggling for their individual survival and, in the case of the larger and more powerful factions, for control of the state itself. Chapter 3 provides an account of the efforts of the regional organization, the Economic Community of West African States, to restore calm in Liberia. Eventually, the political presence of the United Nations was required to broaden the mediating base and take the peace process forward. Chapter 4 describes the Cotonou Agreement, which momentarily brought to an end this first phase of violence. Despite the greater optimism of this period, we argue that in many respects the Cotonou Agreement was fatally flawed in its composition and never had a real chance to succeed. In chapter 5 we show how developments that pre-dated the agreement were highly relevant to its success or failure; for example, Liberia's recent history, political development, and tribal demography. The main purpose of this chapter is to decide whether Cotonou was an inherently flawed process and therefore had no chance of success, or whether it was allowed to founder through mismanagement and ill-judgement. In chapters 6 and 7 we describe the circumstances that influenced the implementation of the first and second Abuja accords, the procedures for gradual demobilization of the factions, and the increasingly vital part played by the regional actors and the United Nations. Chapter 8 examines the developments that moved the Liberian peace process toward a conclusion. It discusses the elections and the prospects for reconciliation and socio-economic reconstruction in the country. In the concluding chapter the study emphasizes the important lessons that emerge from this long and bloody conflict.

Notes

1. John Mackinlay (ed.), *Guide to Peace Support Operations*, Thomas Watson Institute for International Studies, Brown University, Providence, 1996, see pp. 9–21.
2. F. Mezzolama, "Investigation of the Relationship between Humanitarian Assistance and Peacekeeping Operations," Internal Report of the UN Joint Inspection Unit, JIU/REP/95/6, Geneva, 1995, chaps. 2 and 3.
3. See Anthony Clark Arend and Robert J. Beck, *International Law and the Use of Force: Beyond the Charter Paradigm,* London and New York: Routledge, 1994.
4. Alan James, *Peacekeeping in International Politics*, London: Macmillan, 1990.
5. Istvan Pogany, *The Arab League and Peacekeeping in Lebanon*, Aldershot: Gower, 1987.
6. Bruno Simma, *The Charter of the United Nations*, Oxford: Oxford University Press, 1994.
7. Boutros Boutros-Ghali, *An Agenda for Peace,* New York: United Nations, 1992, p. 37.

2

From peace to chaos: The outbreak of conflict in Liberia

Liberia is a small country, both in population and in geographical size. Before the outbreak of the civil war in 1989, the population was only about 3 million and its geographical area about 43,000 square miles. Even in West Africa, where the populations and physical sizes of most countries are relatively modest, Liberia remains one of the smallest countries. However, what the country appears to lack in size and population is made up for in historical distinction: it has the longest history of independent existence in the entire African continent. Its immediate neighbours are Sierra Leone, Guinea Republic, and Côte d'Ivoire to the west, north, and east, respectively.

The Liberian civil war had its roots in the unique circumstances in which the country emerged. Established as a refuge for freed American slaves, it escaped the vicissitudes of European colonialism, only to be subjected to a harsh regime of "democratic feudalism" imposed by a group of freed slaves, the Americo-Liberians, who perpetuated themselves as a ruling class for more than a century. The activities of this oligarchy, its termination, and the military regime that followed, all shaped the future of Liberia and serve to explain the civil conflict that eventually engulfed the country. In this chapter, we provide an overview of Liberia's gradual descent into civil war, tracing the developments from the creation of the country, through the feudal oligarchy of the Americo-Liberians and the emergence of military rule, to the ultimate civil war.

Map 1 **Liberia (Source: graphics by JSCSC Mapping Department)**

The American historical connection

The idea of sending freed slaves to Africa was embraced by two main groups of people in America. The first was the anti-slavery campaigners, who argued that slavery was against the principles expressed in the US constitution, and that people of colour should be sent away to an environment where they would enjoy full civil liberties. Ironically, the second group was proponents of the slave trade, who believed (particularly after the slave revolt of 1800) that the trade was under threat by the growing number of freed slaves, who were liable to incite other blacks. Thus, the defenders of the American Colonization Society (ACS) adopted the argument that colonizing free blacks would protect slavery in the United States and promote Christianity and civilization in Africa, neglecting the argument of the abolitionists.¹ Against the background of this determination, the ACS dispatched a two-man team to the West African coast in November 1817, with the sole aim of finding a suitable home for the freed slaves. Although a permanent settlement was established, this did not meet the expectations of some of the freed slaves and rebellion broke out in 1822 and again in 1824, forcing the ACS agents in charge of the settlement to find asylum elsewhere. The freed slaves wanted not only to be free but also to have an easy life. This tendency and the determination to pursue it were to be important themes in understanding the feudalism that subsequently engulfed Liberia.

By 1824, a new colony named Liberia had been established, and its capital called Monrovia, after the American President Monroe. The national flag was derived from the American flag. This American connection was to mark the beginning of an enduring relationship between the descendants of the slave settlers and the United States of America. It was to serve as the antecedent of the high expectations many Liberians had of the United States when a cataclysmic crisis engulfed their nation in 1987. Without any direct colony of its own in the continent, considerable American goodwill opinion was also extended towards the country, especially at the time when the Cold War dispensation made allies in the third world relevant to global strategic calculations.

The roots of local discontent

Socio-politically, the people of Liberia are divided into two broad groups: descendants of the freed slaves, known as the Americo-Liberians, and the indigenous African population that had historically lived in the area. The former subjugated the indigenous Liberians after a series of wars from 1822 until the early part of the twentieth century.[2] The ethnic composition of Liberia and the political tensions that developed as a result are central to understanding the country's civil war.

Two main factors had long-term implications for the country: the self-perpetuating nature of the institutions and social structures that influenced the administration of Liberia, and the Americo-Liberian treatment of the indigenous population. Americo-Liberians constituted only 5 per cent of Liberia's estimated population of 1.8 million, and about 300 closely knit families formed the ruling elite.[3] The activities of the Americo-Liberians have been well summed up by David Wippman:

[They] created the social hierarchy they had experienced in the ante-bellum (of the United States) but with themselves as the socially dominant, land-owning class. They considered the indigenous population primitive and uncivilised, and treated it as little more than an abundant source of forced labor.[4]

The indigenous Liberians were divided into 16 major groups: Bassa, Dei, Gbandi, Gio (Dahn), Glebo, Gola, Kissi, Kpelle, Krahn (Wee), Kru, Kuwaa (Belle), Loma, Mano (Ma), Mandingo (Mading), Mende, and Vai.[5] The vicissitudes of the colonial division of the African continent meant that some of these ethnic groups were also represented in some of the neighbouring countries. In a number of ways, this was to complicate the role of neighbouring countries in the Liberian civil crisis. Although there were historical rivalries between these groups before the arrival of the Americo-Liberians, the oppression they experienced during the rule of the settlers was to bring them close and resulted in some form of cohesion between them.

Prior to the civil war, power and influence in Liberia focused around three institutions: the True Whig Party, the Church, and the Masonic Temple. The True Whig Party was the ruling party formed by the Americo-Liberians and it produced all the Liberian presidents from the inception of the country until the overthrow of the oligarchy in 1980. The Church and the Masonic Lodge were interwoven because they both provided an avenue for social cohesion for those in the upper echelon of the ruling party. According to Amadu Sesay, the social and political cohesion proved vital to the Americo-Liberians' domination of politics, religion, and commerce.[6] To the indigenous people, however, these institutions were symbols of oppression that consequently became targets for reprisal.

From the beginning, the members of the Americo-Liberian elite had failed to integrate socially, maintaining themselves separately in politics, religion, and education. Ironically, the settlers, who were expected to promote missionary activities in the country, denied citizenship to native Liberians. The latter became citizens only after embracing the adjudged civilized lifestyle of the settlers, having adopted Christianity and denounced paganism for three years.[7] This continued until 1904, when Liberian citizenship was collectively conferred on all indigenous Liberians. However, the fulfilment of these criteria did not guarantee Africans social equality with the settlers. The social segregation of aboriginal Liberians remained. For example, Christian Africans had to enter the home of an Americo-Liberian through the back door.[8]

Settler domination of indigenous Liberians was assisted and prolonged by the flawed political systems in the country. The Liberian hinterland, where the vast majority of the indigenous Liberians resided, was underrepresented in the national legislature until 1964. Yet its residents paid taxes. Prior to 1964, indigenous Liberians did not have the right to vote, and they paid to observe the proceedings of the legislature.[9] The property clause in the constitution further weakened the electoral system – only citizens who owned land were eligible to vote. Yet the government's land-ownership policies had displaced many of the poor. Their traditional farming lands were bought by the comparatively affluent settlers. In some cases, the meagre amounts offered for land were not paid.[10]

Although the True Whig Party dominated Liberia's political scene between 1877 and 1975, it did not make any significant changes to Liberia's oppressive laws. Sesay sees the True Whig Party as

> representing a club of individuals, who were prepared to uphold and advance the privileges enjoyed by the minority Americo-Liberians in the country. All those who were not prepared to "play the game" according to the rules of the party were fenced out of the political, economic and social privileges that the elaborate patronage system could confer.[11]

Americo-Liberian subjugation of indigenous Liberians even included economic exploitation through the "contract" or forced labour.[12] This treatment of the indigenous population became an international concern, and in 1929 the League of Nations investigated allegations of "slave labour" in Liberia. The oppressive policies of the Americo-Liberians continued for so long partly as a result of the inability of indigenous Liberians collectively to oppose the system, given the physical distance between them. The hinterland was largely underdeveloped, with bad roads, a lack of transportation and communication, and no workable programme to achieve unity and development amongst the 16 tribes. A combination of these factors kept the Americo-Liberians in power for 133 years.

A period of gradual reform designed to redress these wrongs was begun in the 1940s under the regime of William Tubman. The process prematurely raised expectations of a more just and socially developed society. It was Tubman who took the first concrete steps to unify the peoples of Liberia. He built roads, schools, and hospitals, particularly in the coastal towns and cities, and promised aboriginal Liberians increased representation in the national legislature. Some commentators have argued, however, that Tubman's attempt to unify Liberians was not the result of altruistic considerations. Rather, he was motivated by political factors, chief amongst which was his need to buttress his weakening support base on the coast with alliances in the hinterland.[13] Others argue that Tubman saw the need to prevent a crisis.

> Keenly aware of this injustice, and the potential danger it posed to security of the nation, the Tubman administration tried to involve the native people in the mainstream of the political and economic life of the nation.[14]

Whatever the reasons behind Tubman's actions, they served to increase the awareness of indigenous Liberians and set in motion the process through which political change would occur. Tubman's "open door policy" was at the core of this process. Under this policy, foreigners were invited to invest in Liberia, including the exploitation of the country's natural resources, with limited preconditions. By 1960, Firestone and the Liberia Mining Company were generating a combined annual pre-tax profit of more than US$32 million.[15] The "open door policy" made capital projects such as the building of roads, bridges, airport, and hospitals possible and it created employment, increasing the earning power of many Liberians. Despite such advantages, however, the Tubman administration did not address the roots of the Liberian problem. The "open door policy" was found to be severely flawed. The Christie concession, for example, which gave mining rights to the Liberia Mining Company for all minerals in particular locations for 80 years from 1945, was strongly criticized for the "shamefully low terms" negotiated by the Tubman regime.[16] Under the terms of the concession, the royalty paid to the Liberian government was fixed at 5 cents per ton for the duration.[17] Tubman's regime resisted the strong opposition to this policy from Liberians who understood its long-term implications, harassing and jailing any visible opponents of the trade agreements.[18] The social barriers between aboriginal and settler Liberians had not been removed, and many of the weaknesses in Liberia's laws and institutions remained. The economic benefits of Tubman's policy had only a selective impact on the population. By 1971 when William Tolbert came to power, 4 per cent of Liberians controlled 60 per cent of the country's income.[19]

Ironically, it was Tubman's educational policies that acted as the real catalyst for political change. His foreign scholarship programme provided the opportunity for many Liberians to study abroad. This broadened their knowledge and understanding and they began to question Liberian laws and the conduct of their government. These scholars would later form groups that would bring serious pressure to bear on the government of the settlers. Such groups included the Movement for Justice in Africa (MOJA),[20] the Union of Liberian Associations in the Americas, and the Progressive Alliance of Liberia. There is no indication that these developments were foreseen by Tubman, who had inadvertently begun the process for major political change in Liberia. When Tolbert assumed office in 1971, he failed to live up to his pledge to carry forward the economic achievements of his predecessor and to work toward the unity of the Liberian people. By this time, there was widespread awareness amongst Liberians of the deplorable state of their economy and the denial of their civil and political rights. Pressure mounted from all groups at home and abroad, demanding changes in the system of government.

Turning the table round: Doe's coup and its aftermath

The military coup that removed Tolbert may have been precipitated by Liberia's economic deterioration. The oil crisis in the early 1970s coincided with the world slump in sales of rubber and iron ore. International aid to Liberia dropped significantly from US$80 million in 1975 to US$44 million in 1976, external debt rose, reaching a record US$168 million in 1976, and inflation reached 11.4 per cent the same year.[21] One of the adverse results of the oil crisis was an increase in the price of local rice – Liberia's staple food. Riots resulted, leading to a clamp-down by government forces and the arrest of key members of the People's Alliance Party. Following mounting pressure, 17 indigenous non-commissioned officers overthrew the Tolbert government, and Master Sergeant Samuel Kanyon Doe emerged as Liberia's new head of state. The coup prevented the process of a deliberate change to a more accountable and responsive civil regime from running its natural course. The impact of this would be felt later when the Doe regime failed to transform Liberia into the plural, truly democratic society that was anticipated by the people.

In 1980 however, it must have seemed to many Liberians as though the indigenous coup had ended the long period of Americo-Liberian hegemony and all the abuses it had brought upon them. Initially, Doe enjoyed the goodwill of the oppressed clans. Dixon aptly describes the joy and expectations of aboriginal Liberians following Doe's rise to power:

> [T]he native population of this country felt that the day had finally arrived for them to enjoy the full right of citizenship in their own country. They thought that their needs and interests which had been long overlooked would now claim the full attention of their government.[22]

However, subsequent events would reveal that Doe's regime was both self-serving and opportunistic. It capitalized on the pressures of an organized outcry against an unpopular regime to create an acceptable motive as well as the opportunity for a military coup that later was used to serve the selfish ends of the ruling elite and their kinsmen.

Not long after assuming office, Doe began to deviate from his stated rationale for assuming power. One by one, his supporters were eliminated – first MOJA, the academic supporters of his coup, then the military. By the end of 1983, all 16 non-commissioned officers who joined his coup had been removed in varying circumstances. Corruption became rife, the economy collapsed, and all forms of opposition were suppressed. Without a legitimate or moral basis of support, Doe exploited his ethnic affiliations to sustain his administration. In a manner as divisive as that of the previous regime, Doe now suppressed other clans in favour of his own Krahn tribe. This factor, coupled with the removal of the common hatred of the Americo-Liberians (which previously united the tribes), re-created powerful and long-standing ethnic divisions. Non-Krahn members of the national army and civil service were often debarred from key positions and emerging rivals were executed or dismissed for alleged coup plots. When the civil war erupted, animosity and a backlash against the Krahn hegemony played a significant role.

In 1984, Doe offered to return Liberia from military dictatorship to civilian rule. Much to the surprise of the Liberian people, Doe, who by now had promoted himself to the rank of General, founded the National Democratic Party of Liberia (NDPL) and announced his intention to contest elections. He increased his age by two years in order to meet the minimum age requirement of 35 years. In the election that followed, the NDPL won 50.9 per cent of the votes amidst allegations of rigging, harassment, and intimidation of opponents. Although there were 11 political parties, owing to the difficult registration procedure only three registered in time for the elections. A notable part of the registration procedure was the requirement to pay a fee of US$150,000, a relatively huge sum of money when Liberia's per capita income was US$400. This was perhaps the least of the problems faced by the parties, whose candidates and members were tormented, coerced, and assaulted by the Doe regime.[23]

Although by 1985 Doe had metamorphosed into a civilian president, his repressive policies remained – for example, the notorious decree 88A, which prohibited "rumours, lies and disinformation."[24] In addition, he did not lift the ban on political parties, for example on the Liberian People's Party and the United Progressive Party, nor did he release all political prisoners. Freedom of speech and expression were almost non-existent as the press was frequently gagged. Newspapers were closed down for publishing reports that portrayed the regime unfavourably, and in some cases pressmen were jailed and tortured, with at least one dying in police custody. The ruthlessness of the Doe regime was perhaps highlighted by the brutal reprisals against all opponents, particularly against those who were in any way implicated in the military coups that took place against the Doe regime. Notable amongst such attempts was Quiwonkpa's failed coup of 1985, when Doe's army killed not only the coup plotters and their families, but over 500 joyous civilians who had taken to the streets in the erroneous belief that the coup had been successful. Above all, the Doe regime is remembered for its atrocities against Liberian citizens, which included looting, rape, arson, flogging, arbitrary arrests, and summary executions by the Armed Forces of Liberia.

The forcible repression that followed the Quiwonkpa coup marks a decisive turning point in the history of Liberia, especially in the countdown to the civil war. Because Quiwonkpa and most of those who joined him in the bid were from the Gio and Mano ethnic groups, the government's retaliatory clamp-down created a disenchanted operational base for a future rebellion among these groups. Although some people in this region escaped to neighbouring countries, those who remained maintained a deep hatred for Doe's government, waiting for an opportunity to express their opposition against the regime. This was to be exploited by Charles Taylor in later years.

By the middle of the 1980 decade, Liberia's history had reached a dangerous impasse. On the one hand there was now a growing awareness of civil liberties but on the other there was ruthless suppression on a wide scale. The question was not whether a violent opposition to the Doe regime would emerge, but when. It came in December 1989. It might perhaps have occurred earlier, but for outside factors such as the implicit support from the United States received by Doe during the Cold War.

A vicious civil war

The civil war that resulted from the invasion in December 1989 of Liberia's Nimba county by a band of rebels known as the National Patriotic Front of Liberia (NPFL), led by Charles Taylor, was among the first to give a true indication of the nature of the inter-communal violence that was to become a characteristic of the post-Cold War era. One key feature of the conflict from the outset was the abandonment of all rules and conventions of war. It was this that lay at the heart of the transformation of this war into a difficult humanitarian emergency, like many other post-Cold War conflicts.

Civilians, who would normally form the core of non-combatants in regular conflicts, were the main targets of the Liberian conflict. The government forces set the precedent, employing terror against civilians. When the rebel forces attacked, Doe's Krahn-dominated Armed Forces of Liberia (AFL) exacted terrible retribution in Nimba county, killing civilians, including women and children, whom they accused of providing support to the rebels. Convinced that Doe was determined to wipe out the Gio and Mano people, who formed a majority in the county, thousands of civilians in the region took up arms against Samuel Doe and actively supported the rebels. However, the rebellion also led to a huge exodus from Nimba to escape Doe's revenge. By October 1990, Liberian refugees in neighbouring states numbered more than 600,000.[25] Although Taylor's first attempt was only a partial success, the cruel overreaction of the AFL caused the local population to support the rebel army. Unfortunately, brutal revenge-reaping was not the monopoly of the AFL; the NPFL in turn terrorized those thought to be Doe supporters and the conflict quickly degenerated into an inter-ethnic slaughter. The Gio and Mano people, along with other ethnic groups, were killed at will by Doe's forces, while the Krahns and their Mandingo allies were butchered by the rebels and their supporters in reprisal attacks.

The targeting of civilians contributed in no small measure to the development of another feature of the war – the use of children as fighters in the campaign of terror. The first wave of child soldiers resulted from the initial AFL atrocities. Several hundreds of children who had lost their families and were displaced in the massacre by government troops joined the NPFL to take up arms against the Doe regime. The composition of the NPFL thus rapidly changed to include children as young as 12 years old.[26] In addition, in the course of the NPFL's counter-terror, many more hundreds of children were forced to join the war. There were also cases where children joined voluntarily because of food scarcities. Much of the available food was controlled by the rebels and those who joined were sure of getting food for themselves and their families.[27]

In addition to the direct involvement and victimization of civilians and the use of children as fighters, foreign relief organizations, the United Nations,[28] churches, schools, missions, and hospitals all became directly involved in the violence.

Perhaps the most notable feature of the Liberian conflict was the proliferation of warring parties and the frequency with which the control of territories changed hands between factions. This proliferation of factions and the warlordism that came with it were to create perhaps the greatest obstacle to peace in Liberia. As the war progressed and as more factions emerged, the leaders of these factions became very powerful, with enormous wealth and influence, and the peace agreements on Liberia inevitably had to take the importance of these people into consideration.

In the early stage of the conflict, there were just two factions fighting against the Armed Forces of Liberia. The NPFL was initially the main rebel faction that challenged Samuel Doe's leadership. Its leader, Charles Taylor, was certainly one of the most controversial warlords created by the Liberian conflict. He was of Americo-Liberian descent, and he first came into the limelight when he served in Doe's government as the Director of the General Services Agency – responsible for government procurements. This public assignment was however to bring him into deep controversy, because he was accused of embezzling money allocated to his department.[29] He fled to the United States in 1983, where he was arrested under the extradition treaty between Liberia and the United States. He jumped bail from a Baltimore prison and made his way through Europe to West Africa, arriving in Côte d'Ivoire, from where he began concerted efforts to oust President Samuel Doe.

The other faction was the Independent National Patriotic Front of Liberia (INPFL), which broke away from the NPFL shortly after the beginning of the rebellion. This marked the beginning of internal splits in the warring factions, a tendency that was to become common in the later stages of the war. The leader of the breakaway faction was "Prince" Yomie Johnson, who was the former NPFL Chief Training Officer. The reasons for the split are numerous, but all centred on the ethnic politics of Liberia, the different perceptions of the factions on what the war should mean, and the personality differences of the respective leaders. Although it was not long before Prince Johnson rode out of the Liberian political scene, he played a major role in the Liberian conflict. He had been Quiwonkpa's aide-de-camp and he fled the country after the failure of the 1985 coup. He was one of the earliest recruits into the NPFL. He is from the Gio/Mano ethnic group, and many of those who defected with him to form the INPFL were also from this group.

The NPFL, which invaded Nimba county as a numerically and militarily weak force, benefited immensely from the display of brutality and indiscipline by the AFL, which brought thousands of additional supporters to the NPFL. Its strength increased and its military effectiveness improved, resulting in early successes and a rapid advance toward Monrovia, Liberia's capital. Although the NPFL cannot be described as a true guerrilla army, given the atrocities committed against the very people it was supposed to be liberating, the NPFL employed some guerrilla tactics that worked in its favour. Taylor began by waging the war against Doe from the remote and difficult countryside. His security in remote base areas, the unidentifiable nature of his troops, and the employment of hit-and-run tactics protected his forces from early defeat by government troops. The bases in the hinterland were also in areas where government troops were unfamiliar with the terrain. Although the AFL was trained for conventional warfare by Israeli and US advisers, the NPFL's weaknesses such as small numbers, poor equipment, and vulnerability also gave it inherent strengths such as mobility, secrecy, and speed, which enabled it to advance rapidly toward the capital.

After taking control of virtually every major Liberian town within the first six months of the conflict, it seemed that it was only a matter of time before Taylor and his men took control of Monrovia and removed Doe from power. This conclusion was reinforced by a sense of panic in the Doe camp after the NPFL successes. After the fall of Liberia's second- and third-largest cities, Yekepa and Gbarnga, and the port city of Buchanan, Doe attempted to appease the rebels, promising not to run for re-election.[30] Doe went as far as promising to declare an amnesty for political exiles, and to lift the ban on three political parties and restructure his cabinet. However, despite these promises and the offer of political asylum by some countries, he stubbornly held on to power.

The expectation that Taylor would soon take control of Monrovia was dashed by the split in the NPFL and the subsequent emergence of Prince Yomie Johnson's INPFL. Although many felt that a war-weary AFL, suffering from tribal divisions and low morale, would soon capitulate, Charles Taylor's problems were also mounting. He was now fighting a war on two fronts. In addition, the NPFL was facing the task of transforming itself into a regular army and fighting in the more densely populated capital, where its speed and mobility would be curtailed and it would face heavier government opposition. Stiff opposition was encountered when it attempted to take over the heavily fortified residence of the president, known as "executive mansion," which was (and still is) by all accounts the main symbol of power in Liberia. The loss of Prince Johnson, one of the NPFL's effective commanders, made the task doubly difficult, particularly when such a formidable force had now become a foe. Many in the NPFL camp referred to Johnson as the "spoiler." With three different factions now struggling for control of power, a stalemate emerged and it promised to be a long, hard struggle, in which many more casualties would be sustained. Taylor however provided a different explanation for his failure to take the executive mansion, arguing that he was persuaded by the United States to halt the NPFL attack while efforts were being made to negotiate with Doe.[31] At the time, it seemed that the state of confusion in Liberia could not get worse, but more rival factions emerged, which served to compound any attempts to make peace in the conflict. These groups, which numbered as many as eight at one stage, and the effects of their influence on the peace process are discussed later in this book.

The "politicians" and the outbreak of the Liberian conflict

Even before the outbreak of the civil war, the political class in Liberia had become confused. The Americo-Liberians, who had dominated the political scene for more than a century, had been replaced by a generation of indigenous politicians who came to power with Samuel Doe during his controversial transition to civil rule. Their lack of experience in the management of the intricacies of politics was further compounded by the outbreak of the civil war. The remnants of the Americo-Liberian political class, on the other hand, were, at this stage of the conflict, cautious about making any declared stand on the conflict. Although Charles Taylor, who started the rebellion, was of their "stock," the extent to which he wanted their political involvement was not clear. Most of the Americo-Liberian politicians had an impression of Taylor as a machiavellian tactician who placed his own ambition and self-interest before any group solidarity. For example, he served in Samuel Doe's government at a time when the administration was not particularly popular among the Americo-Liberians. Thus, from both the indigenous and the Americo-Liberian sides, the Liberian political class was weak at the time the civil war broke out and for some time afterwards. This was to play a major part in the difficulties in the country's search for peace, and also in the setback that the politicians experienced in their comeback bid during the 1997 election that ended the war.

The war economy too played an important role in the peace process in the Liberian conflict. Although Liberia was historically a relatively prosperous country, gaining some wealth from its mineral and agricultural resources, the economy had started a downturn towards the end of Tolbert's regime. Doe's rule further compounded the problem. Liberia's main foreign exports were rubber, timber, diamonds, and iron. A significant percentage of the population was involved in subsistence farming. The economic depression that affected the country from the mid-1980s and the simultaneous increase in the threat against Doe's regime had resulted in the country bartering some of its resources for arms from foreign countries.

Once the war broke out, however, the situation became even worse. Subsistence farming was no longer safe and it became difficult to feed the population. Again, the necessity to finance the war resulted in the warlords exploiting the only viable sources of revenue in the country. In the later stages of the conflict, there were strong allegations that some of the foreign peacekeepers also joined in the exploitation of the Liberian economy. This is discussed later, but it is safe to conclude at this stage that the politics surrounding the exploitation of Liberian resources is one of the most controversial aspects of the conflict, because its ramifications touched all three main participants in the civil war – the peacekeepers, the politicians, and the warlords.

Conclusion

If any conflict clearly demonstrated the withdrawal of superpower interests at the end of the Cold War in African countries, it was the Liberian civil war. During the Cold War, it was inconceivable that the United States would have allowed Liberia to slide into the state of anarchy that now prevailed. In addition to the historical ties, Liberia was a strategic staging post of some importance to the United States. It was being used as a friendly state where it was possible for the United States to establish its Omega navigation stations for the South Atlantic region and a Voice of America transmitter to reach sub-Saharan Africa. The Robertsfield airport in Liberia acted as a stand-by US strategic refuelling and landing site for rapid deployment forces. The United States also had a 500-strong embassy, which acted as the CIA station for the region. Firestone, the world's largest rubber plantation, was operated in Liberia by US interests. Prior to the civil war, almost 5,000 Americans resided in Liberia, including businessmen, diplomats, missionaries, and 160 members of the Peace Corps.[32]

With this level of US involvement and interest in Liberia, it is difficult to dispute claims that Liberia was an ally of some importance to the United States on the African continent. The US government support for the Doe regime strengthened this argument: US aid to Liberia, which was less than US$20 million at the time of the coup, increased rapidly, and by 1985 it was close to US$500 million. It included assistance with interest payments on foreign debts, supplies of staple foods such as rice, and military aid. Doe's troops were trained by the United States, which also built new barracks and supplied uniforms, weapons, and trucks.[33] Doe, in return, closed the Libyan mission in Monrovia and terminated diplomatic relations with the Soviet Union, while establishing relations with the state of Israel.[34] For these reasons, it was expected that the United States would step in to restore order in Liberia, but this did not happen.

The US response to the Liberian conflict was indecisive. Its initial reaction appeared to be pro-Doe, especially given the involvement of Libya on the side of the rebels. The United States was reported to have sent two counter-insurgency advisers, but they were quickly withdrawn after the atrocities committed by the AFL became apparent.[35] Several reasons have been advanced for the failure of the United States to intervene decisively. The Gulf crisis coincided with the war in Liberia, thus diverting US and international attention from the latter. The suggestion is that, but for the Gulf crisis, the United States would have intervened in the Liberian crisis. However, the situation was not so clear-cut. During the first few months of the Liberian conflict, the Gulf War had not developed to its full significance. Thus it appears the United States held back from direct intervention for other reasons, which might include the possible lack of support from the West African sub-region, and the fact that military intervention might not have been a guaranteed success. In any case, it later became obvious that Liberia, or any other sub-Saharan African country for that matter, no longer occupied a significant place in US strategic considerations. The Cold War had ended and Africa's relevance had diminished. Liberians who identified with Americans more than they did with their West African neighbours seemed traumatized by the United

States' apparent lack of interest in the conflict in the initial stages.[36] Enoanyi's remarks emphasize the extent of Liberians' disappointment:

> Liberians – including even the factions involved in the war – continued to hope for the moment when America would step in [and] blow the only whistle that could not be ignored by anyone or group, for an end to the deadly game.[37]

Notes

1. For a full account of the origins of the ACS and the founding of Liberia, see, for example, Amos J. Beyan, *The American Colonization Society and Creation of the Liberian State: A Historical Perspective, 1822–1990*, Larnham: University Press of America, 1991; Tom Shick, *Behold the Promised Land: A History of Afro-American Settler Society in Nineteenth Century Liberia*, Baltimore: Johns Hopkins University Press, 1980; and Yekutiel Gershoni, *Black Colonialism: Liberian Scramble for the Hinterland*, Boulder and London: Westview Press, 1985.
2. Amadu Sesay, "Historical Background to the Liberian Crisis," in M. A. Vogt (ed.), *The Liberian Crisis and ECOMOG: A Bold Attempt at Regional Peacekeeping*, Lagos: Gabumo Publishing Co., 1992, p. 29.
3. Ibid., p. 30.
4. David Wippman, "Enforcing the Peace: ECOWAS and the Liberian Civil War," in L. F. Damrosch (ed.), *Enforcing Restraint: Collective Intervention in Internal Conflicts*, New York: Council of Foreign Relations Press, 1993.
5. W. Ofuatey-Kodjoe, "Regional Organizations and the Resolution of Internal Conflict: The ECOWAS Intervention in Liberia", *International Peacekeeping*, 1(3), 1994; and Joseph Saye Guannu, *Liberian History up to 1847*, New York: Exposition Press, 1983.
6. Sesay, "Historical Background to the Liberian Crisis," p. 31.
7. See Gershoni, *Black Colonialism*, pp. 22–23.
8. Ibid.
9. Sesay, "Historical Background to the Liberian Crisis," p. 34.
10. See Gus Liebenow, *Liberia: The Quest for Democracy*, Bloomington: Indiana University Press, 1987, p. 47.
11. Sesay, "Historical Background to the Liberian Crisis," p. 31.
12. For a discussion of the forced labour or contract, and the effects of this policy, see S. G. E. Boley, *The Rise and Fall of the First Republic*, London: Macmillan, 1984; and Liebenow, *Liberia*.
13. For more on this, see Michael Massing, "Best Friends: Violations of Human Rights in Liberia, America's Closest Ally in Africa," mimeo, 1986.
14. W. Nah Dixon, *Great Lessons of the Liberian Civil War*, Monrovia: People International, 1992, p. 8.
15. Robert Clower, George Dalton, Mitchell Harwitz, and A. A. Walters, *Growth without Development*, Evanston: Northwestern University Press, 1966, p. 133.
16. See Tuan Wreh, *The Love of Liberty ... The Rule of President William V. S. Tubman in Liberia 1944–1971*, London: C. Hurst & Company, and Monrovia: Wreh News Agency, 1976, p. 114.
17. Ibid.
18. Ibid.
19. Joseph Saye Guannu, *An Introduction to Liberian Government*, New York: Exposition Press, 1982, p. 99.

20. For more on the opposition role of MOJA, see Amos Sawyer, *The Emergence of Autocracy in Liberia: Tragedy and Challenge*, San Francisco: ICS Press, 1992, p. 289.
21. Sesay, "Historical Background to the Liberian Crisis," p. 40.
22. Dixon, *Great Lessons of the Liberian Civil War*, pp. 9–10.
23. For details of atrocities committed by Samuel Doe's regime against political opponents and their supporters, see Massing, "Best Friends."
24. Ibid.; and *West Africa*, 16–22 April 1990, p. 612.
25. Figures from UNHCR, Côte d'Ivoire, reported in *Africa Research Bulletin*, 1–31 October 1990, p. 9873.
26. See *Africa Report*, July–August 1990; in addition, *Sky News Special Report*, 7 February 1994, featured NPFL soldiers as young as nine years.
27. Personal interviews with Liberians in Oru-Ijebu (Nigeria) and Monrovia (Liberia).
28. The United Nations pulled out its personnel after its refugee compound was attacked in May 1990 by government troops, who killed and abducted some of the residents. See *Africa Research Bulletin*, 1–30 September 1990, p. 9841.
29. *Africa Research Bulletin*, 15 February 1990, p. 9557 and 15 April 1990, p. 9633; see also *Africa Report*, March/April 1990.
30. *Africa Research Bulletin*, 1–30 September 1990, p. 9841.
31. See interview with Charles Taylor in *The New African*, October 1992.
32. US ties and interests in Liberia are discussed in Michael Massing, "Best Friends"; *Africa Report*, September–October 1990, p. 6; Holly Burkhalter and Rakiya Omaar, "Failures of State," *Africa Report*, November–December 1990, pp. 27–28; and R. F. Zimmerman, *Dollars, Diplomacy and Dependency: Dilemmas of US Economic Aid*, Boulder: Lynne Rienner Publishers, 1993.
33. Massing, "Best Friends," p. 10.
34. Ibid. See also *Africa Report*, September–October 1990, p. 6.
35. *Africa Report*, July–August 1990, p. 49; also, *Africa Report* of November–December 1990, p. 16, reports that, until Doe's army massacred hundreds of civilians in a Lutheran church in July, the US government, with 2,000 marines stationed just off the coast of Liberia, was in fact still considering a face-saving invasion in support of Doe, but was quick to recoil after this incident; see also pp. 27–28.
36. Personal interviews with Liberians at the refugee camp in Oru-Ijebu, Nigeria, for example, confirmed the disappointment of many Liberians that the United States did not "jump" to their rescue. Many admitted that they knew little about their African neighbours before the war, but often looked up to the United States.
37. Bill Frank Enoanyi, *Behold Uncle Sam's Step-Child*, Sacramento: San Mar Publishers, 1991, p. 3.

3
Regional intervention in Liberia

In the absence of decisive action from the United States and the rest of the international community (including the United Nations), and in the face of continued killings and atrocities, it was the Economic Community of West African States (ECOWAS) that took the decision to intervene in the Liberian conflict. At the thirteenth ECOWAS summit in May 1990, a Standing Mediation Committee (SMC) was established to examine ways of resolving first the Liberian, then other conflicts that were brewing in the sub-region.[1] This resulted in the formation and despatch of the ECOWAS Military Observer Group (ECOMOG) to Liberia, with the aim that it would keep an arranged peace between the warring factions. Unfolding events in Liberia and the conduct of the ECOMOG operation in response to these events would later call for the deployment of a United Nations Observer Mission in Liberia (UNOMIL). However, the activities of ECOWAS/ECOMOG and the extent to which the sub-regional response to the situation in Liberia was effectively managed will be the focus of the rest of this chapter.

A number of things should be noted about ECOWAS that will serve to explain the nature of its peacekeeping operation in Liberia. The organization was founded in 1975 primarily to integrate the economic potential of all the countries in the region. Although some clauses of its charter dealt with security issues, it was primarily an economic grouping of regional states. The fact that the security content of the ECOWAS agreement was never used before the outbreak of the Liberian crisis added to the controversy surrounding the despatch of the peacekeeping force, as many argued that ECOWAS had gone beyond its mandate by interfering in the civil conflict.

It is also worth emphasizing the political currents that prevailed in the organization. From its inception and through most of the Liberian civil war, there was a major division between the anglophone and the francophone West African states. The francophone nations were wary about any economic or political link with the anglophone states, especially Nigeria, anglophone Africa's most populous nation and, without doubt, the region's most important nation. It would appear that France, too, shared in this opposition towards Nigeria, and it was some time before the French-speaking West African nations gave support to ECOWAS. All this is important in appreciating the actions taken by some West African countries in the course of the Liberian civil war.

The extent to which the ECOMOG operation would be successful and to which ECOWAS would be able to bring lasting peace and stability to Liberia was determined by a number of factors. Key amongst them were: the mandate; the nature of the peace agreements, and practical problems in their implementation; and structural problems in both the sub-regional organization and the peace force. These are discussed below.

ECOMOG's mandate

Since the conceptualization of peacekeeping in the 1950s, it became fashionable to label multinational forces despatched to conflict areas as peacekeeping forces, even when the activities of these forces could not be described as such – as was often the case with regional responses during the Cold War. This general definition broadened to include the United Nations in the post–Cold War era as fewer and fewer conflict situations now complied with the traditional peacekeeping response. Politicians are said to have a preference for the term "peacekeeping" even when their troops embark on greater use of force, because it has a "favourable resonance."[2] The ECOMOG operation was no exception. It was labelled a peacekeeping force even when there was no indication that it would be able to conduct such an operation. Moreover, it appears there were deeper reasons behind this. It is doubtful that the planners of ECOMOG understood the nature of the conflict they were responding to in Liberia, or the character of the conflicting parties. They simply (at least initially) relied upon the fact that the warring factions, whom they perhaps saw as seriously under-trained and under-equipped, would capitulate in the face of a West African force led by Nigeria.[3]

When the decision was taken to send a peacekeeping force, ECOWAS sources claimed that verbal and written agreements were obtained from both President Doe and Charles Taylor – the main contenders in the conflict, even though by this time the main parties involved numbered three, to include Prince Yomie Johnson. Although evidence of a written invitation by Doe exists, there is none in existence from Charles Taylor, except for a note signed by the Executive Secretary of ECOWAS, stating that Taylor had signed a written agreement.[4] However, it became apparent before the force left for Liberia that Taylor had had a change of heart and was now opposed to the deployment of a West African force, which he threatened to attack if it landed in Liberia. Taylor was particularly concerned that ECOWAS might not be able to effect Doe's resignation. Despite this turn in events, not only was the force labelled a peacekeeping one, but the planners prepared for a peacekeeping operation in Liberia even when there was every indication that the troops might have to use force.[5] However, this may have been done in an attempt (largely by Nigeria) to encourage the regional participants, who might otherwise have been unprepared to commit their men to dangerous missions. Moreover, it was perhaps wiser to reassure the warring factions that ECOMOG was coming to embark on a peacekeeping mission rather than an enforcement one.

Taylor and the National Patriotic Front of Liberia (NPFL) kept their promise to attack the ECOMOG force. Not surprisingly, after suffering casualties during vicious attacks by the NPFL, ECOMOG reacted by swapping its white helmets for green berets. This was now an enforcement operation rather than a mere act of self-defence, as ECOMOG proceeded to drive the rebel forces out of gun range of Monrovia. Their operation was hailed a success by most observers, even if reluctantly in some cases. This intervention restored some measure of order in Monrovia, which was by now virtually uninhabitable, with many streets strewn with dead bodies, and with no electricity or water. Perhaps the most important benefit of ECOMOG's enforcement action was the signing of a cease-fire agreement between the warring factions in Banjul in October 1990. This brought some expectations that Liberia was on the path to lasting peace and stability and that, thereafter, ECOMOG would revert to a peacekeeping stance, interposing itself between the warring factions, patrolling the city, and maintaining checkpoints.

However, a pattern of alternating between peacekeeping and enforcement was to become a key aspect of the ECOMOG operation. The cease-fire agreement was followed by several peace agreements, which were ignored owing to a number of factors that are discussed below. On at least two occasions cease-fire violations escalated into serious conflict, where ECOMOG was mandated to employ enforcement measures. This is discussed in greater detail later.

The peace agreements

Several meetings were organized by ECOWAS on the Liberian conflict. Some of these resulted in the signing of peace agreements, while others played roles in advancing the peace process. The first ECOWAS meeting on Liberia was the one during which the Standing Mediation Committee was established in May 1990. Apart from its decision to establish ECOMOG, this committee also initiated the creation of an Interim Government of National Unity (IGNU). Almost immediately after the Banjul meeting, the NPFL reiterated its determination that there would be no cease-fire in Liberia until Doe resigned. Ironically, President Doe was also against the decision of ECOWAS to create an Interim Government. It was said that Doe considered the imposition of a new government on Liberia while he was still alive to be inappropriate. However, he was willing to go along with the decision, ostensibly to give peace a chance, but in reality because he did not have the domestic base to resist this affront to his authority. On 13 August 1990, ECOWAS came up with "Regulations for ECOMOG," consisting of 45 articles broken down into six chapters.

In October 1990, an "Agreement on Cessation of Hostilities and Peaceful Settlement of Conflict" was signed in Banjul. This agreement is neglected in most analyses of the Liberian conflict, but it was actually the first time that members of the warring factions met to discuss and sign an agreement on the restoration of peace to Liberia. The agreement was signed by the Armed Forces of Liberia (AFL) and the Independent National Patriotic Front of Liberia (INPFL). The NPFL was not represented. Although the meeting was not organized by ECOWAS, the organization seemed to have endorsed it.

In November 1990, there was the first fully convened meeting on Liberia in Bamako, Mali. The details of the agreement are in Appendix 1. Although the Bamako Agreement did not result in any lasting peace in Liberia, it closed the gap that appeared to be opening between the francophone and anglophone countries in the region. It also resolved, even if only temporarily, the problem of the acceptability of ECOMOG. The Bamako Agreement was followed by the Banjul Agreement, signed in December 1990. The main clauses are in Appendix 2. The Banjul Agreement failed to advance the peace process in Liberia, and its imminent failure led the Togolese leader, Gnassingbe Eyadema, to call for another meeting in February 1991. This meeting led to the signing of the Lomé Accord (see Appendix 3). The significance of the Lomé Accord was that it had an "Annex" on how to achieve the cease-fire, which is taken to be part of the agreement. All the faction leaders agreed that it was necessary to brief their troops about the cease-fire modalities and the role of ECOMOG. This was the first time that such a clause was included in a Liberian agreement. During the cease-fire, there would be a clearly stated procedure for reporting violations.[6]

All these peace agreements were flawed. For example, although the Lomé agreement saw disarmament and demobilization as the key to stability, it failed to analyse ways in which they could be effectively achieved. Much was left to the discretion of ECOMOG, which was expected to find the appropriate ways and time to begin disarmament. The agreement also expressly stated that demobilizing troops should be cantoned or encamped,[7] but it did not identify ways in which the full demobilization of troops would be achieved, nor did it make provisions for ways in which ECOMOG could perhaps enforce disarmament if it became necessary, such as cordon and search.

The situation escalated beyond cease-fire violations. Escalation was manifested in several ways. First, the NPFL invaded Sierra Leone, prompting a series of battles with Sierra Leonian forces.[8] Sierra Leone was later plunged into a civil war, with the NPFL supporting the rebel army of Foday Sankoh. Second, was the entry into the war of another faction, the United Liberation Movement of Liberia for Democracy (ULIMO), which was ostensibly "born out of the desire of displaced Liberians to return home and continue their search for democratic freedom."[9] ULIMO was a merger of two distinct movements – the Movement for the Redemption of Muslims, formed by Alhaji Kromah, and the Liberian United Defence Force of General Karpeh. What both groups had in common was their anti-Taylor stance. Indeed, Alhaji Kromah served as a deputy minister in Doe's cabinet while General Karpeh was a close associate of the late president and Liberia's ambassador to Sierra Leone. After serious infighting in the ULIMO, Karpeh was killed and Alhaji Kromah assumed the leadership. ULIMO's entry into the Liberian equation introduced a number of complications, the most important of which was the allegation that the regional peacekeeping force, ECOMOG, had an implicit interest in the formation of the movement and that ECOMOG's arms found their way into ULIMO's hands.

After Lomé, a series of agreements was reached under the auspices of the late Ivorian leader, Houphouët-Boigny, in Yamoussoukro. The agreement that came close to addressing some of the problems and ambiguities of earlier ones was often referred to as Yamoussoukro IV, which emerged from the third meeting of the Committee of Five[10] in October 1991. Accompanying the agreement was a comprehensive programme of implementation and a timetable for cantonment or encampment and disarmament. However, no provisions were made for supporting human and material resources. Much was seen from a military perspective – the major requirement was seen to be the expansion of the

ECOMOG force. There were no provisions for stages beyond disarmament such as demobilization and reintegration. Planners seemed to see the process largely in terms of encampment, disarmament, and elections. If the stages between were in fact organized, they were not carefully outlined, nor were responsibilities for implementing these stages allocated. Not only did this agreement fail to bring the desired stability, attempts to implement it led to a new crisis. About 500 ECOMOG soldiers who were deployed to the hinterland to conduct the cease-fire and demobilization were kidnapped by NPFL troops, who killed six from the Senegalese contingent.

Perhaps the most glaring indication that the Liberian crisis had escalated beyond the negotiating capabilities of ECOWAS diplomatic machinery was the massive attack launched by the NPFL on ECOMOG and Monrovia (known as Operation Octopus) in October 1992. A well-planned NPFL pincer movement was to meet up in the urban fringe with the intention of dislodging the interventionist forces and taking over the capital. The "peacekeepers" were taken by surprise and the advance reached the edge of the city, generating in its wake a string of atrocities and summary executions. ECOMOG had no choice but to revert to a conventional enforcement strategy on a higher scale of intensity than in 1990. After urgent calls for reinforcement, the attack was successfully contained and then turned back.

The most significant lesson that emerged from the failure of Operation Octopus was that ECOMOG did in reality have the capability to take on and defeat the Liberian factions, in particular the NPFL, in a conventional operation. To achieve this, ECOMOG abandoned the restrained and conciliatory approach associated with conflict resolution and traditional peacekeeping. In their tough fight to re-establish a hold on Monrovia they had used powerful and indiscriminate weapon systems against the NPFL and any civil installations where Taylor's fighters sheltered. ECOMOG's impartiality was lost and this was to diminish the chances of a successful peace. NPFL's initial success in flouting the peace agreement was not unconnected with the inexperience of the sub-regional organization in managing an operation of this magnitude and with its inadequate resources for command, communication, intelligence collation, and logistic support.

ECOMOG's operational development

Apart from the flaws in many of the peace documents, there were structural flaws within ECOWAS, the peacemaking body, and its military sub-division, ECOMOG. Primarily intended and designed as an economic organization, ECOWAS did not, and still does not, have a formal organ, akin to the UN Department of Peacekeeping Operations, charged with the task of managing such operations. Structures were not in place for responding to command and control and logistics problems. Closely associated with this problem was the dire financial situation within ECOWAS. The poorly equipped and under-financed Secretariat did not have the assets to conduct a small traditional peacekeeping operation, let alone the type of operation developing in Liberia. Each contributing state was responsible for the maintenance of its troops in Liberia. Given this situation, the ECOWAS Secretariat was unable to control the operation, and the initiative was often hijacked by individual nations (particularly Nigeria, which supplied over 70 per cent of the troops and 80 per cent of the funding for ECOMOG) which not only catered to the needs of their troops but exercised direct command. Thus, even if the agreements had been flawless, the huge military responsibility demanded by a full disarmament and demobilization programme would almost certainly have been beyond the capacity of ECOWAS.

In diplomatic terms, ECOWAS's peacemaking ability was severely weakened by visible divisions within the organization, which invariably influenced the course of the peace process. Prior to 1985, relations between Liberia and Nigeria were cool. Nigeria's civilian regime was opposed to Samuel Doe's coup and even prevented him from attending a summit of the Organization of African Unity in Lagos in 1980. However, the assumption of office by General Ibrahim Babangida in 1985 reversed Nigeria's policy of opposition and improved relations between the two countries. Nigeria became the main source of sub-regional support for Doe and a major ally. When the civil war intensified following Taylor's incursion, Doe paid a visit to Nigeria, allegedly to obtain military assistance. It is widely believed that Nigeria provided support for Doe in the form of arms supplies, before the conflict escalated beyond AFL control. When Nigeria later became a peacemaker in the conflict, it was difficult for Charles Taylor to see the country as a neutral intervener.

Apart from this, Côte d'Ivoire and Burkina Faso were initially opposed to the ECOMOG mission and had supported Charles Taylor's faction, maintaining an arms supply line via Burkina Faso. Côte d'Ivoire was particularly opposed to Doe. President Houphouët-Boigny, whose son-in-law, Tolbert, had been killed alongside his father in the 1980 coup by Doe, was actively hostile. He encouraged another son-in-law, Blaise Compaore, the President of Burkina Faso, to support the NPFL rebel cause. This served to encourage Taylor's intransigence. With such conflicting actions from regional players, any peace overture was bound to encounter difficulty. Signs of progress emerged only later, after an apparent united front in the organization. A Committee of Five was established in July 1991, as an adjunct to the Standing Mediation Committee. It consisted of the heads of state of Côte d'Ivoire (chairman), Guinea-Bissau, Senegal, the Gambia, and Togo.[11] This resulted in the active participation of the francophone countries in the peace process. The Standing Mediation Committee and Committee of Five were later merged and expanded to form the Committee of Nine.

Although ECOMOG was conceptually an altruistic initiative, its underlying politics later became questionable and extremely complicated. Nigeria, the major regional power with a large army and considerable experience of UN peacekeeping, provided the majority of the assets. But to disarm allegations of leverage it surrendered the leadership of the force to Ghana. Although ECOMOG's deployment achieved an intermission in the violence around Monrovia, it was unable to sustain its initiative with much conviction. Poor follow-on logistics and problems of interpreting the mandate diminished its effectiveness, particularly in the initial stages of the operation. During this uncertain and badly coordinated phase of the operation, Doe was kidnapped from ECOMOG headquarters and later killed.[12] Ironically, ECOMOG, which was initially seen as Doe's protector, was unable to guarantee his safety in ECOMOG's heavily fortified headquarters. The embarrassing circumstances of his death forced ECOMOG to reappraise its role and capabilities. General Arnold Quanoo, the first ECOMOG Force Commander, was replaced by Major General Joshua Dongoyaro of Nigeria, a member of the country's ruling military council.

Despite its initial misfortunes, ECOMOG's credibility remained intact. The vacillation and bungling that led to Doe's death were far outweighed by the apparent achievement of reducing the carnage that had so far characterized the Liberian civil war. After a semblance of security and order was re-established in Monrovia, an Interim Government of National Unity (IGNU) was set up to administer the country under Amos Sawyer, a professor at the University of Liberia. Although organized and sustained by ECOMOG to govern the entire country, in reality the writ and presence of IGNU were never established beyond Monrovia. Taylor and the NPFL established a rival government in Gbanga, arguing its legitimacy on the basis that his faction controlled up to 80 per cent of the Liberian land mass.

Major General Dongoyaro has been succeeded by six ECOMOG Commanders, all Nigerian: Rufus Kupolati, Ishaya Bakut, Olatunji Olurin, John Shagaya, John Inienger, and the incumbent at the time of writing, Victor Malu. Their varying degrees of success have been determined by the operational situation in Liberia, but more significantly by politics and power struggles in their home capital, Abuja. In ECOMOG, the success of the Commander was influenced by Nigerian politics and by his political connections and their ability to help him survive. Dongoyaro was vested with the necessary authority through his direct access to the Nigerian President, whose coup plot Dongoyaro had supported and announced. Kupolati did not enjoy such free access to the President, which, along with his preference for compromise and peacemaking with factions, shortened his tenure as ECOMOG Commander. Bakut enjoyed more direct access to power in Nigeria, which possibly accounted for his long stay as Force Commander, despite the fact that his tenure was not significantly effective. Olurin also had direct access to the authorities in Nigeria; in the prevailing crisis in Liberia at the time he assumed command (during Operation Octopus) he held a strong position and was able to act with conviction. Shagaya was made Force Commander at a time when Nigeria was undergoing considerable instability;[13] he became politically isolated and was retired from the military.[14] John Inienger, who held office during the Nigerian unrest arising from the nullification of the June 1993 elections, was left relatively free from interference from Abuja. ECOMOG's current Commander, General Victor Malu, is perceived by all factions, by ordinary Liberians, and by the diplomatic community as a tough-minded, straightforward, "no-nonsense" man. According to Taylor, "there will be trouble in Liberia if there is any attempt to move Malu from the command of ECOMOG at this stage."[15] The US ambassador to Liberia, William Milam, has also acknowledged the effectiveness of ECOMOG as a result of Malu's decisiveness: "every guerrilla knows that if General Malu says he is coming for your gun he means it."[16] ECOMOG's new credibility added to the confidence of Liberians that a new phase in the peace process had indeed emerged. The achievements of ECOMOG under Victor Malu are discussed in chapters 7 and 8.

Once ECOMOG's honeymoon was over and its novelty had evaporated, Liberian perceptions varied. Sawyer's Interim National Government appreciated its efforts,[17] but the NPFL saw it as an attempt to rescue the discredited Doe regime. Taylor did not relax his position even after the death of Doe. Having struggled so hard to overthrow Doe, he was opposed to Nigerian domination in ECOMOG and its support for Doe's forces in the early stages of the conflict. However, NPFL's opposition to ECOMOG varied according to its relationship with each Field Commander. The faction was on relatively better terms with Rufus Kupolati, Ishaya Bakut, and John Shagaya than with Joshua Dongoyaro and Olatunji Olurin.[18] Although the latter had individual styles that did not endear them to the NPFL, there were also military reasons for hatred. Dongoyaro, by re-establishing law and order in Monrovia, had frustrated the NPFL's attempt to seize control in late 1990, and Olurin repulsed the NPFL bid (Operation Octopus) to take over Monrovia in October 1992.

In its attempt to implement its mandate in Liberia, ECOMOG suffered operational problems that were not necessarily different from those encountered by other multinational forces, but were perhaps more acute given the shortage of human and financial resources and the lack of experience. The Executive Secretary of ECOWAS was responsible for directing the operation yet he had no Special Representative in the mission area. The posts of legal and political advisers planned as part of ECOMOG were left unoccupied owing to lack of funds. ECOWAS's failure to maintain a continued political presence on the ground in the area of operation placed a greater burden on the Force Commander, who in most cases performed both political and military tasks. Ultimately, the attainment of peace depended upon the desire of warring factions to resolve their conflict through peaceful means. Despite the flaws in agreements, and ECOWAS's inadequacies, several opportunities were created for the conflicting parties to find solutions to the conflict. After the death of Doe, Taylor's main motive for continuing the war, the NPFL remained unyielding, despite concessions from ECOWAS and the Interim Government of National Unity.

ECOWAS and ECOMOG undoubtedly brought a measure of order and stability to Liberia, but a stronger intervening organization was needed to take the peace process to a higher plane. First, ECOWAS needed a wider mediating base, which would counter Taylor's mistrust of Nigerian domination. Second, it was necessary to build the capacity of ECOWAS to undertake the huge task of effective disarmament and demobilization. The United Nations provided that with its greater political involvement in the crisis after Operation Octopus. The resulting peace agreement in Cotonou in July 1993 provided for the expansion of ECOMOG to include troops from East Africa and the involvement of the United Nations at the operational level, in the form of peace observers and coordination with humanitarian agencies. The nature and magnitude of these activities, and the extent to which their implementation brought success, will be the focus of the following chapters.

Notes

1. The SMC was established under ECOWAS Decision A/DEC.9/5/90. Its members consisted of the Gambia (chair nation), Ghana, Mali, Nigeria, and Togo.
2. See Alan James, *Peacekeeping in International Politics*, London: Macmillan, 1990, p. 9.
3. See C. Y. Iweze, "Nigeria in Liberia: The Military Operations of ECOMOG," in M. A. Vogt and A. E. Ekoko (eds.), *Nigeria in International Peacekeeping 1960–1992*, Lagos and London: Malthouse Press, 1993, p. 220.
4. *Official Journal of ECOWAS*, vol. 21, 1992, p. 5.

5. Interviews with General Williams and with soldiers deployed to Liberia confirm that, in terms of equipment, number of men deployed, and the psychological preparedness of the troops, they were not preparing for battle.
6. On disarmament, the parties agreed that, although it was desirable to disarm immediately, the reality of the situation dictated that it should be done in a flexible manner, according to ECOMOG's appreciation of the security situation. However, a broad procedure was envisaged: the AFL was to assemble at the Barclay Training Centre and Camp Schiefflin in Monrovia; the INPFL was to remain at its Cadwell base in the capital; and the NPFL was to assemble in Firestone, Naama, Salata, Gbata, Gbanga, Zwedru, and Todi-Mesurado. There were to be ECOMOG reception centres at each of the assembly points which would register the troops and classify the sick and wounded. The rehabilitation exercise was to begin at these reception centres.
7. The word *encampment* was used throughout by peace planners and actors in the Liberian conflict. It has the same meaning as *cantonment*, which is more commonly used in other peace operations.
8. *Africa Research Bulletin*, 1–30 April 1991, p. 10072.
9. *Africa Research Bulletin*, 1–30 June 1991, p. 10176.
10. The Committee of Five consisted mainly of French-speaking West African members of ECOWAS. It was established as an adjunct to the SMC. It gave these countries a greater role in the peace process and, perhaps more than this, its establishment created an opportunity for the then Ivorian leader, Houphouët-Boigny, to persuade Taylor to accept the peace plan. The SMC and the Committee of Five would later merge to form the Committee of Nine.
11. *Official Journal of ECOWAS*, vol. 21, 1992, p. 47.
12. For a detailed account of how Doe was arrested, see Iweze, "Nigeria in Liberia," pp. 217–243.
13. This was after the former dictator, Babangida, nullified the June 1993 elections in Nigeria.
14. For more on ECOMOG Force Commanders, see Jinmi Adisa, "ECOMOG Force Commanders," in M. A. Vogt (ed.), *The Liberian Crisis and ECOMOG: A Bold Attempt at Regional Peacekeeping*, Lagos: Gabumo Publishing Press, 1992, pp. 237–270.
15. *Reuters*, 11 February 1997.
16. Ibid.
17. Interview with Professor Amos Sawyer.
18. Discussion with John Richardson, NPFL's representative in Monrovia, 25 and 29 June 1994.

PART II
The Cotonou Agreement

4
The Cotonou Agreement and the inherent obstacles to its success

As noted in the previous chapter, following Operation Octopus and ECOMOG's reprisals mediation continued on several levels – first of all among Liberia's neighbours, including Côte d'Ivoire and the francophone states with French involvement, internationally through the good offices of the United Nations, and regionally by the Standing Mediation Committee of ECOWAS, which organized several peace talks and encouraged the warring sides to meet independently. It was this process that led to the Cotonou Agreement. Signed in July 1993 by Amos Sawyer for the Interim Government of National Unity (IGNU), Charles Taylor for the National Patriotic Front of Liberia (NPFL), and Alhaji Kromah for the United Liberation Movement of Liberia for Democracy (ULIMO),[1] it was the most significant step in the efforts to stabilize the situation in Liberia. The Independent National Patriotic Front of Liberia (INPFL) was no longer involved in the struggle, having been neutralized by ECOMOG during Operation Octopus, and Prince Johnson taken to Nigeria and his followers dispersed. The 19 articles of the Cotonou Agreement covered cease-fire, disarmament, demobilization, elections, repatriation of refugees, a general amnesty, and the issues considered during previous meetings.

Prior to Cotonou, the Yamoussoukro IV Accord signed by the parties in 1991 had also been an important stage in the process towards a settlement. At that time, progress had been blocked by the NPFL's refusal to implement the terms, fearing ULIMO's hidden agenda and continuing to mistrust ECOMOG's Nigerian-dominated motives in Liberia. The NPFL occupied about two-thirds of Liberia, while ECOMOG controlled Monrovia, the capital, and its outskirts. Since 1991 however, a proliferation of guerrilla armies in Liberia had complicated the peace process. By 1993 the United Liberation Movement was established in the two counties on the border with Guinea. Politically, IGNU was effective only in Monrovia under the protection of ECOMOG, and Charles Taylor ruled an area that was beginning to take on the characteristics of an alternative state with its own capital (Gbarnga), police organization, embryo administration, and currency.

With these advantages and with some residual bitterness that the Nigerians had twice thwarted their bids to seize Monrovia, it was to be expected that the NPFL arrived at the peace talks with the aim of reducing the Nigerian domination of ECOMOG. For their part, the Nigerians, with the experience of other interpositional operations, could see that ECOMOG faced a no-win situation. It was not militarily strong enough to subjugate more than a fraction of greater Liberia and its future as a credible instrument of a peace process was now seriously compromised after months of hard fighting against the NPFL. A change of political status was needed from adversary to mediator. This was achieved by the intervention of the Organization of African Unity, which widened the political dimension of ECOMOG by arranging for troops from Uganda and Tanzania to be included. As a result, Taylor appeared to have won a major concession and IGNU, in the weakest bargaining position with its fortunes tied to ECOMOG, was forced to make a number of concessions to placate the NPFL. Although IGNU had proposed that the executive branch of government be made up of the presidency, to be held by nominees of the Interim Government, and two vice-presidents representing NPFL and ULIMO, the NPFL insisted on a five-member Council of State (COS), three of the members to be nominated by the three parties and two others to be selected from a list of nine nominees through a process of consultation.[2] IGNU's proposals to secure its authority during the interim process were not accepted. Perhaps ECOMOG was seeking an exit from the impasse and pressured Amos Sawyer to accommodate the NPFL proposals.

In the substance of the Cotonou Agreement,[3] the cease-fire article appears to be the most important: all subsequent articles relied on it for success. Under the agreement, the expanded ECOMOG and the United Nations Observer Mission in Liberia (UNOMIL) were to "supervise and monitor" its implementation (see appendix 5 for the UNOMIL Mandate). ECOWAS and the United Nations were also mandated to impose a military embargo on the warring factions and to create a buffer zone or otherwise seal Liberia's borders to prevent cross-border attacks and importation of arms. All sea and air ports of entry were also to be monitored. Violations of the cease-fire agreement included importation of arms and ammunition; attack against the position of any warring faction by another; and recruitment and training of combatants.

Disarmament, covered in Article 6, required each warring faction to list all weapons and ECOMOG was given the authority to disarm combatants and "non-combatants" and to conduct searches to recover lost or hidden weapons. The success of this plan relied on the full disclosure of men and weapons. The ultimate sanction was that ECOMOG could forcibly disarm the factions,[4] raising NPFL fears that ECOMOG might forcibly implement the Agreement and one day attack with a view to eliminating them from the Liberian equation. Cotonou also provided for general and presidential elections approximately seven months from the signing of the Agreement (in February/March 1994).[5] The Transitional Government would then disband and a democratically elected president and national assembly be sworn in to run Liberia. The Agreement also provided for the repatriation of all Liberians who had fled the country during the conflict to take part in the electoral process.

An important factor was the greater participation of the United Nations in the politics of peacekeeping in Liberia. Before the Agreement, the United Nations had limited its involvement in the Liberian crisis to the platitudinous condemnation of the war in the General Assembly or occasionally at the Security Council. With the Cotonou Agreement, the United Nations decided to become practically involved in the Liberian crisis. The United Nations Observer Mission in Liberia was established under Mr. Trevor Gordon-Somers, the Special Representative of the Secretary-General. A Chief Military Observer, Major General Daniel Opande, from Kenya, was later appointed for UNOMIL.

Cotonou marked a substantial departure from the Yamoussoukro process. ECOMOG's role was reduced to implementing the peace accord in close association with the United Nations' observer teams, which conferred a more convincing impartiality on its supervisory role (whereas the Yamoussoukro IV Accord had made ECOWAS solely responsible). The ECOMOG peacekeeping force was expanded and made theoretically less Nigerian in its constituency with the addition of units from other ECOWAS Member States and troops from outside the West African sub-region.[6] In order to monitor the cease-fire prior to the arrival of ECOMOG and the United Nations Observer Mission, a Joint Cease-fire Monitoring Committee was to be established, comprising representatives from the three parties, ECOMOG, and an advance team of the UN Observer Mission.[7] ECOMOG's absolute authority in its supervisory role was diminished by constant emphasis in the Agreement that all procedures of the peace process would be jointly observed and organized by UNOMIL.

This should have encouraged the NPFL to submit itself more readily to the conditions relating to disarmament and encampment. Although the parties were to hand over weapons to ECOMOG (in its expanded form), this process was now to be monitored and verified by UNOMIL in a way that went far beyond the Yamoussoukro IV Accord.[8]

The Cotonou Agreement was welcomed by all the sides in the Liberian conflict. The three warring sides saw it as a major step forward in the resolution of the conflict. The NPFL was particularly content to see that it incorporated the United Nations and reduced the authority of ECOMOG. IGNU, although losing some ground, still felt satisfied that concessions had been made to bring peace to the country.[9] Alhaji Kromah, on his part, must have considered his inclusion as a recognition of the role his new movement could play in the future of the country. In Monrovia, there was for a while an air of optimism generated by the successful conclusion of the Agreement. It was, however, a dangerous optimism that concealed unrequited political interests and seemed to bring on a myopia that encouraged some to ignore the possibility of the factions rekindling the terrible passions that long-standing rivalries would in due course unleash.

Obstacles to success

On the face of it, the Cotonou agenda of disarmament, demobilization, and elections seemed to address the principal afflictions of a very disordered state. However, after more than a decade of a brutal repressive dictatorship followed by three years of inter-communal violence, there were by now deep wounds in Liberian society that would take years to address and generations to heal completely. The institutions of the state had collapsed. Power had slipped from the grasp of central government into the hands of a proliferating number of warlords. The economy lay in ruins. The institutions that, rightly or wrongly, had held the state together in the past were now shattered and, on its own, their resuscitation would be a meaningless exercise. The Liberian identity had eroded and in its place a more impractical state structure had emerged without a corporate nationality and disposition to be governed. What were the principal elements of this new identity that would be key determinants in any durable peace solution?

Factions

Although the prospects for a peaceful settlement were improving in Liberia, the majority of territory and real power still lay in the hands of the factions. At the signing of the Cotonou Agreement in July 1993 the country was, broadly speaking, divided into three factional areas controlled, respectively, by the Armed Forces of Liberia (AFL) in close co-operation with ECOMOG, the United Liberation Movement of Liberia for Democracy (ULIMO), and the National Patriotic Front of Liberia (NPFL). In 1994 a fourth area was already beginning to develop within the NPFL territory under the emerging Liberian Peace Council (LPC), which considered itself beyond the authority and scope of the peace agreement. As the peace process took shape, factional structures began to erode and sub-divisions proliferated, in particular within ULIMO. Although an accurate assessment of their strength and location was required by UNOMIL, directly after the signing of the Cotonou Agreement, in order to organize the demobilization process, in Liberia no one, not even the factions themselves, possessed accurate information about their organization. The declared strengths (discussed later) were almost certainly misleading and errors were exacerbated by the ephemeral nature of factional sub-units. In UNOMIL, monthly fluctuations were expressed territorially on a small-scale map (see map 2). This was probably as reliable as any method of relative strength assessment. Although the territory held by each faction altered every month, in principle the mean average of these fluctuations confirmed and emphasized that beyond the urban fringes of Monrovia the Liberian countryside was not controlled by ECOMOG. For this reason, the good conduct and continued support of the factions were crucial to the success of the peace process.

Although in most cases the factions (with the exception of the LPC) were represented in the Transitional Government and legally might be expected to conform to the articles of the Cotonou Agreement, in reality beyond Monrovia they acted autonomously. Their behaviour was unpredictable and at every level faction leaders reacted more readily to immediate local pressures regardless of whether their actions might jeopardize the success of the peace process. There were several reasons for instability within the factions. Each faction included an array of differently composed sub-units in which there were wide disparities in age, experience, and motivation.

For example, during the early stages of the civil war, displaced youths, traditional hunters, and deserters from the Liberian defence forces all joined Charles Taylor in the NPFL, regardless of ethnic background. Some were professional army officers expensively trained in the United States, others were jungle dwellers without any education whose main contributions were their innate fieldcraft and survival skills. More than 6,000 child fighters joined the factions, many of them in order to survive the consequences of family separation.[10] Some of the children inter-

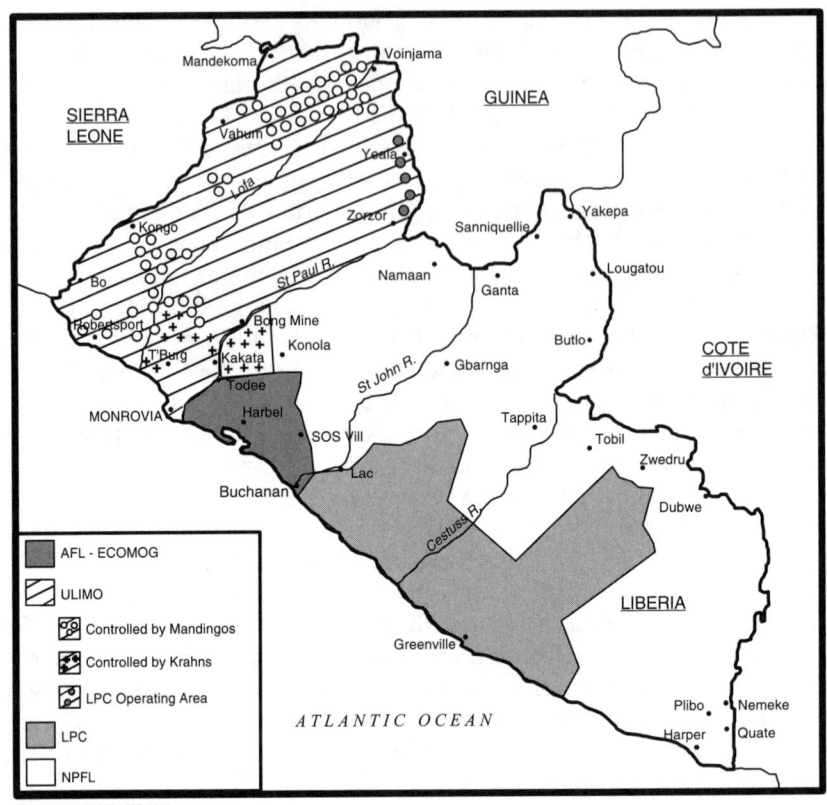

Map 2 **Areas controlled by factions, June 1994 (Source: UNOMIL HQ briefing, June 1994; graphics by JSCSC Mapping Department)**

viewed claimed to have carried automatic weapons from the age of 10. Fighters expected hardship, sleeping in the field and living hand to mouth for extended periods. Most did not receive a cash salary – their food and essential survival needs were "found" from local sources. Looting captured houses was seen as a legitimate reward for months, sometimes years, of extreme hardship.

Within a faction, smaller sub-units frequently formed, dispersed, and reformed in new configurations. As a consequence, command structures were largely ad hoc except for the key appointments. In common with many so-called terrorist "armies," the Liberian factions were made to seem much larger by the transient presence of local fighters whose status was decidedly part time. At the fighting edge, the abundance of "generals" and field-ranked officers did not signify their real command status. For example, in any faction, a gang of five to ten youths operating a road block might be commanded by a "colonel." At the highest level, principal commanders in factions varied in their motivation and education. Some from professional civilian backgrounds prior to the war were ideologically motivated and received military training abroad. On the whole, those in this category disassociated themselves from the routine looting and savagery committed against civilians. But others, less educated and more venally inclined, indulged their reputations for brutality, adopting ghoulish nick-names, wearing piratical dress, even using human remains as warning symbols at road blocks. Success and influence depended more on a commander's power in his own right as a dominating personality in the faction hierarchy than on his capabilities as a military leader. Consequently, in some cases well-trained and motivated officers were subordinated to the lawless and bizarre elements in a faction.

As a result of this fragility of command and the need to respond to local pressures, no faction could be regarded as consistent or as a reliable exponent of a coherent policy in its likely reaction to a given event. A faction leader's power and ability to control could be exercised only down as far as his most reliable field commanders. Beyond that limit, at a local level the gangs of youths who made up a field commander's "unit" responded unreliably to orders, perhaps because they were out of contact, but more likely because their immediate concern was focused on local issues and survival needs. As the overall threat to a faction decreased, as it did in some areas after Cotonou, cohesion reduced. Locally, gangs and individuals began to search for food, gainful employment, or opportunities for looting. Even in NPFL-held territory, where unit cohesion was better than in other factions, unofficial road blocks increased on the road to Gbarnga, despite Taylor's instructions that they should be removed; youths searched vehicles and demanded payments or favours for onward passage. Loss of control on this small scale had wider implications. As time passed, decisions to disarm and participate in the peace process had devolved downwards, out of the grasp of the faction leaders, to the autonomous gangs and individuals in the field who loosely comprised each faction. Although UNOMIL negotiators found widespread exhaustion in April/May 1994 and an eagerness to turn in weapons as part of the peace process, locally fears for individual security and the need to stay armed in a weapon-carrying environment proved stronger than the dictates of the Cotonou peace plan and in some cases even stronger than orders to disarm from faction leaders themselves.

Civil disruption

The degree to which civilian communities had disintegrated and moved from their original homes acted strongly against the chances of a successful peace settlement. By 1993, 700,000 Liberian refugees were living in the neighbouring states of Côte d'Ivoire, Ghana, Guinea, Nigeria, and Sierra Leone. These people had not settled and during the Cotonou "process" still planned to return as soon as security permitted, thereby introducing a sizeable factor of uncertainty into Liberia's demography in terms of the timing of their move and final destinations. As many as 150,000 threatened to start moving back before official repatriation began.[11]

Within Liberia itself, large numbers had fled from the immediate violence around their homes and regrouped in temporary camps, urban areas, and newly erected shelters in rural areas that they deemed to be safer. More than 500,000 were estimated to have moved from threatened villages in rural areas to the comparative security of Monrovia. The population of Monrovia was shown as having increased from 300,000 before the civil war to 900,000 in May 1994.[12] As the violence between the factions continued, the displacement of communities within Liberia increased, with dramatic numbers moving from county to county: 150,000 relocated in Upper Lofa, 40,000 in Grand Bassa, and 10,000 in Bong.[13] Since these figures became available in 1994, further displacement was anticipated. During the hardest months of the crisis in 1992, "nobody was starving" according UN relief officials.[14] Nevertheless, in April 1994, as many as 1.4 million were receiving humanitarian assistance of some kind, mostly in food supplements.[15]

The fracture lines of the civil upheaval ran through every echelon of society. In villages and communities, youths had left school and university to join factions. Families separated by the suddenness of the NPFL advance on Monrovia in October 1992 during Operation Octopus were still attempting to regroup themselves. The remains of old people left behind in the rush to flee were now being found as young survivors returned to their homes. Faction fighters who left their villages to seek survival or the opportunities of loot might not be received with much enthusiasm in the communities they abandoned. Many were known to have committed serious crimes; some would be regarded as having betrayed their families and communities by leaving them during the most hazardous stages of the civil war. Few were left unscarred by the civil war; for both the victims and the perpetrators, violence had a price to pay. Relief workers reported a "false normalcy" returning to urban areas, encouraged by shops, cinemas, bars, hotels, and public transport having resumed services. These outward signs encouraged an artificial sense of post-violence euphoria, but the real damage in terms of inter-communal animosity remained largely unaddressed. The psychological impact of the war remained, because people were waiting to take revenge.[16]

The extent to which the civilian elements of the population, who were not part of the factions, were still armed was hard to assess. A senior NPFL general maintained that in his area of responsibility weapons were retained in every village and these constituted a considerable reserve call-out capability in an emergency.[17] Weapons were not normally carried openly, but professional military staff interviewed in both UNOMIL and ECOMOG agreed that firearms continued to be important for individual survival. They were not kept as symbols; in particular instances when examined they were found to be in good working order, well maintained, and handled with a degree of assurance and skill. "It is my life; take this and I am dead," one young fighter said to us. Unarmed civilians became prey to armed youths in search of food and essential needs. Unprotected vehicles were hijacked, unprotected houses looted. In a lawless society, a group or community might organize collective protection for themselves, but after four years of civil war weapons had proliferated and become essential to individual survival.

A war-damaged economy

Although violence continued throughout the period of the Cotonou peace process, causing population displacement and civilian casualties, a key factor in Liberia's long-term transition towards a peace settlement would be its ability to resuscitate the economy. As the relief systems – provided to a large extent by UN agencies and non-governmental organizations – became more capable of coping with the emergency needs arising from day-to-day inter-factional conflict, a change of emphasis was needed towards rehabilitation and reconstruction. But a real shift away from hand-to-mouth survival techniques, which added to the instability, depended on the state's capacity to employ a population relocated after repatriation or freed from the need to fight for its survival. In these circumstances, humanitarian emergency measures had to take account of, and wherever possible be coordinated with, community development and long-term reconstruction.

Three-quarters of Liberia's economy was traditionally based. Despite efforts prior to the civil war to diversify the monetized balance of 25 per cent, Liberia's economy had relied narrowly on the export of crude iron ore, rubber, and timber. Rubber, with almost half of the land cultivated for its long-term production, had been the most important cash crop, generating the second-largest earnings after iron ore. Both were sensitive to falling prices in the world market. Foreign investment sustained 70 per cent of the rubber estates; foreign capital, management, and technical assistance would be needed to restart and maintain iron ore production.

Several major obstacles lay in the path of a successful restart. Most of Liberia's main money-making installations either had been lying idle or were severely damaged; substantial financial and technical resources would be needed to refurbish them. Besides the erosion and decay that was endemic to a tropical climate, the majority of the plant had been looted. Reports from UN observers, foreign technical assessments, and our own observations confirmed that systematic looting had reduced or in some cases completely removed Liberia's production capability, particularly from the iron ore mines and their related infrastructure. Plant, vehicles, generators, tools, copper cables, and even building materials had been systematically stripped from all principal installations in Monrovia. Port facilities at Buchanan, Robertsport, Greenville, and Harper were reported to have been looted. Liberia's international air terminal, Monrovia-Roberts, had been severely war damaged; the airport building and cargo-handling facilities lay gutted, and only its main runway was intact. Apart from random mining and some bridge damage, Liberia's rail lines were largely undamaged. Although this list is incomplete it serves to show that without massive foreign investment Liberia's economy and its infrastructure could not be restored or restarted.

Foreign investors were in no hurry to assist. Key installations, for example the Firestone rubber plantation and factory at Harbel and the iron ore port handling facilities at Buchanan, were still at the interface between factions during the Cotonou process. When we visited Firestone in June 1994, the plantation areas were occupied by military sub-units from ECOMOG, AFL, LPC, and NPFL. Parts of the plantation changed hands on a weekly basis, and, although the factory was in good condition, the collection of latex would first of all have required the re-establishment of a vehicle fleet, which had been removed by looters. Firestone managers would need to be guaranteed effective security before they could begin to exploit resources and operate cargo vehicles. In addition to the problems of securing an area in which to operate safely, foreign investors were also deterred by the Liberian political and social environment. "Fiscal indiscipline," inadequate legal protection, and over-bureaucracy combined to create an unattractive climate for investment.[18] Together with low expectations of any rescue plan, a debt of US$3.5 billion would be inherited by a newly formed national government. Without the security of a successful cease-fire and disarmament programme, this debt would be impossible to repay.

Notes

1. The witnesses to the agreement were President Soglo of Benin Republic, who was ECOWAS chairman, Dr. James Jonah, who represented the UN Secretary-General, and Professor Canaan Banana, who stood in for the OAU Secretary-General.

2. See Peace Talks on Liberia, Geneva, 10–17 July 1993, Draft Agreements [undated], cited in Marc Weller (ed.), *Regional Peace-keeping and International Enforcement*, Cambridge: Cambridge University Press, 1994; *British Broadcasting Corporation Summary of World Broadcasts Third Series ME\1744*, Part 4, Africa, Latin America, and the Caribbean, 19 July 1993, p. ii.
3. The full Agreement is in Appendix 4.
4. See Article 7.
5. Article 16 (3).
6. Article 3 (2). However, Article 3 (1) stressed the fact that the parties recognized the neutrality of ECOMOG, but this was a reference to the reconstituted ECOMOG in para. 3 (2).
7. Article 3 (3).
8. Articles 6 (1–7) and 7 (1–3).
9. Discussion with Professor Amos Sawyer.
10. UN Document S/1994/463, dated 18 April 1994, *Third Progress Report of the Secretary-General on the United Nations Observer Mission in Liberia*, para. 27.
11. Ibid., p. 39.
12. UNICEF, *An Orientation Guide to Liberia*, 1994, p. 9.
13. S/1994/463, paras. 31–39.
14. Hiram Ruiz, *Uprooted Liberians: Casualties of a Brutal War*, Washington, D.C.: US Committee for Refugees, 1992.
15. S/1994/463, p. 31.
16. Ruiz, *Uprooted Liberians*, p. 11.
17. NPFL Commander of South Eastern Districts interviewed at Gbarnga, 29 June 1994.
18. UNDP 1994 Draft Programme, *Liberia: Rehabilitation, Reconstruction and Long-term Development*, p. 6.

5
Why Cotonou failed

Between the effective date of the Cotonou Agreement and the proposed programme for the completion of elections in September 1994, several progressive stages of restoration had to be successfully completed. These actions were linked, so that the success of one led to another (see fig. 5.1). For example, the return of refugees and displaced people required the establishment of a workable degree of individual security and freedom of movement in the areas concerned. But workable levels of security relied first of all on a successful disarmament that actually diminished the power of the factions and sub-factions, and ultimately removed it, preventing autonomous gangs from extorting a living from those who attempted to follow more lawful and productive lifestyles. Disarmament on such a scale needed the prospect of viable rehabilitation. The disarmed fighter had to have alternative means of survival – a job, a house, and a social structure to which he could return or at least the realistic expectation of developing one. Jobs and houses relied on a resuscitated economy, but would-be investors needed the guarantee of a workable level of security as a sine qua non for any kind of rescue plan.

The stages in the peace process could not succeed in isolation. Furthermore, in every case they involved the support of all the Liberian parties involved, whether the Transitional Government, the factions, or the traditionally organized elements of the civil population, as well as an effective leadership to coordinate their efforts. When the Cotonou Agreement was signed there was widespread exhaustion and a disincli-

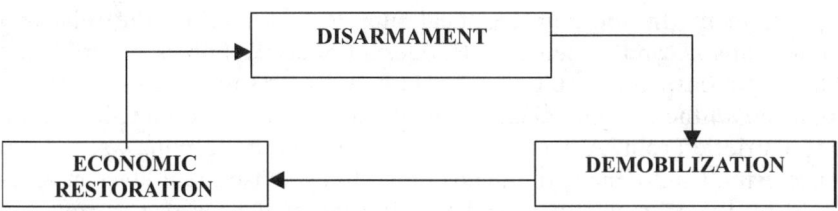

Fig. 5.1 **The link between disarmament and economic restoration**

nation among fighters to go on living indefinitely like wild animals in the fringes of the countryside. But there were many reasons why the provisions of the Agreement might be ignored by Liberian communities, especially those living far beyond the protection and influence of the forces that were promising peace. The peace process needed to be energized by outside forces, that is the United Nations, regional forces, and non-governmental organizations (NGOs). Progressing from "cease-fire" to "elections" also required a degree of coordination between these external players, first to agree the prioritization of immediate tasks and secondly to elicit the assistance of the right combination of aid and restructuring organizations essential to a particular element of the process. The central question in this chapter is whether the endemic Liberian problems, discussed in chapter 4, were so overwhelming that any peace process would have failed. Or were the conditions in Liberia just viable for a successful peace process and it was the ineffectiveness of ECOMOG, UNOMIL, and the intervening relief agencies that failed to deliver the momentum and energy for the peace plan to succeed. Was Cotonou after all just a stage in a larger process or a viable peace process in itself?

Fundamental flaws in the Agreement

The Cotonou formula (disarmament–resettlement–elections) was derived from previous inter-communal conflict resolution attempts, its prototype being the Zimbabwe (Rhodesia) Independence Agreement of December 1979.[1] In essence, the concept was to freeze hostilities by a cease-fire, reduce the capability of the factions to continue fighting by regrouping them into cantonment sites, impose arms embargoes, resettle the displaced elements of the population, and, in the relative calm achieved by these measures, conduct an election. The Zimbabwe/Rhodesia example relied on a risky and experimental programme of cantonization and disarmament, which succeeded because contiguous regional powers, exhausted by years of insurgency, pressured their client factions towards a settlement. In addition, logistical support provided by the relatively more capable and undefeated Rhodesian Security Forces ensured that the Commonwealth monitors, whose job it was to supervise these events, reached *all* the designated cantonment sites *in time* to receive the incoming Patriotic Front. A decade later in Cambodia the formula was far less successful. Cantonment site teams failed to establish themselves in areas held by the Khmer Rouge and the disarmament process was reversed when that faction failed to disarm and others re-armed to protect themselves in an atmosphere of mutual distrust. For different reasons the formula also failed in Angola, and the full extent of disarmament is still a source of discussion in the context of Mozambique. Nevertheless Cotonou followed this procedure. Running in parallel were plans to organize the election and restore displaced elements of the civilian population to their original villages and communities. Although conceptually this arrangement had the appearance of a workable peace process, in practice it turned out to be fundamentally flawed.

During the period between the start of the agreed cease-fire regulations and the successful conclusion of the elections, the essential elements of an interim administration were to be provided by the Liberia National Transitional Government (LNTG). Its authority was to extend throughout the territorial limits of Liberia. This body was a successor to the previous Interim Government of National Unity, described above. Although it now represented elements of all the parties to the dispute, the LNTG's ability to extend its authority beyond Monrovia was in reality extremely limited. Despite its newly acquired inclusive composition, the LNTG's authority in real terms had not been increased and, as before, the administration's reach and authority relied entirely on the supervisory presence of ECOMOG.

In view of the Monrovian administration's lack of effectiveness and limited reach, a more universally competent authority would be required to coordinate the separate but related modalities of the peace process. Although Cotonou did not explicitly confer this coordinating role on UNOMIL's Special Representative of the Secretary-General (SRSG), Mr. Trevor Gordon-Somers, it was assumed by many, de facto, to be the case. Liberian officials felt that the SRSG would "ensure that each group played its role in co-ordination and collaboration with one another in accordance with the provisions of the Agreement."[2] UN staff documents also reflected a political/military coordinating role for the SRSG within the UN structure (see fig. 5.2). Under previous arrangements, coordination had relied on the personality of Ross Mountain, the United Nations' resident representative in the preceding structure known as the United Nations Special Coordinating Office for Liberia.

However, compared with similarly appointed interim authorities, for

Fig. 5.2 **UNOMIL organization** (Source: "UNOMIL Standing Operating Procedures," [1993], Part 2, Section 3, Annex A)

example Lord Soames in the Zimbabwe/Rhodesia settlement or Mr. Akashi in Cambodia, Mr. Gordon-Somers held a much less powerful executive position that reflected the unique constituency of UNOMIL and its relationship with the other factions in the peace process. Unlike his predecessors, in the event of UNOMIL's role being challenged or his officers becoming exposed to danger, Gordon-Somers would have to rely on the military support of ECOMOG, a force palpably not under his control or even within his influence. At the crucial point of interface with the ECOMOG Field Commander (see fig. 5.3), Gordon-Somers' precedence was unclear; what was certain was that the ECOMOG Field Commander held final authority over his own force and could decide on a case-by-case basis whether he wished to protect UNOMIL. Many Liberians saw UNOMIL as subordinated to ECOMOG. For them the signs were visible in day-to-day events on the street. They saw UNOMIL vehicles stopped and searched at ECOMOG road blocks. UNOMIL was also required to observe the curfew times, and influential Liberians asked how UNOMIL could be "verifying" their activities when ECOMOG was free to act without witnesses, for example during the hours of darkness.

By its explicit failure to address this question of ECOMOG and UNOMIL's mutual security modalities, the Cotonou plan separated the coordinating element of the peace process (which de facto was to fall into the lap of the United Nations) from responsibility for security and civil order, which rested with ECOMOG. The Field Commander was to "create zones or otherwise seal the borders ... to prevent cross-border attacks, infiltration or importation of arms."[3] Although in the text of the Agreement the functions of coordination and security seemed to be dovetailed together, in reality they were not. Moreover, when compliance

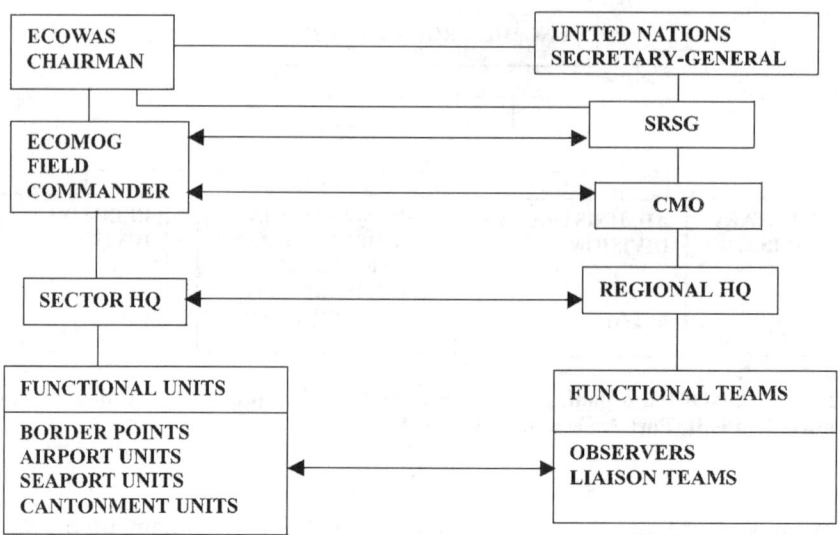

Fig. 5.3 **Reporting relationship of UNOMIL and ECOMOG (Source: "UNOMIL Standing Operating Procedures," [1993], Part 2, Section 3, Annex H)**

with the provisions of the Agreement was threatened, ECOMOG's peace enforcement powers included the right to self-defence and the "obligation to ensure the security of UNOMIL observers and other UN staff present in the area."[4] Implicitly the SRSG assumed the role of overall peace process coordinator, and explicitly his authority and security were underpinned by ECOMOG, but nowhere did the Agreement explain how this could work. Who should decide when, where, and, above all, how ECOMOG was to support the UNOMIL teams? There were foreseeable difficulties in these arrangements. At crucial moments the SRSG might not be able to influence ECOMOG to come to his rescue; in any case ECOMOG's writ and presence did not extend beyond Monrovia. The apparent clarity of the Agreement and the continually emphasized relationship between ECOMOG and UNOMIL whereby ECOMOG's specified activities were "to be monitored and verified by the United Nations observers" concealed problems of command and the reliability of the ECOMOG/UNOMIL linkage. These manifested themselves later when UNOMIL teams were seized in Tubmanburg and Gbarnga and held by the warring factions. In particular, it was not specified under what procedures and precisely how ECOMOG troops could come to UNOMIL's assistance; there were also areas in which the United Nations was operating without ECOMOG's protective cover. In a newspaper interview in February 1994, Arthur Dennis of the LNTG implied that this contingency would not arise because they would deploy "always in concert."[5] In reality, by the time he gave the interview UN observers had already deployed without ECOMOG cover.

Although the Schedule of Implementation (Article 12) allowed a degree of flexibility in setting the timing of the various stages of the peace process, this provision was to some extent disarmed by Article 16. It stated that the "transitional Government shall have a life span of approximately six months commencing from the date of its installation" and that elections "shall take place approximately seven months from the signature of this Agreement." The vagueness of the word "approximately" contrasts with the finite period implied by time limits set in the article. Both injunctions relied on unanimous interpretation by the factions and a best-case-scenario outcome with regard to the administrative arrangements prior to the election. If these failed to meet the seven-month deadline or the parties failed to agree on the implications of the word "approximately," there was no obvious fall-back position.

In his interview on 4 February 1994 Arthur Dennis was alert to the lack of any provision in the Agreement for the organization of a "new national army in Liberia." He asserted that, regardless of its omission from both the Cotonou Agreement and the text of S/RES/866, which spelled out UNOMIL's mandate,[6] this requirement was reflected in UNOMIL's tasks during the preceding negotiations. Moreover, during the Geneva peace talks in July 1993, a list was circulated to the conference that included the need "to monitor and verify the formation of a new model army."[7] In its translation to the Cotonou text however, the item from the Geneva version seems to have been forsaken in favour of the list of UNOMIL tasks published in S/RES/866. Neither its Standing Operating Procedures (SOPs) nor the United Nations' official brief reflect a role for UNOMIL in the formation of a new army in Liberia.

The procedures for elections were not covered with much rigour. Article 15 leaves it to the LNTG and the Elections Commission to "work out the modalities for the participation of observers and monitors" and confirms that the parties have agreed that the elections should conform to accepted codes of conduct. No solution was given for the related problems of population displacement, voter registration, and the provision of an electoral law to define the rules of the contest and the nature of its constituent voting districts. Although a successfully held election was central to the peace process, its organization and control had been delegated to a semi-autonomous Elections Commission. It was unclear how this untried, ad hoc body would relate to, or become part of, the overall structure of agencies and military units that would have to provide security, logistical support, and all the communications needed to promulgate its proposed election plans.

It is a characteristic of inter-communal peace negotiations that the politicians and actors who facilitate the successful signing of a peace agreement in the short term often exercise a degree of myopic optimism over detail lest the discussion become interminably bogged down in practicalities. Even the exhaustively negotiated Paris Agreements for the Cambodian peace process were fatally reliant on a best-case-scenario outcome on matters of disarmament. In the Cotonou Agreement, with a wave of the negotiators' "magic wand," factions would become disarmed, displaced populations resettled, voters registered, and elections held. Such optimism had to be underpinned by a strong and flexible interim authority. In the event of delay and opposition, the process had to survive the less carefully negotiated parts of the process and, where necessary, circumnavigate and redesign them to keep up the momentum. The structure of the relationship between ECOMOG and UNOMIL was too fragile to provide for a strong and flexible interim authority; there were, however, plenty of other reasons why a best-case-scenario might not be expected.

Disarmament

In the past, negotiators of inter-communal conflict have set great store on "disarming". In the planning process it has been the key to success, but in the epilogue it is often the principal reason for failure. Despite the enthusiasm of third-party negotiators to disarm the parties involved, few inter-communal conflicts have experienced verifiably successful disarmament. Even in peace processes where the final outcome has been apparently "successful," subsequent investigation has shown that the most powerful factions cheated on the process, reserving a military capability until the outcome was clear.[8] For several reasons it is now questionable whether the instinctive urge to have warring factions disarmed as soon as possible is not counter-productive to the overall effort to establish conditions for a lasting peace process. No territory, or its population, that has been used as a war zone for several years can expect to be completely disarmed. There will be too many residual weapons caches to monitor, and consequently it will be impossible to guarantee that factions could not swiftly re-arm when the need arises. Nor can disarmament be conducted in isolation. First there must be convincing reasons to disarm and an environment in which weapons become redundant, rusty, and unserviceable impediments to the more important problems of finding shelter and gainful employment. This is likely to happen only when individual security can be assured by a higher authority or regime in which individuals do not have to fend for themselves. It is in a collapsed state that a supergang or military force, which is superior to the sum of all the parties in the immediate area, possibly nationwide, can establish itself. In some cases the regime that provides this condition may not be democratically elected, and may even behave in a brutal and unjust manner. The question that the designers and negotiators of a peace process have to decide is whether it is easier to bring a despotic regime into a peace process than the array of sub-factions and local gangs spawned by a partially successful disarmament process that has robbed the district of its supergang, which previously guaranteed individual security.

In Liberia there was no convincing supergang or pervasive nationwide military force. Only the factions acting within their own areas could exercise this stabilizing condition locally. In Gbarnga, for example, the NPFL had established the embryo of an alternative state within Liberia. Gbarnga began to take on the functions of a capital, with Taylor's staff and HQ compound assuming a presidential character. Livestock presented by regional heads of state grazed on the lawn and a "presidential" guard supervised security around the HQ. In Gbarnga town, goods were traded for the NPFL's own currency and, considering the circumstances, there were reasonable arrangements for policing, security of vital installations, a civil radio station, and a hospital. However, by the summer of 1994 the lessening or removal of the threat to the NPFL's survival also diminished Taylor's control. For all the faction leaders, the prospect of being able to regulate the possession and carriage of weapons even within their own areas was fast decreasing, as the result of eroding coherence, sub-divisions, and intra-factional rivalry. Individually, the unpaid faction fighter still needed his personal weapon. Without it he could not obtain the necessities for his own survival, and should he manage to scrape an honest living from the land he became vulnerable to those who were still armed.

In the Liberian context it might have been useful to learn from the Cambodian and Angolan failures. It may be more realistic to accept that, without the interim presence of an effective third-party military force or even, in the worst-case scenario, a supergang to ensure individual security, disarmament is not a viable concept at national level. Individual security may be possible only under the aegis of each faction. This must lead to the unusual view that, instead of negotiating to weaken the factions by disarmament, stability may be improved in the short term by encouraging factions to be stronger and more centrally controlled. Rather than attempting to disarm in isolation, it is probably more fruitful to create an environment in which weapons become increasingly less important to individual survival. In the case of Liberia, this meant improving other conditions that were linked to security, the economy, and reconciliation, and at the same time increasing the tempo of political exchanges between faction leaders rather than relying on their proxy representatives in the LNTG.

Although the details of the overall security under which demobilization could operate seemed unresolved, the plan itself was well conceived. In particular there were well-developed arrangements to provide for the rehabilitation and personal needs of each fighter, which in many ways were considerably more advanced than previous disarmament programmes by UN and regional forces. The rehabilitation plan recognized the psychological dislocation of young Liberians who had left school to train and be indoctrinated as faction fighters. It also took account of the resentment and hostility that they would experience on their return to their original communities. In many cases the communities themselves had been uprooted and dispersed so that reorganization became impossible. In a sense, the civil war set off a social revolution in Liberia that destroyed many of the traditional structures of tribe and community without providing a workable alternative.

The unsettled bands of young men who roamed the roads and villages in Monrovia and in the NPFL areas as a consequence exerted a destabilizing influence. There were also the problems of revenge taking. To address these obstacles, UN programmes and national organizations were given the task of reintegrating the demobilized ex-combatants. Teams visited villages and communities in anticipation of the arrival of the returnees, explaining the problems of reconciliation and attempting to purge the residual inclination for violence and revenge.[9]

Owing to the lack of Liberia-wide security and the failure of ECOMOG companies to reach all their agreed locations, disarmament and demobilization sites were not opened in all of the areas originally proposed. On arrival at an established site, fighters received clothing, rations, digging tools, and transport to a community of their choice. After an initial flow of personnel and weapons from each faction (except for the LPC), disarmament had come to a standstill by June 1994 apart from a small trickle of variously motivated fighters heading for Monrovia. The lack of accurate information about the factions, or their disregard for truthful declaration, is demonstrated by the huge disparities between the estimated figures for disarming personnel, weapons, and ammunition and the actual figures (see table 5.1).

The disarmament process on which so many other mechanisms of the peace process relied never seemed likely to succeed at any stage. The figures shown in table 5.1 convey the extent to which the aspirations of the process failed to match reality. Power had not been transferred from the hands of the factions to a newly convened pan-Liberian authority. It has not been possible to investigate conclusively the reasons for the failure of the process. Those who did demobilize seemed to have planned for

Table 5.1 **Disarmament statistics, 22 June 1994**

Faction	Personnel		Weapons		Ammunition	
	Estimated	Actually handed over	Estimated	Actually handed over	Estimated	Actually handed over
AFL	8,037	755	1,921	1,078	85,413	151,062
NPFL	35,000	741	3,500	562	–	1,284
ULIMO	10,500	769	3,520	378	–	78,096

Source: data supplied by UNOMIL office in Liberia.

the next stage of their life and had aspirations for employment or resettlement. The corollary may be that the majority did not have such prospects, and it was more secure for them to remain in the factions. It is not clear to what extent the failure to provide for a "new national army" in the Liberian reconstruction plans added to the fear that demobilizing the factions would lead to greater anarchy. Taylor himself voiced this anxiety,[10] but it is doubtful whether at grassroots level the perception of a security vacuum would in itself have deterred young men from coming forward.

ECOMOG

Since its initial deployment in August 1990, ECOMOG performed many different roles and its strength and deployment altered accordingly. In summer 1994, when the Cotonou-related study took place, ECOMOG troops could be seen as peacekeepers; they moved in small infantry groups, with arms slung on the shoulder and not "at the ready" in a manner that signals aggression. But many remember them in a more offensive mode when they advanced, supported by tanks and light howitzers, along the roads leading out of Monrovia. During Operation Thunderbolt in April 1993, ECOMOG troops fought their way towards Buchanan, their fire power boosted by Guinean 122 mm multi-barrelled rocket launchers and naval gunfire from Nigerian warships standing offshore. Ground attack aircraft were also used to attack Gbarnga. After Cotonou, the force reorganized into three groups: a Ground Task Force for the security of Monrovia, 15 ECOMOG Brigade on the Gbarnga axis, and 7 ECOMOG Brigade on the Buchanan axis. Although close-support artillery and light tanks were still present in 1994, they were less evident in Monrovia, where urban security was the primary role. Naval patrols

Table 5.2 **ECOMOG strength, in June 1994**

Serial	Contingent	Officers	Soldiers	Total
1	GAMCON	1	9	10
2	GHANCON	73	1,048	1,121
3	GUCON	140	440	580
4	LEOCON	16	348	364
5	MALICON	3	7	10
6	NIGCON	442	7,489	7,931
7	TANCON	41	733	774
8	UGACON	53	731	784
	Total	769	10,805	11,574

Source: ECOMOG Headquarters, Monrovia, June 1994.

continued to monitor traffic in and out of Liberia and there were occasional incidents when boats attempted to run the blockade.

In its post-Cotonou manifestation, ECOMOG was acting in a policing role and in some cases seemed more alert to the long-term consequences of losing local support. Its narrowly Nigerian-dominated West African composition could be shown to have been diluted by the addition of Tanzanian and Ugandan battalions and a large contingent of Ghanaians. However these alterations were to some extent cosmetic. Strength returns still showed a Nigerian domination of the force (see table 5.2), not only in terms of numbers (approximately 8,000 Nigerians out of a total of 11,500 troops) but also in the key appointments. As a result, much depended on the personal qualities and approach of the Force Commander. Without an ambassadorial presence to give political guidance or lead in the constant round of negotiations, professionally he was a lonely figure. Ostensibly he received his instructions from the distant ECOWAS HQ in Lagos whence the Executive Secretary General might issue instructions, but this rarely happened. More frequently directions came from the Chiefs of Staff conference that was held in the contributing nations' capitals on a rotational basis each month. In reality, however, the Force Commander himself had the most direct influence on the conduct of ECOMOG, and in 1994 there was no micro management from distant national HQs. The Force Commander received vaguely worded political directives and translated them into action on the ground.

For some, ECOMOG is part of Liberia's problem and for others it is the solution. Judged by NATO standards it had serious weaknesses as a military force and, according to the criteria set by Cotonou, had not delivered its agreed targets to deploy Liberia wide. ECOMOG barely controlled a third of the country, its troops occupied weakly constructed positions along the main highways, and there was no presence in depth between posts. Poor logistic supply, poor living conditions, poor motor transport, poor communications, intermittent pay and personal mail, and a high incidence of malaria were sources of discontent among units in the field. But over and above the problems of troops in the field, a potential source of unhappiness in most armies was the more fundamental problem of ECOMOG's impartial status. It was expecting a great deal for the negotiators of Cotonou to imagine that ECOMOG, after two years of unrestrained combat against the NPFL, could, by including an additional two battalions from East Africa, somehow have assumed an impartial status in Liberia. Cotonou came too soon after the fighting around Monrovia; it was impossible to restore mutual trust between the NPFL and ECOMOG, particularly for the Nigerian staff officers, who still regarded their former adversary with some caution.

Although the tension was principally between the NPFL and the Nigerian elements of ECOMOG, general disquiet about Nigerian activities in Liberia was also increasing. Liberians had always regarded Nigerians with a degree of caution (which softened, only for a moment, for Nigeria's success during the 1994 Soccer World Cup). This caution had been exacerbated by the behaviour of Nigerian troops in Monrovia. The NPFL alleged sizeable arms and ammunition sales by individual Nigerians to factions. There were also wider allegations of systematic looting of Liberian installations involving the removal of very large amounts of equipment that would have required the use of sea transport and therefore connivance at a senior level. Finally there were allegations of Nigerian support for the LPC faction, allegations that were made not only by the NPFL, which could be expected to make them, but also by UN officials and reliable correspondents. The seriousness of these allegations for the future of ECOMOG in Liberia was not so much that they might or might not be true, but that a growing body of Liberians and international civil servants *believed* they were true. This growing lack of faith in Nigeria's motives would in due course become a disabling factor in the search for peace.

On the other hand, many Liberians continued to see ECOMOG as a solution and argued that Nigerian domination was the price of effective intervention. Nigeria was the strongest military power in West Africa and the Organization of African Unity (OAU). It supplied the majority of fighting and logistical assets because no other OAU country was able or willing to do more. Its domination of ECOMOG was to be expected and the pervasive presence of Nigerian staff officers was essential if the ships and aircraft under command were largely Nigerian. The same principle dictated the command structure of the coalition forces in Desert Storm, which were dominated and controlled by the United States. Many Liberians were saved by the arrival of ECOMOG in Monrovia and its subsequent operations to arrest the NPFL advance on the capital in 1992. In 1994, relief operations continued and a workable level of security prevailed in the areas held by ECOMOG, but it did not extend with any assurance into areas held by the factions. Although a poor military force judged by NATO standards, ECOMOG had been militarily quite successful in Liberia, demonstrating that in unrestrained conflict it was superior to the sum of the factions deployed against it. This had been a significant factor in the development of the Yamoussoukro and Cotonou peace processes. Monrovians are only half joking when they say that UN observers in their expensive vehicles came as tourists to their country and that it was in fact ECOMOG that had to tackle the problems of the city. It was true that, post Cotonou, ECOMOG failed to deploy to its agreed areas, but with only 11,000 troops this task would have been extremely difficult in a best-case scenario and impossible against local opposition. The problems of alleged corruption and clandestine support were less easy to ignore. Even if the allegations were untrue, they nevertheless eroded, and would in due course destroy, Liberian confidence in a Nigerian-dominated solution; if they were true, they had a much wider implication for the credibility of any future Nigerian-led response to the region's growing list of impending disasters.

UN coordination

Although the SRSG's office may have seen itself as the coordinating instrument between the various agencies of the United Nations, possibly extending to the NGO community, there was no evidence of an overarching plan published by the SRSG's office that focused the disparate elements of the relief community within Liberia towards the achievement of an overall long-term strategy. In view of the six- to seven-month transition period between the signing of the Cotonou Agreement and the elections, the time to achieve the necessary conditions for successful disarmament, rehabilitation, and resettlement and to conduct an election was impossibly short, and the manifest impatience of the Security Council took no account of the slow-moving pace of events in Liberia. To be effective, any plan had to be agreed and promulgated directly after Cotonou, not in mid-summer when the transition period was almost over.

Among officials in the United Nations' HQ at Mamba Point in Monrovia, there was an awareness of the scope of the problem as well as of the political difficulties of achieving a coordinated response. After Cotonou, Liberia needed to move out of its hand-to-mouth emergency response phase towards recovery mode. It was true that civil violence continued and there was still a requirement for humanitarian relief efforts to cope with the victims of dislocation and inter-communal fighting. Nevertheless, response mechanisms had become more orderly and systematic. Between the bouts of intense violence, traffic returned to the streets, goods were displayed for sale, and business entrepreneurs began to return from overseas in an opportunistic manner. These locally encouraging, although superficial, developments and the imperatives of the peace process itself dictated the need for a "recovery plan" as opposed to ad hoc, independently managed progressions in each of the strands of relief activity that contributed to overall recovery. Although funding from international resources was assured (for example after the 21 June 1994 meeting at Abidjan), it seemed to rely on unfounded assumptions about Liberia's ability to organize its own recovery. In practical terms a plan was needed; it had to integrate funding efforts and regional and corporate interests at a strategic level with tasks at an operational level; in particular, it had to achieve a marriage of interests between the relief providers and the political and military imperatives of the peace process. In several areas, coordination failed.

The coordination of security for disarmament and related humanitarian/reconstruction efforts was essential to success. In a recent conflict zone such as Liberia it was important for the UN installations and the staff who operated them to be protected. Although ECOMOG had ostensibly agreed to do this for the demobilization process, it was possible to deduce from their lack of enthusiasm for extending their deployment directly post Cotonou that ECOMOG units would not spread out Liberia wide (see map 3), in step with the plan for demobilization and elections. It is not clear to what extent a new UNOMIL demobilization plan was developed in view of this consideration, or whether UN security planning became a reactive, damage-control process that took place on a day-to-day basis. Each disarmament and demobilization site was supposed to be protected by an infantry company, complete with personal weapons, provided by ECOMOG; in reality some sites never received this protection (see map 4). Although in locations where ECOMOG sub-units were deployed their presence was reassuring, when armed factions interfered with the sites and with the staff responsible for the peace process, which they did in June and September 1994, ECOMOG infantry failed to protect them. The arrangements between UNOMIL and ECOMOG provided only for "consultation" and "reporting procedures." UNOMIL documents acknowledged that the line of command would be separate, which invited doubts about who could call out ECOMOG to launch an effective rescue. On paper, the disarmament plans seemed to be well conceived and the supporting rationale for rehabilitation and reconciliation programmes better thought out than in the past. They failed because the environment for disarmament and rehabilitation was not sufficiently

Map 3 **ECOMOG deployment, June 1994 (Source: UNOMIL HQ briefing, June 1994; graphics by JSCSC Mapping Department)**

established. In some communities, locally arranged "food for work" programmes were successful, but these were isolated and failed to spread into an area-wide trend that could have fuelled a wider desire to disarm. Perhaps with better funding and a more intrusive mandate it might have been possible to connect these nascent attempts to achieve local stability towards longer-term economic resuscitation and disarmament. In the event, lack of coordination between relief providers and political elements of the intervening agencies may have contributed to the gridlock from which it was impossible to generate a convincing climate and momentum for disarmament.

The political negotiators who envisaged a continuum of peace-restoring activities from Cotonou to the proposed September 1994 elections also assumed as much about the executive capabilities of the LNTG

Map 4 **UNOMIL deployment, June 1994 (Source: UNOMIL HQ briefing, June 1994; graphics by JSCSC Mapping Department)**

as about the forces of harmonious cooperation among the relief and reconstruction agencies. As early as May 1994, UN officials could identify serious obstacles to an autumn election. Between 700,000 and 1.2 million Liberians were still displaced and there were no practical methods to enable them to register or vote in foreign countries where they resided in camps. Nor was it possible to assume that the population remaining in Liberia was still located in its correct constituencies. National records had been destroyed, the 1985 electoral boundaries were invalid, and there was no way of assessing who was eligible to vote. Even the electoral system itself and the principles of representation to be adopted remain unresolved; Liberians, it was felt by some, would vote for candidates not for parties, but the electoral concept that was emerging did not seem to address this likelihood. Professional UN staff in the UN offices at Mamba

Point in Monrovia felt that the ad hoc Liberian Elections Commission had neither the expertise nor the executive energy to tackle these problems by September 1994, and to be fair it would have needed superhuman organizational skills to succeed in these circumstances. The question was whether these problems could have been resolved by identifying and tackling them at an earlier stage in the Cotonou–elections continuum.

The weakness of the interim government also had an impact on the prospects for economic recovery. Humanitarian relief and long-term restoration were controlled by third-party agencies. Any plan that successfully moved Liberia towards recovery would have to harness the array of third-party resources and organizations to an overall strategy. In spring 1994, relief activity, although apparently achieving the telegenic qualities and sense of immediacy needed for donor titillation, was acting against Liberian interests for long-term recovery. Short-term emergency relief distribution of dry rations was discouraging the development of more ambitious plans to return to subsistence agriculture. A coordinated strategy was needed to wean the displaced element away from short-term expedients and to push for an overall resettlement campaign that gradually transferred them from one system to another. Emergency aid was generating a dependency on systems and programmes that were too sophisticated and could not be sustained once a Liberian administration took them over. Although UN officials at the highest level saw the need for a plan that integrated the functions of UN agencies, bilateral relief organizations, and local and international NGOs, they were unable to provide the necessary direction or coordination. The pressure of events after Cotonou, their own lack of authority over the more independent-minded elements, and their inability to step back from day-to-day pressures to take a more long-term view all combined to prevent the United Nations from assuming this role. In the eventual circumstances of the collapse of the Cotonou peace process it is probably true to say that even in the most propitious planning circumstances this initiative would have been unsuccessful because of the overwhelming nature of the "Liberian factor." The endemic problems that lay beyond the control of any intervention were not ready to be resolved; perhaps Cotonou is after all just a chapter on a much longer path to recovery.

Lessons of Cotonou

The lessons of Liberia's failure to achieve a peace process are universally relevant, above all for future complex emergencies, and especially for those that comprise the same mix of civil violence, collapsed government infrastructures, and humanitarian disaster on a wide scale. Although

Liberia received scant attention in comparison with Rwanda, Somalia, and the former Yugoslavia, the elements of all these emergencies are similar. In Liberia's case, instead of third-party intervention by UN forces, intervention was provided by a sub-regional force. Commentators have so far failed to make the comparison that in its relative strength, role, and mandate ECOMOG has similarities to UN forces in Bosnia, Somalia, and Rwanda. Although Cotonou has become just another chapter in the Liberian peace process, the lessons have a wider significance both for the United Nations at large and for future pan-African disaster response.

The lack of a strong executive capability in the field

In Liberia, as in other recent UN peace supervisory experiences in Bosnia and Somalia, the reaction and support of the warring factions in the crisis area were crucial to the outcome of the peace process. In this case, a successful peace process would have acted against the interests of the warlords, who were certain to lose their individual power and status as a consequence of a state-wide election that restored a monopoly of power to state level. The consent of the warring factions was therefore not an anticipated factor in the recovery process. At the same time, the international community had turned its back on Liberia as far as offering the military protection that would be needed in an environment where local consent was unreliable. The forces in ECOMOG lacked a nucleus of effective military capability that is normally provided by more powerful nations, which in this case had failed to support the peace process except through the NGOs. This meant that the activities of all the response agencies in the crisis would take place in the grey zone between peace-keeping and peace enforcement. They would always be operating from positions of weakness, a prey to the day-to-day caprice of the factions.

Despite the uncertain and dangerous conditions, the Liberian process had adopted a calendar for actions that had an almost ritual quality, as though each event would inexorably lead towards a successful conclusion. In reality, however, these UN mandates did not have the self-fulfilling qualities sometimes attributed to them by organizing staff in New York. The absence of a cut and dried peace treaty that could run smoothly to its conclusion needed the United Nations to provide a strongly proactive executive capability in its field HQ that allowed senior officials to do more than just react to events. A staff was needed to think ahead, investigate options, plan, and above all promulgate ideas and ensure that they were being followed. Despite the energy and very high standard of the tiny nucleus of key officials and military staff in Monrovia, UNOMIL did not have sufficient executive capability actively to oversee the process and keep up its momentum. UNOMIL was established on the wrong assumption that its small numerical presence limited it to a commensurately insignificant role, whereas in reality UNOMIL HQ influenced a much wider span of events.

In early 1994 it was already clear that many assumptions about the continuum of events from Cotonou to the September 1994 elections were incorrect, but no restructured plan or realistic coordinating strategy could be promulgated to exploit the areas of success that emerged and maintain the momentum of the peace accord. When Cotonou began to slow down, there was no capacity to allow key UN officials to disengage from day-to-day damage control and look ahead and plan effectively.

The absence of a success strategy

Relief providers and UN officials acting in this complex emergency faced challenges that no longer responded to the tried formulas. There were so many disparate elements in international, regional, and local response packages that individually they acted against each other in the long term. Although there was a widely recognized need for coordination that overrode the selfish interests of individual agencies, there had been depressingly little evidence in the Cotonou period in Liberia that any effective institution could be vested with sufficient authority to coordinate efforts in the field. The superficial structures for coordination that emerged in Liberia, as in other relief theatres, collapsed under the strain of the irreconcilable interests of individuals and their parent institutions.

Donors developed funding campaigns that were geared to respond to short-term, high-drama humanitarian emergencies; there was no evidence of the change in funding tactics that would be needed to sustain a conflict resolution process in a strategically less important area that could take decades to achieve success. For example, the public were willing to sponsor a hospital rebuild once, but not again and again as the front lines shifted and it was overrun and looted for a second or third time. In view of these universal problems, now re-emphasized by the Liberian experience, it had to be concluded that, although the international community was still willing to respond to complex emergencies, albeit with varying degrees of conviction and generosity, it had no strategy for success. Such a strategy would require each agency and military unit to devolve an element of its individual authority and subordinate some of its interests towards achieving long-term goals.

Misconceptions about disarmament

In common with Somalia, Bosnia, and Angola, the Liberian experience demonstrated that some UN officials and internationally respected diplomats involved in designing and negotiating the peace process cherished idealistic views about the value of disarmament per se. Events in Liberia have re-emphasized the previously understood lessons regarding the problems of insisting on disarming factions without anticipating the consequences of a partial disarmament. In Liberia it was demonstrated that disarmament could not take place in isolation from prevailing conditions in the area. Unless faction fighters had reasonable expectations of employment, shelter, a community structure, and personal security they would probably retain their weapons and remain as part of a local gang. As a rule, disarmament planners should not have attempted to disarm factions until they had organized effective state-wide security or at least the guarantee of achieving it. In the uncertain period after the reduction of hostilities, a failed or half-successful disarmament encouraged a proliferation of smaller groups at local level. These lawless gangs became harder to bring back into the disarmament process than their parent factions, however despotic and inhumane the leaders of the main factions were.

Inadequacies of the regional response mechanisms (ECOMOG)

Military analysts, particularly in NATO, tended to disparage regional attempts such as ECOMOG to intervene in conflict resolution on the grounds that regional forces could not deliver what NATO experts regard as the minimum standards of effectiveness required for the task. There was a danger that the international community's failure in Liberia would be interpreted unfairly to reinforce this fallacy in the case of ECOMOG. In the African context, ECOMOG's intervention was the lesser of two evils. ECOMOG demonstrated a rough-and-ready capability to take on the factions and restore a relative degree of order. In this way it was a vital element of the peace process. But even in the most optimistic circumstances ECOMOG did not have sufficient forces in Liberia to maintain a reasonable level of security and deploy to all the proposed encampment areas for disarmament. In addition, ECOWAS failed to provide an ambassadorial figure in Monrovia to assist in the negotiating and political processes that involved the intervening regional forces.

At the time of Cotonou it seemed that ECOMOG might in due course fail to meet the criteria for a successful peacekeeping force because of its overt and clandestine involvements in Liberian affairs. In particular, Nigeria jeopardized its impartial status in Liberia and diminished its regional credibility as a future leader and organizer of an African response mechanism by failing to take action to disprove the allegations of looting in Liberia or to discipline those involved and by its active support for the Liberian Peace Council faction.

The failure to negotiate a viable peace formula

Cotonou contained all the ingredients for its own failure and it seemed that the negotiators had repeated many of the mistakes of past UN experience. The talks were characterized by a collective desire to deliver a favourable outcome at any cost and this urge seemed to outweigh the more important need to address practical details on the ground. Too much credibility was given to respected figures who, in the changed circumstances of civil war, no longer controlled events on the ground and consequently could not deliver vital elements of the agreement. There was a lack of attention to detail regarding the election, the methodology of demobilization, and arrangements for security in the new Liberian government. The drafters of the Cotonou Agreement assumed too much about the effectiveness of the Liberian interim administration, the strength and deployment intentions of ECOMOG, the mechanisms whereby ECOMOG would protect UNOMIL, and above all the preconditions needed to achieve successful disarmament. These omissions have been noted from previous negotiating experience and are not peculiar to Liberia. It is a depressing conclusion, especially for research efforts such as this one, that the international civil servants and respected diplomats concerned approached this particular problem with a narrow view of recent history that excluded its obvious lessons.

The aftermath of failure

Immediately the Cotonou accord began to fail, countries in the region started considering how best to rescue what might be saved. The general belief among ECOWAS members was that they had identified some of the problems in the previous peace processes, and that it would be possible to build on the goodwill and optimism that characterized Cotonou. Both ECOWAS and the Liberian warring factions still had diametrically opposed views about the failure of the Cotonou Agreement. This was to be reflected more strongly in the first agreement signed after Cotonou – the Akosombo Agreement.[11]

The Akosombo Agreement was organized by the Ghanaian President, Jerry Rawlings, in September 1994. Like Cotonou, the accord got its name from the town where it was signed. In its stipulations, the Akosombo Agreement was unambiguous in its claim that it was only to supplement the Cotonou Agreement, and not to replace it. The main intentions were to remove potential obstacles from the clauses of the Cotonou Agreement and to give the LNTG and the warring factions greater participation in the management of transition efforts in the country.

The main clauses of the Akosombo Agreement were: the reformation of the Armed Forces of Liberia, the involvement of the AFL in the management of the accord, and the reorganization of the decision-making structures. On the question of reforming the AFL, the parties to the accord believed that the AFL would require complete restructuring if it was to cope with the challenges of post-war reconstruction and become a durable force. This same approach underlined the decision to involve the armed forces in the activities of ECOMOG and UNOMIL in Liberia. Apart from wanting to initiate the post-war process in Liberia, another reason for reforming the Liberian armed forces and bringing them into the peace plans was to increase the number of armed personnel who would participate in the disarmament and demobilization arrangements.

But the Akosombo Agreement's greatest impact was in the modifications it made to the decision-making process. Unlike the Cotonou Agreement, which required decisions to be reached by consensus, decision-making under Akosombo was on the basis of a simple majority. The transitional assembly was also expanded with the inclusion of one member from each of the 13 counties. The Agreement added a balancing arrangement to prevent any abuse of power: where a ministry was under the executive control of one of the factions, the other two factions would be allocated to the deputy posts. The life-span of the accord was to be 16 months.

The Akosombo Agreement lasted only three months before the need arose for further discussions to clarify and expand some of its provisions. The main reason for this was the proliferation of factions. Not long after the signing of the Akosombo Agreement, both ULIMO and the NPFL fragmented into two factions each. ULIMO split into ULIMO-K (under Alhaji Kromah) and the Roosevelt Johnson faction, known as ULIMO-J. In the NPFL, Lavel Supowood, Tom Woewiyu, and a number of key members broke away to form the Central Revolutionary Council of the NPFL (CRC-NPFL). A number of new factions also emerged. These included the Liberian Peace Council (LPC), under George Boley, the Lofa Defence Force (LDF), and the Liberian National Conference (LNC). It was the desire to get all these new factions on board the peace process that led to the calling of another meeting in Accra, Ghana.

The Agreement on the Clarification of the Akosombo Agreement was signed in December 1994,[12] as was the Acceptance and Accession Agreement, which allowed the new factions to commit to the Akosombo Agreement and its Clarification.[13] The Accra Clarification reaffirmed the importance of the Cotonou Agreement and the amendments made to it in Akosombo. The major clauses concerned the membership of the Council of State, the appointment of ministers, and the establishment of safe havens for the encampment and disarmament of factions.

The most controversial of these clauses, which almost made the signing of the agreement impossible, dealt with the composition of the new Council of State. It was agreed that the membership of the Council should consist of representatives of the NPFL, ULIMO-K, AFL/Coalition, and the LNC, and a traditional chief selected by the NPFL and ULIMO. Taylor and Alhaji Kromah represented the NPFL and ULIMO-K, respectively. Getting representatives for the AFL/Coalition, however, created some difficulties. General Hezekaih Bowen represented the AFL, while Tom Woewiyu was made representative of the Coalition forces (ULIMO-J, LPC, CRC-NPFL, LNC, and LDF). The NPFL however objected to the nomination of Tom Woewiyu, as a former NPFL member. The bickering became more intense, and President Rawlings sent them back to Liberia. These developments set the scene for a further three years of negotiation towards achieving an effective peace process.

Notes

1. J. A. S. Grenville and B. Wasserstein, *The Major International Treaties since 1945: A History and Guide with Texts*, London: Methuen, 1997, pp. 329–335.
2. Arthur Dennis of the LNTG Ministry of Defence quoted in *The Facts*, 4 February 1994.
3. Cotonou Agreement, Article 4 (3).
4. UN Doc. S/RES/866 (1993), section 12, is the overarching authority; an internal memo "UNOMIL Mission Report," 20 August 1993, explicitly states ECOMOG's obligation.
5. *The Facts*, 4 February 1994.
6. See Appendix 5.
7. *The Facts*, p. 5.
8. John Mackinlay's investigations of the Zimbabwe/Rhodesia settlement show that both factions of the Patriotic Front set aside elements of their forces, which were brought into the peace process only after the disarmament. In Cambodia and Angola, most parties practised set-aside policies to a greater or lesser extent.
9. Professor Delvin Walker, an agriculturalist of Cotlington University College, Gbarnga, remained on the campus after it became the NPFL training centre and was able to use his first-hand observations of youth indoctrination as a basis for UNOMIL's rehabilitation programme when he became its Deputy Reintegration Coordinator in 1993.
10. Charles Taylor, NPFL president, interviewed at Gbarnga, 30 June 1994.
11. See Appendix 6.
12. See Appendix 7.
13. See Appendix 8.

PART III
The Abuja accords

6
Abuja I: Plans for disarmament, demobilization, and reintegration

The Abuja agreements of August 1995 and August 1996 turned out to be the most successful of the agreements: they resulted in the greatest level of disarmament and demobilization since efforts to restore peace in Liberia began in 1990, and paved the way for the elections that were held in Liberia in July 1997. The period following the 1995 Abuja Agreement saw the establishment of a comprehensive disarmament, demobilization, and reintegration plan, which later stalled in the crisis that erupted in Monrovia in April 1996. Nevertheless, the agreement was brought back on track in August 1996, and resulted in the disarming and demobilization of over 70 per cent of the combatants of warring factions.[1] With this unprecedented level of disarmament, demobilization, and reintegration and the most promising progress toward elections, Abuja can be said to have been successful in propelling Liberia towards peace and stability.

This was possible not because Abuja differed sharply from Cotonou or because the problems encountered during earlier agreements had all disappeared – indeed, the crisis during April 1996 (to be discussed later) indicated that the process was by no means a smooth one – but because a number of factors not previously present emerged to contribute to the measure of success enjoyed during the implementation process. These factors, the surrounding circumstances, and the remaining flaws in the process are the focus of chapters 6 and 7.

Abuja I supplements and amendments

Despite the assumption that disarmament was the key to success, and despite the negotiated progress made towards disarmament and demobilization under the Cotonou, Akosombo, and Accra accords, it was the physical implementation of the Abuja accords that generated the political momentum and commitment that were lacking in previous agreements. There was by now a deeper understanding of what disarmament and demobilization would require in practical terms, a general recognition of what the role of different actors should be, and how the process could be secured and sustained. These factors had been lacking in the past, particularly the insight into the real needs of disarmament and demobilization in the context of Liberia and the political and military assets that determined success.

The first Abuja Agreement[2] was intended to supplement the Cotonou, Akosombo, and Accra accords. There were no changes to the disarmament and demobilization plans agreed in Cotonou and amended in Akosombo. The real contribution of the first Abuja Agreement was in securing the agreement of conflicting parties on the membership of the new Council of State, a factor that had been a stumbling block after Accra. Under Abuja, the parties agreed on a six-member Council of State: Charles Taylor (NPFL), Alhaji Kromah (ULIMO-K), George Boley (Coalition), Oscar Quiah (LNC), Chief Tamba Taylor, and Wilton Sankawulo. Sankawulo was appointed Chairman of the Council;[3] the remaining members were to be Vice-Chairmen of equal status.[4] Being constituted by the top leadership level of each faction gave the Council the power and authority it had lacked in previous reconciliation attempts.

The activities of the Elections Commission were to be jointly monitored by ECOWAS, the Organization of African Unity, and the United Nations.[5] The Transitional Government was to be installed within 14 days of the agreement and thereafter remain in office for 12 months.[6] The provision of the Cotonou accord that officials in the Transitional Government wishing to contest the elections should vacate office remained. Such candidates or their parties were to nominate their replacement in the Council.[7] Furthermore, the Chairman of the Council of State was ineligible to contest the first presidential and parliamentary elections.[8] The fact that the Abuja Agreement was signed by all the parties concerned and that the Council of State, with its greatly enhanced authority, was installed thereafter gave the peace process a momentum not attained after Accra. It was therefore possible to begin to tackle other issues of disarmament and demobilization that had been put on hold when progress was stalled after Accra.

Planning for the peace process

The agreement in Abuja created a climate for success but progress was largely the result of the planning in the few months preceding the agreement, set in motion by the Ninth Progress Report of the UN Secretary-General in February 1995.[9] Perhaps the most significant development was the recognition that previous attempts to achieve a peaceful conciliation had been flawed. Abuja I also displayed a greater understanding of the needs of the process. Achieving disarmament and reconciliation was seen to require a number of carefully planned procedures, in which the roles played by different parties – technical, political, and financial – were clearly outlined and the tasks of the different players properly coordinated. By June 1995, a Task Force had been set up, and its duty was to "review operational concepts, plans and programmes for the disarmament, demobilization and reintegration process." Membership of the Task Force included representatives of the government of Liberia, ECOMOG, UNOMIL, UNDP, non-governmental organizations, and donors. It was the first effective effort to coordinate the activities of the different organizations and agencies that would play a crucial role in the peace process. Although this Task Force was already in place by June 1995, it was unable to make any impact because the detailed plans for moving from disarmament to reconciliation could not function in isolation from an overall peace process. The lack of progress on the political aspects of the peace process – evidenced by failure to agree on membership of the Liberia National Transitional Government (LNTG) after Accra – meant that the peace process was stalled until after the breakthrough in Abuja in August 1995.

A coordinated peace process

Two key factors became evident during the implementation of Abuja. First, all the participating agencies operated from a near common perception of what the process of disarmament and demobilization would entail. Second, there was an indication that the agencies involved in the peace process recognized that their roles and tasks were interdependent. Thus the success of one was dependent on the success of the others. Disarmament was seen as "the formal organised disengagement or dissolution of all units and personnel of the various warring factions from military and or war-like activities,"[10] the key element of which was seen to be the physical separation of arms from combatants and units. The common aim in demobilization was the "deliberate dismantling of military command and power structure of the warring factions."[11]

There was a consensus amongst the different agencies (e.g. the LNTG, UNOMIL, and ECOMOG) that this process would be implemented through the cantonment or encampment of combatants, after which disarmament and demobilization would occur.[12] This was no different from the provisions of Cotonou, but what was new was the detailed process through which this could be achieved. There was a common approach in which, nevertheless, each agency had specific tasks and its own concept of operations. The process entailed a sequence of events, the main aspects of which were:

1. Disengagement of combatants
2. Verification (of disengagement)
3. Identification and preparation of safe havens
4. Identification and preparation of assembly sites
5. Identification and preparation of encampment sites
6. Deployment of faction fighters to safe havens
7. Deployment to assembly sites
8. Deployment to encampment sites
9. Disarmament by ECOMOG and verification by UNOMIL
10. Demobilization of faction fighters
11. Reintegration of fighters into the civil community

However, there were variations in the time that some agencies had allocated for specific phases of the operation, particularly how long fighters were to spend in encampment. For example, according to the ECOMOG plan, disarmament of troops at the encampment sites was expected to last 60 days, after which ex-combatants would be handed over for demobilization. The LNTG, on the other hand, wanted each fighter to be processed within a two-week period to avoid holding them in encampment sites for too long. As a result, efforts were made to rectify the time discrepancies between ECOMOG and UNOMIL.

Within this process, each agency's role and responsibility in implementing the process were clearly outlined – a departure from previous attempts. The common perception of what the process should entail was supported by a clear definition of what the role of each player would be and how these roles were related to the overall process. However, the question remained: to what extent were the individual agencies, supplied from international, regional, and local sources, able to provide these functions? Was each one adequately equipped and motivated to perform its tasks? Each element of the peace process is analysed below.

ECOMOG

The primary task of providing security for the whole of Liberia and of disarming non-combatants was given to ECOMOG. Disarmament was to be done in stages, from the verification of disengagement of combatants to the disarmament stage as explained above. ECOMOG had to conduct an assessment of the number of troops it would need to carry out its task at each level. ECOMOG's concept of operations required the maintenance of a Force Headquarters and the deployment of troops to 9 safe havens, 10 assembly sites, 10 encampment sites, and 13 main points of entry along Liberia's borders, at airports, and at seaports.[13] This needed about 12,000 men in 16 self-supporting battalions, at a time when the force consisted of only about 8,000 troops.

UNOMIL

In the overall disarmament, demobilization, and reintegration process, UNOMIL's major task was to begin at the demobilization stage, although it was also required to verify the stages up to disarmament. In addition to the preparatory work leading to the demobilization stage, UNOMIL, in concert with individual NGOs, was to undertake the primary responsibility for transforming the combatant into a civilian. This was to be done in stages: interview and establishing a "combatant profile," providing combatants with a package of essential needs (civilian clothing, health checks, food, a resettlement package), transportation of ex-combatants to their "home region," and plans for reintegration into their communities.

UNDP and reintegration

The interdependent roles of the different agencies were reflected in the overlap of their tasks. Efforts to begin reintegration of ex-combatants could only be an indication of the successful implementation of other phases. In Liberia, there were no effective plans for reintegrating ex-combatants into their communities in the months before the first Abuja Agreement – many of the tasks ended at the demobilization phase. However, the UNDP developed a concept of how reintegration should come about and what it should entail. Although the United Nations and other NGOs were to take part in the earlier stages of demobilization (such as health checks and treatment, counselling, skill and literacy training), the period of encampment would provide an opportunity for them to prepare for the reintegration of fighters into civil society. It was anticipated that, during this time, "relief and development agencies would quickly be moved into position in the rural sector and help to create new employment and income generation activities."[14]

The demobilization and reintegration of child soldiers were given special attention at the preparation stage. In planning for the reintegration of child soldiers, the United Nations Children's Fund (UNICEF) operated from the assumption that this class of fighters should be treated not as adults or "soldiers with a cause," but as victims.[15] It was argued that, for the demobilization of child soldiers to be successful, it must be linked to long-term reintegration initiatives. UNICEF saw "community-based strategies" as the most effective way of reintegrating child soldiers, rather than strategies that would entail the removal of child soldiers to institutions outside of the local community. Families and communities were also recognized as requiring assistance in the reception of child fighters back into society. Activities such as counselling should take place within communities rather than institutions, to facilitate and enhance the full reintegration of child soldiers.

The LNTG

The role played by Liberia's National Transitional Government grew as the peace process advanced. In addition to plans for restructuring the Armed Forces of Liberia (AFL), its role was broadened under Akosombo to include joint verification of the disarmament process. The LNTG was also concerned with the "re-adjustment of former combatants, and their re-integration into normal community life." Toward this end, it established a National Readjustment Commission. Its task, amongst other things, was to "formulate basic policy-guidelines and provide general direction for the management of Re-adjustment Programs approved and adopted by the Government for the re-integration into normal life of the combatants and non-combatants affected by the civil conflict." The government of Liberia indicated a preference for disarmament and demobilization camps to be used as "transit centres," where an ex-combatant would be "processed" in 14 days. It was considered essential during this period to record an ex-combatant profile to enable the government to determine an appropriate "social service plan." The government also aimed to provide a cash-for-guns benefit in the belief that this would act as a catalyst to the process of disarmament and demobilization. Several areas of activity were identified for the government's reintegration plan, with incentive opportunities intended for the short and the long term. The major problem with these plans, however, was that, although the government of Liberia had been given a huge role to play in the reintegration of combatants into civil society, it lacked the resources to carry out these plans. It would have to depend on outside agencies and organizations in order to implement the plans.

Coordination

In addition to identifying a joint concept of operation and clearer delineation of tasks for the different agencies, efforts to achieve coordination at different levels set the scene for effective implementation of a disarmament and reintegration process. The establishment of the Task Force and regular meetings was one way to improve coordination. Perhaps the most noticeable effort at other levels was the attempt to improve coordination and cooperation between ECOMOG and UNOMIL, which had obvious coordination problems during the first attempt to implement the Cotonou Agreement, as indicated in earlier chapters. For example, steps were taken to correct this previous lack of coordination, particularly at the working level, through proposals that a Joint ECOMOG–UNOMIL Coordination Cell be established at the ECOMOG headquarters[16] or that there should be an exchange of liaison officers.[17] The Special Representative of the Secretary-General (SRSG) confirmed the implementation of the Joint Coordination Cell.[18] In addition, plans were made for weekly coordination meetings at headquarters level, and twice-weekly meetings at sector level.[19] Further evidence of improved working relations between ECOMOG and UNOMIL was the greater interest and involvement shown by UNOMIL in enhancing ECOMOG's capability to implement its concept of operation. UNOMIL, supported by the SRSG, was involved in assessing and reviewing the logistics requirements that would make it possible for ECOMOG to implement its mandate. This requirement was presented to potential donors at a conference on assistance to Liberia held in New York on 27 October 1995.[20]

The pledges of aid that resulted from the conference can be linked to another issue that enhanced progress during the implementation of Abuja. The greater display of unity by ECOMOG and UNOMIL made it easier to enlist international donor support for ECOWAS. This factor seemed to create its own momentum, which linked aid to progress. The international community's technical and financial assistance was becoming critical to the success of the peace process. Financial assistance was also offered to other parts of the process, where an increased level of coordination was also apparent during Abuja. Efforts to expand and strengthen coordination mechanisms during the implementation of Abuja resulted in the appointment of a Humanitarian Coordinator, who was charged with the task of supporting and coordinating "the efforts of the operational agencies of the United Nations" (for example, UNICEF, the UN High Commissioner for Refugees, and the World Food Programme).[21] In addition, the Humanitarian Coordinator was required to generate increased participation by the Food and Agriculture Organization, UNDP, the World Health Organization, and the United Nations Educational, Scientific, and Cultural Organization in providing relevant assistance, as well as providing support for the activities of the wider humanitarian community, including NGOs. A Humanitarian Assistance Unit was established, consisting of two offices: the Humanitarian Assistance Coordination Office (HACO), which was to provide support for the Humanitarian

Affairs Coordinator; and the Demobilization and Reintegration Office, which was responsible for organizing and coordinating demobilization and reintegration services. This office and its component parts, along with the UNOMIL offices, were all located at the Hotel Africa building after the April 1996 crisis.

There was evidence of greater coordination in other areas, particularly in terms of achieving greater involvement of the Liberian parties themselves in the peace process. For example, after the signing of the first Abuja Agreement, a National Disarmament and Demobilization Commission (NDDC) was established, which was to support the activities of the Liberian Refugees Repatriation and Resettlement Commission (LRRRC) and the National Readjustment Commission (NRC). These initiatives were indicative of the fact that longer-term reintegration activities were being prepared. Attempts to achieve greater participation of the Liberian factions and to coordinate their roles were also evident in the establishment of the Disarmament Committee, whose membership included the LNTG, UNOMIL, representatives of the different factions, and ECOMOG, which chaired the committee.[22]

Apart from the progress in coordination between the agencies and peacemakers, there were noticeable improvements in the organization of some key actors in the process. ECOWAS, for example, made efforts to improve the ECOMOG command structure, through the appointment of a Special Representative of the Executive Secretary, who was supposed to coordinate political aspects of the peace process, working closely with the SRSG in Liberia.[23]

The peace process also saw unprecedented progress in cooperation between the factions and ECOMOG in its role as a peace force. In response to a request for information regarding their troop strength, preferred locations for assembly, number of weapons, minefield location, and prisoners of war, the factions furnished the Disarmament Committee with a list of preferred assembly sites and their troop strength. The information provided on their troops showed the following strengths: NPFL, 25,000; AFL, 8,734; ULIMO-J, 7,776; ULIMO-K, 12,460; LPC, 4,650; LDF, 750.[24] Map 5 shows the designated disarmament centres.

The reality: Gaps between planning and implementation

However, the Abuja I peace process did not progress beyond this point. Despite the visible efforts to generate momentum amongst the international agencies and strengthen disarmament, demobilization, and reintegration procedures, there was no movement toward peace between the warring factions, which, with few exceptions, did not disengage. For

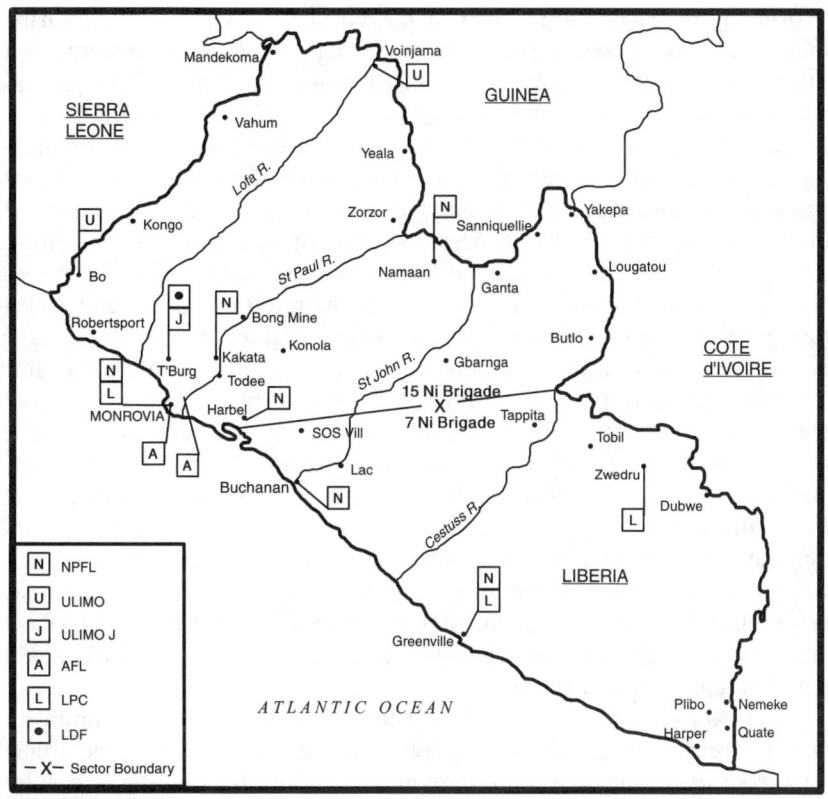

Map 5 **Designated disarmament areas, 1996 (Source: UNOMIL HQ briefing, 1996; graphics by JSCSC Mapping Department)**

example, although ULIMO-J had fully disengaged from Bong Mines and removed its checkpoints in Kakata and the NPFL had also disengaged from Bong Mines, ULIMO-J and ULIMO-K did not disengage from Tubmanburg. The ULIMO leaders revealed that, owing to mutual distrust, they could not disengage in the absence of an ECOMOG deployment in the areas concerned.[25] The result of this continued distrust and confrontation was that the other phases that were to follow disengagement, such as the assembly, encampment, and disarmament and demobilization phases, could not begin. Without disarmament and demobilization, the prospects for reintegration were very poor because it could be attained only after fighters had been disarmed or at least encamped, so that the local areas could be secured and opened up to enable relief and development agencies to move freely to establish economic activities.

In many respects, the progress achieved in the phases of the disarmament and demobilization process was cosmetic. Although a structure was put in place, with procedures and tasks properly delineated, in practice the means to implement this process were absent. There was still a lack of financial and manpower resources to carry out the tasks of encampment, disarmament, demobilization, and reintegration. ECOMOG was under-funded and under-staffed. It needed a total of about 12,000 men to implement its part in the general concept of operations but its troop strength was instead reduced to 7,269 after the withdrawal of the East African troops. Furthermore, other logistics requirements (communication, transportation, spares) were grossly inadequate to enable it to carry out its mandate in Liberia. As indicated earlier, such logistic constraints had contributed in part to the failure to implement the Cotonou Agreement. UNOMIL also required an increase in staff strength, as well as an adjustment of its mandate in order to implement its task effectively. Although an increased level of financial assistance was later forthcoming from international donors, this was not available during the period immediately following the signing of the first Abuja Agreement. There was a time gap between planning the peace process, the request for assistance, and the eventual manifestation of that assistance. The last two occurred long after the signing of the agreement, thus disastrously delaying implementation of the process.

The resource gap was a significant factor in the failure of demobilization and reintegration. The period of encampment was seen to be crucial for the successful reintegration of combatants and for long-term stability in the country. In the proposal for two to four months of encampment, it was hoped that fighters would have been properly separated from the command structure of their factions and could be psychologically prepared for a civilian lifestyle or at least for another vocation. In some cases they would be demobilized and re-formed into new units in preparation for retraining as a regular security force – army, police, and immigration. However, there was no funding to maintain the encampment sites for the proposed period or, indeed, for a shorter period of time. Indeed, the resources that would become available to support the process of disarmament and demobilization could sustain fighters in the encampment sites for only six hours. This was a huge shortfall in expectations. This six-hour period now involved physical disarming, interviewing, and the provision of a incentive/resettlement package, which would include: a plastic cup and plate, a spoon, a bucket, two cooking pots, soap, a towel, either a hoe or a cutlass for those whose final destination was in the rural areas, and an educational package for those under the age of 15.[26] The time now allocated for the execution of this process was a huge reduction from the incentive and resettlement process envisaged under Akosombo. Even then, this tiny package was not readily available immediately after Abuja I. Thus, although the LNTG had a conception of what the process of reintegration should entail and made plans on paper for the reconciliation and reintegration of both combatants and community members, it was impossible to achieve this without adequate resources. Turning these plans into reality was dependent on the goodwill of the international community and other donors, for the Liberian government was not in any position to generate revenue.

In the absence of the required resources to implement the planned encampment, demobilization, and reintegration, spontaneous disarmament became the only practical option. There was an indication that as many as 70 per cent of the combatants were willing to disarm if they had the chance to do so.[27] However, there was some reluctance on the part of the planners to embark on spontaneous disarmament, given the possible risks that this option entailed. For example, there was the risk of releasing potentially dangerous people into society without any rehabilitation.[28] Planners nonetheless recommended that, although spontaneous disarmament should not be encouraged, it should be conducted if fighters, particularly children, came forward to hand in their weapons.

In addition to the shortage of financial and manpower resources, some of the major issues that partly prevented progress after Cotonou and Akosombo remained. The absence of a process to provide an effective national army, police force, immigration service, and customs meant that there was no alternative vocation for the combatants to pursue, particularly in the city, where the opportunities for income-generation programmes readily available in the rural areas were severely limited.

However, these particular problems were only manifestations of a much greater stumbling block, which alone was impeding the peace process: the refusal of the conflicting parties to move toward a peaceful solution. The fact that the implementation of the first Abuja Agreement was halted by more cease-fire violations revealed that the entire peace process was absolutely dependent on the desire of the conflicting parties to see them succeed. Either they were unwilling to pursue a peaceful settlement or they were not confident that the circumstances were yet right to put too much trust in the peace process. After Cotonou it was the latter, but in the improved climate of the Abuja process their real motives were unclear. Indeed, progress after Abuja I was largely related to the superficial momentum generated by peacemakers and other external actors who had a role to play in this peace process; beyond this, there was little progress. More significantly, while national and international agencies attempted to put effective machinery in place so that peace might be attained, the warring parties failed to make the concessions needed to underpin a workable peace process.

The failure of Abuja I

A number of events signalled that the first Abuja Agreement was on the road to collapse. The first was the increasing number of cease-fire violations, following the signing of the agreement, which made the planned disengagement of combatants impossible. The second was the incident in Tubmanburg in December 1995, which led to the death and injury of some ECOMOG troops. The breakdown of security gradually escalated and culminated in the April 1996 crisis, when violence erupted amongst warring parties following attempts by the Council of State (instigated by Taylor and Kromah) to arrest one of the warlords, Roosevelt Johnson, for murder. The result was a new crisis characterized by widespread looting and arson in Monrovia.[29] The looting affected indigenous Liberian offices and foreign agencies alike. The materials intended for use in the disarmament and demobilization process, stored in warehouses in the capital, were completely looted. The Liberian capital had not witnessed the level of destruction that occurred in April 1996 throughout the preceding six years of civil war. The new crisis in effect put paid to efforts to implement Abuja I and set the peace process back a few paces.

Notes

1. *Agence France Press* (AFP), 7 February 1997.
2. See Appendix 9.
3. *Abuja Agreement*, 19 August 1995 (hereinafter Abuja I), Part II, Section A, paras. 1 and 2.
4. Ibid.
5. Abuja I, Section C, Article 15.
6. Ibid., Section D, Article 16, paras. 1 and 2.
7. Ibid., Article 16, para. 3.
8. Ibid., Article 16, para. 4.
9. *Ninth Progress Report of the Secretary-General on the United Nations Observer Mission in Liberia,* S/1995/158.
10. National Readjustment Commission, "Plan for Disarmament and Demobilization," 1995.
11. Ibid.
12. ECOMOG, Disarmament Concept Paper, 1995.
13. See S/1995/158.
14. UNDP, Draft Reintegration Concept Paper on disarmament, demobilization, and reintegration, 1996.
15. UNICEF, Demobilization/Reintegration: Child Soldiers Concept Paper, 1996.
16. S/1995/158, para. 32.
17. *Thirteenth Progress Report of the Secretary-General on the United Nations Observer Mission in Liberia,* S/1995/881, 23 October 1995, para. 30.
18. Interview with the Special Representative of the UN Secretary-General, Liberia, January 1997.

19. S/1995/881, para. 30.
20. Ibid., para. 38.
21. Ibid., para. 40
22. UN-HACO, *Liberia Disarmament and Demobilization Plan*, 19 October 1996; and S/1995/881, para. 31.
23. S/1995/881, para. 11.
24. S/1995/881.
25. S/1995/881, para. 18.
26. UNOMIL, Demobilization Concept Paper.
27. Ibid.
28. UNDP, Reintegration Concept Paper.
29. For a comprehensive account of the events leading up to the April 1996 crisis and its immediate impact, see *West Africa*, 24–30 June 1996.

7
Abuja II

After the collapse of Abuja I, attempts to restore the momentum of the peace process in Liberia resulted in the extension of the Abuja Agreement of August 1995 with a revised schedule of implementation. The extended Abuja Agreement (referred to as Abuja II) was signed in Abuja on 17 August 1996. Despite the serious challenges which had derailed the preceding arrangement and the emergence of new ones, this agreement was implemented and resulted in the disarmament of about 23,000 combatants,[1] something that had seemed impossible only a few months earlier. This was all the more significant when the circumstances of this achievement are closely examined: Abuja II seemed to have succeeded without a process of assembly and encampment, using a tighter implementation schedule, a sharply reduced demobilization period, a stringent, almost non-existent incentive and resettlement package, and without any substantial reintegration plans. This chapter discusses the terms of the agreement, the implementation problems, and the factors that brought about the achievement of a level of disarmament that peacemakers had only dreamed of for seven years.

The agreement

Abuja II sought to bring the first Abuja Agreement back on track. The first agreement was retained in its entirety without any amendments.

It was agreed that it would remain valid for a further nine months, from 21 August 1996 to 15 June 1997, but its implementation schedule was revised, as shown below:[2]

20–31 Aug. 1996	Cease-fire, disengagement of factions from checkpoints and combat positions.
1 Sep.–30 Nov. 1996	Delivery of logistic supplies by the international/donor community to ECOMOG.
20 Aug. 1996–31 Jan. 1997	Verification of cease-fire and disengagement by ECOMOG, UNOMIL, and LNTG.
3–10 Oct. 1996	Situation assessment meeting in Liberia by Chairman's Special Envoy with ECOMOG, UNOMIL, representatives of donor community, and LNTG.
12 Oct. 1996–31 Jan. 1997	Recce mission by ECOMOG and UNOMIL of arms collection centres.
4–8 Nov. 1996	Committee of Nine[3] ministerial meeting in Monrovia.
7 Nov. 1996–31 Jan. 1997	Deployment of ECOMOG to agreed safe havens by Committee of Nine.
22 Nov. 1996–31 Jan. 1997	Disarmament, demobilization, and repatriation.
6–13 January 1997	Verification visit to Liberia by Chairman's Special Envoy with ECOMOG, UNOMIL, representatives of donor community, and LNTG.
20 Jan.–15 April 1997	Preparations for elections.
10–15 March 1997	Committee of Nine meeting, Monrovia.
17–24 April 1997	Assessment visit to Liberia by Chairman's Special Envoy with ECOMOG, UNOMIL, representatives of donor community, and LNTG.
30 May 1997	Election day.

In addition to this revised implementation schedule, the Heads of State and Government of the Committee of Nine sought to put certain measures in place that would guarantee the compliance of the factions with the peace process. It was agreed that any faction found guilty of "acts capable of obstructing the peace plan" would have invoked against it the following measures:
- travel and residence restrictions
- freezing of business activities and assets in member states

- exclusion from participation in the electoral process
- restrictions on the use of the airspace and territorial waters of member states
- expulsion of members of the families of the Liberian leaders and their associates from the territories of member states
- request for the UN Security Council to impose visa restrictions
- restrictions on imports from Liberia
- invocation of the OAU 1996 Summit Resolution which calls for the establishment of a war crimes tribunal to try all human rights offences against Liberians.[4]

Although many commentators argued after the signing of Abuja II that these measures would deter Liberian faction leaders from further "derailing" the implementation of the peace plan, it is difficult to determine the effect the sanctions have had, if any. Member states were also urged to maintain the arms embargo on Liberia, and the right of ECOMOG to ensure strict compliance with the arms embargo was reaffirmed.

A number of other issues were also addressed at the Abuja II meeting. It was noted that the Council of State (COS) was not particularly effective. A new Chairman, Ruth Perry, was appointed to head the Council. It was recommended that ECOMOG's strength should be increased to about 18,000 troops in order to implement the peace plan effectively. Concern was also expressed that Liberian security agencies were strongly connected to the warring factions. The Committee of Nine supported the proposal that the armed forces and security agencies be restructured to reflect geographical and ethnic balance, and noted a British government offer to sponsor a programme to train the cadre of military instructors around which a new national army could be organized.

Implementing the peace process after Abuja II – surrounding circumstances

The materials and goods intended for demobilization and reintegration, stored in three warehouses, were completely looted, along with vehicles and equipment, during the April 1996 crisis. This meant that the prospects for the peace process were even worse than had been anticipated during the original planning period. Workers in the humanitarian/relief community were forced to abandon their tasks in Monrovia. UN staff contracts were terminated, with the exception of 10 UNOMIL and 15 civilian staff.[5] After the crisis subsided, attempts were made to recruit new staff, propose a new budget, and submit requests for the purchase of vehicles and equipment. Given the bureaucracy within the United Nations, these plans had not been completed when Abuja II was signed.

Table 7.1 **Troop pledges to ECOMOG, January 1997**

Country	No.
Ghana	760
Burkina Faso	320
Niger	500
Mali	612
Gambia	67
Côte d'Ivoire	90

Source: Interview with ECOMOG Chief Operations Officer, January 1997.

Table 7.2 **ECOMOG troop strength, January 1997**

Serial	Contingent	Officers	Servicemen	Total
1	GAMCON	1	9	10
2	GHANCON	65	775	840
3	GUCON	60	514	574
4	LEOCON	14	360	374
5	MALICON	8	3	11
6	NIGCON	390	6,407	6,797
	Total	538	8,068	8,606

Source: ECOMOG Headquarters, Monrovia, January 1997.

The relief community had suffered a loss of confidence and morale after the destruction of 6 April.

ECOMOG however suffered the least because its premises were not looted during the crisis. It had the added advantage that much of the assistance pledged by the international community following the October 1995 conference had only just begun to materialise after April 1996. The assistance rendered to ECOMOG was to include US$30 million from the United States, trucks from the Netherlands, vehicles from Germany, and communications equipment from the United Kingdom.[6] Furthermore, Belgium, Denmark, and the Netherlands were willing to support two additional contingents from Ghana and Burkina Faso.[7] However, these battalions were weak owing to inadequate troop strength, communication equipment, and transportation, which had not been resolved at the time of the signing of Abuja II. Despite pledges to contribute troops to boost ECOMOG's strength (see table 7.1), the force consisted of only 8,606, two-thirds of the required 12,000 (see table 7.2 for a breakdown of this figure as at January 1997). UNOMIL was similarly not at the desired strength (see table 7.3).

Additional ECOMOG troops were not forthcoming until February 1997, when the United States conducted a strategic airlift operation to

Table 7.3 **UNOMIL strength, March 1997**

Country	Military observers	Others	Total
Bangladesh	7	7	14
China	7	–	7
Czech Republic	5	–	5
Egypt	14	–	14
India	14	–	14
Kenya	13	–	13
Malaysia	3	–	3
Nepal	6	–	6
Pakistan	14	–	14
Uruguay	2	–	2
Total	85	7	92

Source: *22nd Progress Report of the Secretary-General on Liberia*, March 1997.

move 560 troops from Ghana and 600 from Mali, and 100 medical personnel from Côte d'Ivoire, to reinforce ECOMOG.[8] Despite this augmentation, the implementation of Abuja II commenced with an extreme shortage of assets.

Given the lack of resources, the procedure for the peace process was modified significantly from that contained in the plans before and after Abuja I. Encampment could not be realistically conducted given the acute shortage of funds and inadequate troop strength from ECOMOG and UNOMIL. In addition to the lack of resources, the LNTG also expressed doubt about the encampment of fighters. It saw a danger in concentrating all the fighters together into encampment sites since this might encourage collective lawlessness after the international community left.[9] It was thought that there were other hidden reasons why faction leaders discouraged encampment.[10] The overall time spent by a fighter at the site of disarmament and demobilization was significantly reduced from what was originally anticipated. Plans were made to disarm and demobilize 59,370 fighters at 12 demobilization sites, at an average of 100 fighters per day, over 84 days, with each fighter staying a maximum of 12 hours at the site, except in cases where lack of transportation resulted in overnight accommodation.[11]

Each demobilization camp was expected to have representatives from the LNTG (NDDC), UNOMIL, ECOMOG, the Humanitarian Assistance Coordination Office of the United Nations Department of Humanitarian Affairs (UNDHA-HACO), and United Nations and non-governmental humanitarian organizations. The National Disarmament and Demobilization Commission (NDDC) was in charge of the pre-registration phase, which was meant to occur at least one week prior to the commencement of demobilization. The pre-registration form for each fighter to be demobilized was to be provided by the NDDC at least a day prior to the demobilization of that fighter. Disarmament was to last 5–10 minutes per fighter. It was to be undertaken by ECOMOG and verified by UNOMIL. Each fighter was expected to surrender one weapon. ECOMOG would separate ammunition and weapons and ensure their security. Trucks would be present at each site to remove the ammunition from the vicinity of the fighters and the demobilization site. A record of the type of weapon submitted by the fighter and its level of serviceability was to be kept for later verification by the United Nations.

After handing over their arms to ECOMOG, the fighters would be interviewed by HACO for an estimated 10 minutes per group of seven fighters. Thereafter, the process of registration by HACO was to last 20–30 minutes per group of seven fighters. Detailed records of fighters were obtained, after which an identity card was issued to each fighter (a process of 5–10 minutes). A profile of each ex-combatant was then prepared, with guarantees of confidentiality. Information contained in the profile would include details of education, training, family, and religion, amongst other things. The need for counselling was to be determined during such interviews. Detailed interviews were to be conducted for child soldiers, followed by a medical examination by UNICEF and WHO in collaboration with the Liberian Ministry of Health. Children returning home (rather than going to institutions) would receive one month's food ration supplied by the World Food Programme and delivered on site. Adult fighters were to receive a medical examination with the cooperation of the LNTG Ministry of Health, lasting 20 minutes per group of five fighters. There was the possibility that counselling on AIDS, sexually transmitted diseases, and alcohol abuse would be provided, and condoms distributed to each fighter.

After the process described above, the fighters were to go to the distribution section. Plans were made for those who chose to return directly to their homes to receive one month's supply of food at the demobilization site. Fighters who planned to go directly to bridging projects or farms were to be given "promissory notes," depending on their immediate future plans. For example, blue notes were given to those who chose to join food-for-work programmes, pink notes to those who required agricultural kits, red notes to those going back to communities awaiting the food-for-work programmes, and yellow notes to those needing extended medical attention at a referred hospital. At the end of the process, ex-combatants were to be transported to a final destination of their choice or to their town of origin.

Not much emphasis was given to reintegration during the implementation of Abuja II, which focused more on disarmament and demobilization in the few hours earmarked for the process for each fighter. A reintegration plan had been considered whereby, on the arrival of fighters at their home town, they would report to a special centre to be included in a detailed reintegration plan.[12] These centres were not just for fighters but also for the displaced and returning refugees.[13] This plan was, however, abandoned after the April 1996 crisis. In January 1997, the only available reintegration programme for ex-combatants was a three-month bridging programme after demobilization, which was just starting on a small scale. Reconstruction teams would go around seeking to engage demobilized fighters in projects such as road clearing and bridge mending.

The disarmament and demobilization process

In these circumstances, it was a great achievement that a measure of disarmament and demobilization was achieved. The patience and enthusiasm displayed by faction leaders and their fighters in the first few days after the start of the process raised the hopes of peacemakers and the Liberian community at large that the country was finally on the road to stability. By 28 November, six days after the process began, 1,815 combatants had been disarmed and demobilized.[14] By 14 December, 22 days after the programme began, 4,733 fighters had been disarmed, more than the total number disarmed during the period between 1994 and 1996. At this point the progress of the first few weeks of disarmament and demobilization began to slacken, and the initial enthusiasm shown by the factions waned. Figure 7.1 analyses the gradual decline. On closer examination, many of the weapons handed in by the fighters were unserviceable, which meant that the serviceable weapons were still at large and therefore the factions were retaining the potential to return to an active status. By day 50, on 12 January 1997, with 19 days to the end of the stipulated disarmament period, only 6,826 of the expected 60,000 had been disarmed.[15] A breakdown of the figures for the various disarmament sites is provided in table 7.4. What accounted for the slump in progress? Were these factors political or operational? Can the initial enthusiasm of the factions to disarm be re-created? If so how?

Threats to progress

A number of factors accounted for the slump in progress. First, the fighters mistrusted each other. In Zwedru, for example, the LPC was reluctant to disarm because it knew that the NPFL was maintaining a group of fighters just outside the area.[16] In Voinjama, the ULIMO-K voluntarily disarmed in September 1996 and was attacked by bandits shortly afterward. ULIMO-J complained that, in Tubmanburg, some fighters were

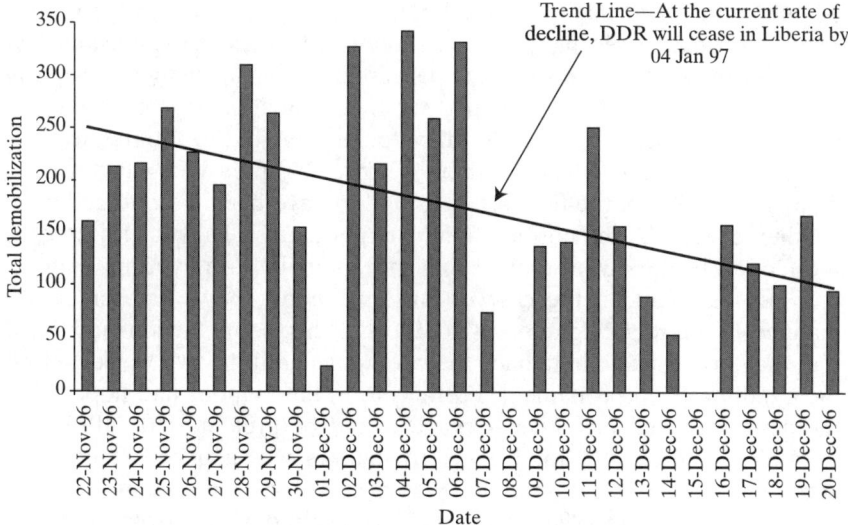

Fig. 7.1 **Trends in disarmament, 22 November–21 December 1996 (Source: UN office in Monrovia)**

Table 7.4 **Demobilization statistics, January 1997**

Site	No. demobbed	Children		Adults	
		Male	Female	Male	Female
Monrovia	2,365	847	2	1,511	5
Camp Namaan	1,611	446	2	1,158	5
Tubmanburg	201	66	1	132	2
Camp Schiefflin	623	51	0	572	0
Kakata	442	109	0	333	0
Zwedru	242	173	0	69	0
Voinjama	596	132	1	451	12
Buchanan	439	98	1	340	0
Bo Waterside	62	30	0	29	3
Tappita	245	40	1	201	3
Total	6,826	1,992	8	4,796	30

Source: UN office in Monrovia.

attacked on returning to their village following disarmament and demobilization. The possibility of being vulnerable to attack by other fighters led many to hold on to their weapons as discussed above. Second, many fighters were discouraged by the fact they had to walk long distances before reaching disarmament sites. Third, faction commanders remaining in the field were personally reluctant to disarm. Many of them were unsure of their future and thus prevented fighters under their control from disarming. In some cases, fighters were threatened with severe punishment if they disarmed individually without permission. Fourth, the figure of nearly 60,000 fighters originally provided by the combatants in the estimates prior to the process was now in dispute. In their bid to intimidate their opponents and not to expose their weaknesses, they had inflated their figures. In addition, the factions were said to have been discouraged from coming forward by the notion of one gun per man.[17] This was rejected by the faction leaders, who argued that in a guerrilla army you never have one gun per man; in the case of large weapons, they were sometimes manned by up to six fighters. In addition to this, some factions indicated that they preferred to hold back their weapons until the two weeks before the deadline for disarmament. Furthermore, the factions had hoped that the assistance and incentive package would be greater. The NPFL, for example, claimed that food given to fighters was a poor incentive. It gradually became clear that this was a common view amongst all the warring parties. The 1996–7 package was vastly different from the situation in 1994 after Akosombo. Above all, the peacemakers and the Liberia community were agreed that the real incentive should be peace, although the feeding programme would be continued until the bridging projects had taken off fully.

Of all the factions, the NPFL seemed to have the most difficulty with the effects of the peace process. A major issue was the unrealistic desire of the peacemakers to have total disarmament before proceeding to other stages of the peace process.[18] The clause of the agreement requiring faction leaders who wished to contest elections to resign from the Council of State and then nominate a replacement was seen to be flawed by the NPFL, because there were no guarantees that elections would be held and any faction leader who resigned might find himself waiting for elections indefinitely. Lastly, the NPFL was concerned with the issue of a status of forces agreement with ECOWAS, which remained unsigned despite the agreement after Akosombo that it would be signed. The NPFL was uncomfortable about the possibility of ECOMOG remaining in Liberia indefinitely without any conditions for its withdrawal. It was concerned that the existing loose arrangement would undermine Liberia's sovereignty.

Positive developments

Attempts were made to address some of the issues that threatened to stall the peace process. Operational problems were addressed by ECOMOG in a number of ways. First, a buffer zone was created between ULIMO-J and ULIMO-K at Lofa Bridge and in Tappita, to allay the fears of the

Table 7.5 **Revised estimates of faction strength, January 1997**

Faction	Estimated strengths of factions		Fighters disarmed	
	Original	Revised	No.	% of estimated strength
National Patriotic Front of Liberia (NPFL)	25,000	12,500	11,553	92.42
ULIMO	12,460	6,800	5,622	82.68
Armed Forces of Liberia (AFL)	8,734	7,000	571	8.15
ULIMO-J	7,776	3,800	1,114	29.32
Liberian Peace Council (LPC)	4,650	2,500	1,223	48.92
Lofa Defence Force (LDF)	750	400	249	62.25
Total	59,370	33,000	20,332	61.61

Source: UN office in Monrovia.

LPC. Second, trucks were sent deep into faction areas to pick up fighters and take them to the disarmament sites. The Cease-fire Committee asked factions to resubmit the numbers of fighters in their faction. The revised figure, totalling 33,000, was accepted by the Committee, although many in the Liberian community were sceptical, still suspecting that the numbers were inflated. Table 7.5 gives a breakdown of the new figure. In addition, the Committee never did expect total disarmament but thought that a high percentage of disarmament would be satisfactory.[19] It was agreed that, after the deadline of 31 January 1997, ECOMOG would enforce disarmament.

The last week of the disarmament phase saw a rush by armed factions to disarm. The 31 January deadline was extended by one week, to accommodate those who had a "last-minute" change of heart. By the end of this period, more than 20,000 of the 33,000 fighters declared by the factions had been disarmed. This was welcomed as a significant achievement in the peace process. As it turned out, none of the peacemakers expected that 100 per cent disarmament should be achieved before election plans could begin.

A number of aspects of the demobilization process aroused considerable concern about the future of Liberia. In what is perhaps the best analysis of the process, Jeremy Armon noted that, although the exercise began in November 1996, the bulk of the disarmament did not begin until mid-January 1997, with the majority of the fighters demobilized after 14 January 1997.[20] More important, however, was the comparison between the demobilization behaviours of the warring factions. Armon noted that the extent of the demobilization by the two warring leaders who had signalled an intention to contest the elections – Taylor (NPFL) and Kromah (ULIMO-K) – was particularly impressive. Despite the fact that the two leaders controlled an estimated 60 per cent of the fighters, they accounted for 84 per cent of the disarmed fighters. The response from the LPC and ULIMO-J, whose leaders had not signalled any interest in election, was not as impressive. Another issue with possible long-term implications is the geographical discrepancies in the demobilization figures. In areas relatively pacified by ECOMOG or a single warring faction, demobilization was more successful than in resources-rich areas that were at the time of the process then militarily contested.

On the whole, the Abuja II Agreement advanced the Liberian peace process and set the country on the path to a successful election. What had proved difficult in previous agreements – disarmament and demobilization – was achieved with significant success under the Abuja II accord. All these achievements were made possible not only by the contents of the accord, but also by the changes in the attitudes of all the parties to peace. For example, the warring factions became less intransigent in their demands; Nigeria became less controversial in its leadership of ECOMOG; the peacekeeping force became more focused; and ECOWAS stood firm in its resolve to hand down heavy penalties for non-compliance with the agreement. The road towards a final settlement seemed clear.

Notes

1. *Reuters*, 1 and 7 February 1997; *Agence France Press* (AFP), 7 February 1997.
2. See *Final Communiqué of the ECOWAS Meeting on Liberia*, which was the fourth meeting of the Heads of State and Government of the Committee of Nine, Abuja, 17 August 1996; see Appendix 10.
3. The Standing Mediation Committee and the Committee of Five were later merged to form the Committee of Nine.
4. *The Inquirer* (Liberia), 23 August 1996, p. 7.
5. Interview with the Political Affairs Officer, UN-HACO, January 1997.
6. Interview with the SRSG, January 1997.
7. Minutes of the meeting between the relief community and the US Ambassador to Liberia, William Milam, 30 July 1996.
8. AFP, 16 February 1997.
9. Interview with the Chief Demobilization Officer, UN-HACO, Monrovia, January 1997.
10. Ibid.
11. UN-HACO, *Liberia Disarmament and Demobilization Plan*, 14 November 1996, p. 4.
12. Interview with the Chief Demobilization Officer, UN-HACO, Monrovia, January 1997.
13. Ibid.
14. UN-HACO in Liberia, *Demobilization Bulletin*, Day 7, 28 November 1996.
15. UN-HACO in Liberia, *Demobilizaiton Bulletin*, Day 50, 12 January 1997.

16. Interview with the Political Affairs Officer, UN-HACO, Monrovia, January 1997.
17. Ibid.
18. This view was strongly expressed during an interview with representatives of the NPFL at their Monrovia radio station in January 1997.
19. Interview with the SRSG and UNOMIL Chief Military Observer, Monrovia, January 1997.
20. Jeremy Armon, "The Disarmament Exercise in Liberia," Paper presented at the Foreign and Commonwealth Office Discussion on Liberia, 1997.

8
Towards a settlement

Although the Liberian crisis had reached great depths of human suffering with untold loss of life and national resources, by the summer of 1997 even the most hardened pessimist could see important changes that told of a new era. These changes were in attitude as well as in tangible development. Much depended on the outcome of the elections. Previous UN peace settlements had failed because the rituals of a state election had failed to restore power and a monopoly for violence to state level. In many collapsed states, unless the victor of the election can also bring with him his own means of sustaining himself in power, no real transfer of authority will take place. Case history shows that, unless the elected head of state is also a major power broker in his own right, that is to say almost certainly the leading faction in any conflict, there is little chance that the state can move from emergency and conflict to a period of peaceful reconstruction. In Liberia's case, all hopes seemed to be pinned on Charles Taylor and his National Patriotic Front of Liberia (NPFL). A political solution that could not include him was almost certain to fail.

It was true that past attempts to return to peace and carry out state elections had failed hopelessly. Now several factors had changed. For the first time Charles Taylor demonstrated that he trusted the peace process and saw the possibility of an election that could recognize his true power. Because in the past he did not have this confidence, he had failed to relinquish his grip on his NPFL fighters, who, in the event of an electoral failure, provided him with an essential safety net from which he could return to the struggle as strong as ever. In 1997, he allowed sizeable elements of the NPFL to disband. What had caused this turn-round? The most significant change in attitude was regional. ECOMOG, particularly the Nigerians, had for seven years opposed the NPFL. But by 1997 their attitude had completely altered. This provided an important confidence-building factor for both the NPFL and the ordinary Liberians who in the past had been caught at the interface of these opposing forces. However, winning the election was only the first step on a very long road. Case history demonstrated that plenty could go wrong, even in a country like Zimbabwe where the structures for governance and state security were largely intact at the time of hand-over. In Liberia, the inter-communal wounds were much deeper and even the most basic instruments of government had been destroyed and would have to be re-established. This chapter describes some of these events and issues on Liberia's road to recovery.

Elections

On 19 July 1997, Charles Taylor won the Liberian elections with a convincing 75 per cent majority that ruled out the need for a second ballot. However, despite this apparently favourable result for Liberia's future political stability, the election organizers and the participating parties had had to endure many anxious moments and a general postponement of the elections before reaching this successful outcome. A number of unresolved issues prevented elections from taking place on 30 May 1997 as planned. First of all, sections of the 1985 constitution needed amendment. If, for example, the 10-year residency clause had not been revised, it would have been impossible for Taylor and other presidential candidates to contest elections. Secondly, the composition of the Elections Commission was undermined by the looming prospect of a deferred election date. The United Nations proposed that the commission should consist of 10 members – 7 representatives of the political parties and various Liberian groups, and 3 international representatives, who had no voting rights.[1] This would replace the Elections Commission established in 1994, which was composed more narrowly of representatives of the armed factions. In the aftermath of previously failed election programmes, an alliance of seven political parties and many ordinary Liberians demanded a more effective, independent electoral commission, fearing that a commission without credibility would not inspire international donors to fund the elections.[2] Charles Taylor was initially opposed to the suggestions that sections of the constitution should be amended and that three international representatives should sit on Liberia's Elections Commission. He maintained that this would undermine Liberia's sovereignty.[3] Election experts cited the examples of South Africa and Mozambique, where successful elections were conducted with international officials on the electoral commission. Plans also needed to be made for the return of refugees from other West African countries, to enable them to exercise their right to vote; alternatively, arrangements had to be made for them to vote in the host countries.

Although none of these issues had been resolved, faction leaders who wanted to contest the elections were expected to resign from the Transitional Government. This requirement raised a number of concerns. It appeared that more time was needed, making the 30 May election date unrealistic. If the electoral problems were left unaddressed and the elections went ahead, it would be difficult to gain the confidence of the Liberian populace in the peace process. On the other hand, if Taylor, Kromah, and other warlords resigned from the Transitional Government and elections were then postponed indefinitely, this would leave these powerful men in limbo and deprived of institutional power. There was a danger they would return to their factional power base. Delay could thus cause the peace process serious difficulties. Many Liberians and members of the peace forces were afraid of the consequences of a disillusioned Charles Taylor returning to the bush if he felt isolated from the peace process. So much seemed to depend on Taylor. He was the candidate most prepared for the May elections and, with so much campaign machinery already in place in anticipation of the end of the disarmament period, he would not take kindly to a postponement of the May date. This view was also reflected in Nigeria and other ECOWAS countries, which wanted to conclude the Liberian peace process successfully, albeit for different reasons. In ECOWAS there was a common desire to put an end to the costly peace operation, which was now in its seventh year; successful elections might bring this chapter to a happier conclusion, especially for Nigeria where the Abacha regime needed to improve its international standing.

Apart from these procedural issues, many of the political parties themselves appeared to be largely unprepared for a May election. Thirteen parties registered for the elections. Three were formed by former warlords: the National Patriotic Party (NPP) by Taylor, the All Liberia Coalition Party (ALCOP) by Alhaji Kromah, and the National Democratic Party of Liberia (NDPL), now led by George Boley, but founded by the late President Doe. Of these, the NPP was best organized for an election. The NPFL had maintained a dual organization for several years, with shadow government officials and military infrastructures. The organization included a headquarters in Gbanga and its own press unit and radio station, which broadcast to the entire country. It was therefore easier for the NPFL to transform itself into a political party, a process that began after Taylor's move to the state capital, Monrovia, in 1995. During this process NPFL recruited some of the best political and economic advisers in the country. ALCOP and NDPL did not have such a sophisticated approach, and in each case the time between the end of the disarmament phase and the election date was insufficient to build an organization to challenge Charles Taylor's. For the civilian political parties, which either had lost their support base (in the case of the old parties) or did not have the time to begin to build one, the prospects for reorganization were even worse. Presidential candidate Ellen Johnson-Sirleaf of the Unity Party had barely returned from the United States in time to organize a campaign. The other parties were the United People's Party (Liberia's oldest opposition party), the Liberian People's Party, the Progressive People's Party, the Liberian National Union, the National Reformation Party, the Free Democratic Party, the Reformation Alliance Party, the People's Democratic Party of Liberia, and the Alliance of (two) Political Parties.[4]

The greatest concern to ordinary Liberians was that, if a strong winner did not emerge amongst the presidential candidates, the country would again be torn apart along factional lines. In particular, many were concerned that, if Taylor was not victorious, he would take up arms again. Although press reports suggested that many Liberians would vote for Taylor out of fear, it was also true that many Liberians were attracted to Taylor; he was a charismatic leader who appealed to young supporters. Although it was thought that Ellen Johnson-Sirleaf would provide tough opposition for him, taking the ballot to a second round, Liberia's teenage population has few or no memories of pre-war politicians whose support base had by now been completely eroded, and Taylor seemed to be on course for victory in the elections.

For several practical reasons the elections were postponed until 19 July 1997. This afforded the other parties a little more time to prepare for the elections. Unfortunately, West African neighbours that sheltered Liberian refugees had refused to allow polling to take place within their borders, so arrangements had to be made to allow those who wished to vote to return to Liberia. July was however the latest date that could be set if Charles Taylor's confidence in the peace process was to be retained. Even after the extension, many political parties were not ready for the elections. Taylor was now aware of his massive advantage over the other parties and he was keen not to lose it. Last-minute efforts by some candidates to postpone the elections for a second time invited harsh statements from Taylor, who warned on the state radio on 8 July that, if the chairman of the Independent Elections Commission attempted to postpone these elections, "only the angels, not even ECOMOG could protect him."[5]

The United Nations and the West African peacemakers appeared to differ over whether or not to hold elections on 19 July. The United Nations was concerned that the elections might be rushed and thus fail to allow other political parties to be better prepared. On the other hand, the West Africans, particularly the Nigerians, felt that, given time, the increasing US interest might displace ECOWAS's initiative and influence in the process. Observers had their own interpretation of events. The United States was seen to be more favourably disposed to Ellen Johnson-Sirleaf and would have preferred that she and her party had more time to prepare for the elections. The Nigerian-led ECOWAS, on the other hand, appeared to support Taylor, perhaps because his victory would be the only way to ensure that Liberia did not return to a state of war, allowing the ECOWAS countries to withdraw their troops.

In the event, Charles Taylor won a landslide victory, the National Patriotic Party (NPP) winning 75 per cent of the votes cast. The elections were based on proportional representation. On 24 July 1997, when Taylor was declared the winner, the NPP had won 468,443 of the 621,888 votes.[6] Ellen Johnson-Sirleaf came closest with 59,557 votes, or 9.6 per cent. The remaining 11 contenders won less than 10 per cent of the votes cast. Henry Andrews, chairman of the Independent Elections Commission, estimated the polling day turnout at just under 90 per cent of the 700,000 registered voters, surpassing the 1985 turnout.[7] With this margin of victory, Taylor took near total control of Liberia's bicameral legislature. His NPP won 21 of the 26 Senate seats, and 49 of the 64 seats in the House of Representatives. Taylor's closest opponent, Ellen Johnson-Sirleaf and her Unity Party, won 3 seats in the Senate and 7 in the House of Representatives.[8] Alhaji Kromah's All Liberia Coalition Party (ALCOP), won 2 Senate seats and 3 House of Representatives seats. The Alliance of Political Parties, led by Cletus Wotorson, and Baccus Matthews' United People's Party each won 2 seats in the House, while the Liberian People's Party of Togba-Nah Tipoteh won only 1 seat in the House.[9] Only 6 of the 13 political parties that stood for election won seats in parliament. The rest did not meet the minimum requirement of 0.6 per cent of votes to obtain a seat.[10]

The elections were monitored by about 500 international observers, including 300 from the United Nations and 50 from the European Union. The monitors declared that the elections were generally free and fair, although Johnson-Sirleaf complained that her party's election observers were manhandled by NPP supporters at the Bong County polling stations, and that Taylor voters had the active backing of the Nigerian ECOMOG soldiers also charged with the security of the polling area.[11] ECOWAS and the United States responded differently, possibly as a result of their positions on the election dates and the preparation of candidates. In a joint statement issued on behalf of the United Nations and ECOWAS, UN spokesman Fred Eckhard declared the elections free, fair, and credible, arguing that there were no reports of irregularities or incidents that could have affected the outcome of the elections.[12] Although the United States declined to take a position after the Unity Party's allegations of irregularities, it urged the international monitors to investigate the claims.[13] The US State Department later endorsed the Liberian elections, describing them as generally free and transparent, while noting that there were allegations of misconduct and other administrative deficiencies stemming partially from the constraints of time, weather, and logistics.[14]

Taylor's landslide victory gave confidence to many ordinary Liberians, who were convinced that a clear winner and strong leadership would be crucial to reconciliation efforts. The result had ensured that the biggest warring party, which had the capability to bring Liberia to its knees, would now not return to the bush. In addition, the size of Taylor's majority meant that he could push through his policies, including his plan to restore Liberia to the US dollar standard, without any serious opposition. However, there was a fear that a strong government might ultimately strangle any meaningful opposition. The elections were only a first part of the democratic process. They did not guarantee a fair and accountable government. Much depended on Taylor's policies for reconciliation and rebuilding. His early gestures were conciliatory and included plans to retain many of the ministers of the interim cabinet.[15]

Liberia's new national armed forces

A lasting peace required the rebuilding of Liberia's armed forces within the framework of an overall reconstruction plan. Taylor's plan was to train a 10,000-strong army and police force. However the fact that a framework for rebuilding the Armed Forces of Liberia was not included as part of the Abuja II peace plan raised concern that Taylor's government, in the absence of a strong opposition, might be tempted to rebuild Liberia's armed forces to reflect NPP, rather than national, interests. Avoiding the pitfalls of pre-war Liberian armed forces in terms of recruitment, tribal affiliation, and social education, civil–military relationships would be one of the keys to building a stable environment. Although most of the external actors in Liberia conceded that reforming the armed forces was the duty of the government installed after the election, each actor was considering its own unilateral action. Perhaps the most discussed of these options was the possibility of integrating the armed forces of all the warring factions.

Creating a new national armed force from warring factions had its own difficulties. Although this was done with considerable success in Zimbabwe, there were important differences between Zimbabwe and Liberia. In Zimbabwe, there was a structure upon which the integrated army was to be modelled. Although the Smith government had been politically defeated, the Rhodesian security forces were tactically unbeaten. They were also an operationally effective force with well-established structures. To provide a robust nucleus for the future based on these structures, President Mugabe asked the Commander of the Rhodesian Army, General Peter Walls, to continue the management of the integrated army of Zimbabwe. This principle could not be applied in Liberia, where the national armed forces had been torn apart and depleted by failures of every kind. As a result, the Liberians took the rebel forces more seriously than the AFL.

In Zimbabwe, the political arrangement that ended the war allowed for an orderly transfer of the guerrillas from their bases in Zambia and Mozambique to the assembly camps. Here, under all-party supervision, the process to recruit Zimbabwe's new armed forces was begun. The Lancaster Agreement that ended the war in Zimbabwe had already committed the warring factions to the creation of the new national army. This made it possible for President Mugabe and Mr. Nkomo to discuss the details with all their guerrillas and to brief them about all the steps to be taken in that direction. The stages of the peace process were monitored and supervised by General Peter Walls, Lookout Masuku, and Josiah Tongogara, the commanders, respectively, of the Rhodesian Army, ZIPRA, and ZANLA. This made it possible for them to explain the details of the integration exercise to their respective forces.

In the case of Liberia there was no formal recognition of these problems, which were to make the process of organizing a defence force much more difficult. A number of problems confronted any attempt to integrate the warring factions. The first arose from the fact that the war had divided society, so that not all the warring factions would be willing to cooperate and integrate their fighters to form a new national army. From the demobilization figures discussed earlier, it can be seen that the fighters of the LPC and ULIMO-J had not shown any deep interest in demobilizing. Their lack of enthusiasm for joining a national army matched the lack of enthusiasm shown by their leaders for contesting the presidential elections. If ULIMO-J and the LPC, both of significant strength, refused to join in the exercise, they could undermine the entire integration effort.

A second problem centred on the need for an external moderator that could monitor the reorganization process. In Zimbabwe this role was played by the British Military Advisory Team. From the experience of Zimbabwe, an external supervisor required three things to be successful: credibility, resources, and determination. Credibility was needed to reconcile the conflicting interests of all the factions impartially, resources were required to support the retraining programme and offer professional advice at every level, and, above all, determination was essential to ensure commitment till the end. In the Liberian situation, getting an external moderator with these three credentials would be difficult. ECOMOG, which seemed to be the most likely candidate for this assignment, appeared to be tired. After seven years in Liberia, with all the attendant financial drain, the peacekeeping mission was looking for a way out. There was a fear that such an open-ended commitment would be likely to bring it once again into confrontation with the recalcitrant factions. Most ECOMOG officers were not willing to consider such an option. However, this position appears to have altered with the successful staging of elections and the emergence of a strong leader. With renewed confidence, ECOMOG committed itself to remaining in Liberia for six months after the presidential elections to assist in the rebuilding of a new armed force and to provide security during this period.

At this stage it was not known how many of the factions would react to some of the steps that would be required in any efforts to harmonize their interests. At the outset there were too many self-styled "generals," all with ranks conferred on them by their faction leaders or more often by themselves. It was inevitable that many of them would have to lose these ranks, including many of the senior officers of the AFL who were too young and inexperienced. Equitable restructuring involving widespread demotion, however carefully conducted, was bound to be universally unpopular and, without the overwhelming supervisory presence of a more powerful "moderating" force, almost impossible to achieve. There was also the problem of demobilization. In the previous attempts at integration, this had always been a contentious issue. It was certain that only a few of those who volunteered to join the new Liberian army would be needed in what it was hoped would be a smaller peacetime requirement. The criteria for selection would have to cater for the political peculiarities of the situation. It was not known how this could be agreeably achieved. In previous more successful examples, the selection criteria and the numbers and proportions to be selected were agreed long before the armed forces restructuring process was begun.

Reconstruction

There were many pressing issues that the Taylor government had to address almost immediately if the reconciliation process was to gain impetus. The process involved a substantial international effort as well as a massive and essential element of Liberian involvement. Coordination was to be a major challenge. The list of rebuilding priorities included:
- rebuilding the economy
- the resettlement of refugees and displaced communities
- the reintegration of "war-affected" children, youths, and women
- facilitating the return of professionals and skilled labour, skills development, and job creation
- training programmes for non-combatants
- the restoration of basic social services
- rebuilding schools
- income-generation programmes for local communities
- redeveloping the media
- strengthening law enforcement institutions and building civil administration.[16]

The economy

In 1987 Liberia's main exports were timber, iron, rubber, and diamonds. The economy had started its downward plunge even before the war and the situation was further aggravated by the crisis. Apart from the fact that there was no effective central government to control the management of these resources, the war had destroyed much of Liberia's industrial infrastructure. Added to this, illegal mining of resources went on throughout the war. All the warring factions had participated in illegal mining of resources. Figures quoted from the US State Department[17] noted that, between 1990 and 1994, Liberian diamond exports averaged US$300 million annually. Annual timber and rubber exports during the same period averaged US$53 million and US$23 million, respectively. The same source alleged that iron ore exported between 1990 and 1993 averaged almost US$41 million. The US State Department confirmed that virtually all these revenues found their way into the private accounts of the warlords. Debilitated by this illegal extraction of its wealth, Liberia became unable to feed its citizens or to export its commodities and generate its full potential output.

Social infrastructure

The impact of the war on social infrastructure was more difficult to quantify, especially when much of it could not be reduced to statistics.

Certainly schools, hospitals, and other public utilities were destroyed, but another less definable aspect of societal life had also suffered considerably as a result of the war: moral values. Prostitution, until recently a problem that had been ignored, now had long-term implications for the country. The problem was rooted in a reversal of responsibility that had occurred as a result of the war. Children had developed too fast. To survive under conditions of severe danger and hardship, in many cases without their parents, children now had to act as adults, males joining the rebel groups and females taking to prostitution. The war had produced child soldiers and child prostitutes. In addition to demobilizing the factions, the international community had to plan how to "demobilize" Liberia's youth. By the middle of the 1990s, Liberia was completely unable to face the future without considerable external support.

Social and economic reconstruction

The UN agencies and international non-governmental organizations were expected to perform the bulk of the socio-economic reconstruction of Liberia. In most cases, their efforts had started during the war, with the hope that the provision of a crude semblance of socio-economic well-being would assist in reconciliation. Some of the previous peace agreements, especially the Cotonou and the Abuja agreements, specified roles for these organizations and agencies in assisting Liberia's reconstruction. In some cases, as in the Cotonou accord, these were tied to disarmament and the demobilization process. For example, Section H, Article 9(2) (see Appendix 4), called on the United Nations and other international organizations to programme and finance the process of demobilization, retraining, and rehabilitation of all former combatants so that they could return to normal community life.

UN agencies had been operating in Liberia even before the arrival of UNOMIL. Notable among these organizations were the United Nations Children's Fund (UNICEF), the World Food Programme (WFP), the United Nations Development Programme (UNDP), the UN Humanitarian Assistance Coordination Office (UN-HACO), the Food and Agriculture Organization (FAO), and the United Nations High Commissioner for Refugees (UNHCR). The UNHCR catered for the refugees, while UNICEF worked on demobilization, taking care of child soldiers. The WFP distributed food aid and the FAO assisted Liberians to get back to their real capacity of food production. In many cases these organizations had worked in harmony with ECOMOG and UNOMIL.

However, a number of factors weakened their capacity to operate effectively, including inter-agency rivalry. Like other foreign organizations in the country, the United Nations suffered during the resurgence of violence in April 1996. UN offices were destroyed and property looted. In most cases UN agencies had to move. Even UNOMIL moved from its Mamba Point apartments to Hotel Africa on the outskirts of Monrovia. After the crisis, the UN agencies targeted essential services to improve malnutrition, alleviate hunger, provide emergency health services, prevent epidemic diseases, and provide basic education and basic operational support services. However, there was a lack of cooperation between the UNOMIL office and many of the humanitarian organizations. This was a significant limitation during demobilization, which involved a number of organizations in the same phases of the process. Under the Abuja accord, a number of agencies were nominated to participate. It is also alleged that the United Nations failed to cooperate with the National Disarmament and Demobilization Commission, a body charged with collecting data on disarmament and demobilization.

In a crisis that among other priorities focused on the problems of children, the United Nations and its agencies could not agree with some NGOs and bilateral relief organizations on what constituted a child and what should be done in the rehabilitation of children. Under the UN convention, anybody under the age of 17 is considered a child. The European Union (EU), however, argued that, if children could be fighting at the age of 12 and 13, some of them would be more realistically regarded as adults seeking gainful employment rather than children returning to school. Most agencies have also been criticized for focusing mainly on relief and failing to create the capacity for the country to get back on its own feet, thus causing dependency on foreign assistance. Failure by some important agencies to deploy to areas in the south-east part of Liberia had condemned people in these areas to suffer neglect at the hands of the warring factions.

Non-governmental organizations

The number of local and international NGOs fluctuated each month with the surge and ebb of violence. Some were very brave and penetrated, at great risk to themselves, to hostile areas such as Buchanan, Tubmanburg, Harbel, Tappita, and Greenville. NGOs were on the whole critical and suspicious of the Nigerian military presence in Liberia. Some NGOs came into serious confrontation with ECOMOG and the United Nations. Tension escalated and, in the case of ECOMOG soldiers, led to attacks on NGO convoys, particularly during "Operation Octopus." ECOMOG for its part counter-accused the NGOs of white-washing the activities of the NPFL and even, it was alleged, running weapons into Liberia for them. NGOs also resisted and evaded the efforts at overall coordination of the demobilization phase by UN-HACO. Whatever the rights and wrongs of this dispute, the overall result was a reduction in the efficiency of the international restoration effort at its interface with the Liberian population. However, despite these problems of rivalry, many agencies operated successfully.

After the elections, the problem was to move from relief to rebuilding programmes. The EU was particularly successful in this respect. Its three-man team arrived in the country in November 1996, working mainly on the Micro-project Programme of Reintegration and Resettlement. It established 12 ex-combatant programmes, and by mid-January 1997 had provided jobs for 874 people. It identified 15 micro-projects, including rebuilding schools, agricultural production, sanitation, and well rehabilitation, where the basic objective was to move forward from temporary work programmes to rehabilitation and resettlement for ex-combatants. In its programmes, the EU tried to mix ex-combatants with non-combatants. This was with the intention of breaking the command structure of the former combat organizations. As of mid-January 1997, the EU was working in 8 of the 13 counties in Liberia, and aimed to cover at least 11 before the end of the year.

ECOWAS, in contrast, had not taken any active role in addressing the long-term socio-economic problems of Liberia. The attention of the organization had been primarily on the peacekeeping mission. The main reason for this was that most of the countries in the region did not have the economic resources to sponsor long-term assistance for Liberia, their resources having been depleted by involvement in the peacekeeping activities. In public, ECOWAS maintained that the entire issue of post-war rehabilitation was the prerogative of the new government in Liberia and that West African countries could help, in their individual capacities, in the long-term reconstruction of Liberia. In private, however, many felt that Liberia should better look to Western Europe and the NGOs for any enduring relief.

Local NGOs have also played a most important role in the reconstruction of Liberia. Perhaps the most important of these is Susukuu, a development NGO formed by Dr. Togba Nah-Tipoteh. Although the organization was established in 1971, its activities were most felt during the war, when it focused on stimulating the flow of international assistance to Liberia, on reconstruction of social infrastructure, and on the rehabilitation of former combatants through training, counselling, and education. Susukuu was able to influence many of the combatants to disarm. The organization started the "School for Gun" programme, whereby child soldiers would be given support to return to school in exchange for the return of their guns. The programme showed enormous early promise, but the renewed hostilities in April 1996 set things back considerably. Other efforts by Liberians include the National Volunteer Programme, formed by local people but supported by UN agencies and international NGOs, and the Special Emergency Life Food (SELF).

With the end of its war, Liberia was confronted with the difficulties of post-war reconstruction. Although the nature of the problem was clear both to the new government and to the international community, it proved difficult to find the funds to carry out reconstruction. Although the international community sympathized with Liberia, the extent to which it was willing to back this up with financial assistance was not certain at the time Taylor took power. The realization by many that the absence of external aid for reconstruction might lead to the renewed outbreak of conflict created concern about the prospects for stability in Liberia. The new president, however, made a resolute promise to Liberians and to the international community that attempts would be made to make Liberia a success story.

Notes

1. *Reuters*, 7 February 1997.
2. Ibid.
3. Ibid.
4. For a discussion of many of these parties and their candidates, see *West Africa*, 14–20 July 1997. See also, *Agence France Press* (AFP), 17 July 1997.
5. *Reuters*, 22 July 1997.
6. AFP, 24 July 1997. Also *Reuters*, 24 July 1997.
7. *Reuters*, 24 July 1997.
8. *Reuters*, 26 July 1997.
9. AFP, 26 July 1997.
10. Ibid.
11. Associated Press, Liberia, cited in *BBC Focus on Africa*, 24 July 1997.
12. Ibid.
13. *BBC Focus on Africa*, 21 July 1997.
14. AFP, 24 July 1997.
15. AFP, 27 July 1997.
16. See UNDP, *Peace Activities and Programme*, Liberia, 1996.
17. In Jeremy Armon and Andy Carl, "The Liberian Peace Process 1990–1996," in *Accord: An International Review of Peace Initiatives*, London: Conciliation Resources, 1996.

9

Conclusion: Some lessons from the Liberian experience

In the worst moments of Liberia's agony there were many who sought to marginalize the importance of what was happening there. This collective failure to address the seriousness of Liberia's internal conflict was facilitated by its comparative global isolation and its proximity in time to the Gulf War. Nevertheless the lessons of the Liberian tragedy are important both for the region and for the wider community of northern states. Liberia has the features of a post-Cold War complex emergency and the international response to it. If the international community is to improve its understanding of these crises, the lessons of Liberia's experience have a wider global significance.

Liberia's has been the trauma of a country that in effect collapsed, resulting in the massive displacement of the population both within the country and to neighbouring countries. It was not just a military crisis, but a crisis that affected the entire civilian population, with the greatest weight of the disaster bearing on the children. Several armed factions contested the future of the country, resulting in a situation where power devolved into the hands of sub-state actors – not politicians and statesmen accustomed to the use of power, but traders, petty criminals, and religious bigots. The intensity of the crisis led to the dispatch of the first regional peacekeeping mission in the aftermath of the Cold War, followed by the first involvement of United Nations military observers cooperating with the regional peacekeeping operation. Few global conflicts have all these characteristics, although some are present in virtually all complex emergencies. What were the universal lessons of this experience?

Recognizing the locus of power

Throughout the conflict there seemed to be a continuous, wishful lack of appreciation of the centres of effective power in Liberia and who controlled them. The early chapters of this book have described a gradual collapse of government. The native Liberian communities had been led to expect a brighter era ahead in which their ethnicity and social needs would be recognized. In the late 1980s, when they began to realize that Doe's government would fail to deliver on these expectations, these communities moved beyond the reach of the central government. In 1990 as the state broke apart, its centre of gravity sub-divided and passed into the hands of sub-state actors.

Despite this inexorable devolution of power from the capital into the hinterlands of NPFL and ULIMO held areas, regional powers such as Nigeria, together with officials from ECOWAS, the United States, and the United Nations, kept up the fiction of the Liberian state. Visitors from abroad could for most of the crisis travel to Monrovia and, as long as they remained within the envelope of comparative security created by ECOMOG troops, imagine that they were living in a damaged but functioning state. But ECOMOG's power to maintain an area of comparative tranquillity around Monrovia was transitory and dependent on several external factors, such as the cohesion of regional support and the continuing supply of funds, mainly from Nigeria. ECOMOG constituted a considerable drain on its West African contributors, its artificially supported environment around Monrovia was a very short-term affair, and ECOMOG had an exit strategy in sight throughout.

The reality was that beyond the envelope of ECOMOG's security lay other sovereign powers. To the north for example, in "Taylorland," was a rival capital, Gbarnga, with its own currency, radio station, police, hospital, and an embryonic crude government emanating from Taylor's villa, which communicated both internally to his subordinate commanders and to the world beyond. The mistake that recurred like a constant theme through every stage of the peace process until the final Abuja negotiations was to maintain the fiction that Monrovia was still the central and most significant actor. In reality the power to bring the settlement to a successful conclusion had passed into the hands of the warlords. A successful peace process would have to, first of all, fully recognize that situation and, secondly, devote much of its substance to addressing the concerns of the warlords rather than the effete needs of the Americo-Liberian politicians in Monrovia.

Despite this, there were several peace negotiations at which the key power holders in Liberia were not effectively represented. Instead, the discussion went on between Monrovia-based politicians who could not in reality deliver the conditions of a peace process from the faction-held hinterlands. There was also a general failure to understand how power ebbed and flowed within the factions themselves. During a lull in the fighting when the threat to the overall security of a faction was diminished and negotiations might be taking place, the constitution of the factions themselves would alter. At local level, a faction's constituent bands would move away from the control of the warlord as they scoured the countryside to sustain themselves with food and money. If a faction leader was absent for long periods, it became more difficult to deliver the faction as a reliable participant in a peace process. Although the peace process was organized and hosted with a considerable degree of altruism in its early phases, there was a lack of awareness of how power was constantly changing hands in Liberia. The intervening powers cherished an idealistic view of a return to the previous order, to statehood, and there was a general failure to recognize how power, despite the efforts to disarm and to demobilize, remained in the hands of the warlords. This wishful misapprehension is a constant theme not only in the Liberian tragedy but also in other responses to complex emergencies in the post–Cold War period.

The lesson for impresarios of future peace processes is that they must have access to a constant source of reliable information about who wields the power in the absence of state government. Once the new centres of power have been identified, peace-organizing governments must be prepared to communicate and deal effectively with these leaders. In some cases it will be difficult to organize reliable communications to them on a day-to-day basis. Many of the faction leaders involved in the peace process will have committed serious war crimes. But unless power can be forcibly removed or diverted from them, which is very seldom the case, even after an apparently successful process of disarmament and demobilization, it is hard to see how they can be excluded from a peace process if they continue to have the power to sabotage its success.

State failure brings massive social change. In Liberia, the failure of the state launched social changes that were almost revolutionary in their scale and impact. The factional violence had direct consequences for the civil population, because it was impossible to remain neutral or detached from what was happening. As warring factions moved around to assert themselves in greater Liberia, the civilian population fled before them, migrating in massive numbers. A high proportion moved into the urban areas, particularly into the ECOMOG security envelope, where they could subsist with the help of the NGOs and not become a part of the fighting. Others fled across adjacent borders or took to the bush, where they managed to live hand to mouth until it was safe to return to their homes. In this process of constant upheaval on a massive scale, social structures began to collapse. The hierarchies of the family, the village, and the clan in many cases could not survive the constant stress of migration and violence. The population had been uprooted in every sense, and a considerable element of its youth criminalized by its experience of factional violence. Education at every level had been in abeyance for several years, releasing a tide of boys and even children to become participants in factional violence. Armed with AK47s, these young faction-fighters overturned traditional social structures and found themselves in a position to dictate to older generations who once regulated society. This trend was exacerbated in urban areas. The lesson for the organizers of the peace process was that they were dealing with a new social order. It would be impossible to resuscitate the structures of the past. They had to recognize that the failure of the state had much wider social implications. It had left a vacuum in the social structure and they would have to design their immediate and long-term responses accordingly.

Implementing the peace process

From a strictly local vantage point, there was very little reason why the surviving faction leaders in Liberia would want to submit themselves to the peace process. In their own environment they controlled all the most important life-sustaining resources. They more or less commanded a monopoly of military power in their own area, they could control the civilian population as they desired, and in most cases they were exploiting all the raw materials and commercial opportunities that existed locally. For example, Charles Taylor's personal fortune in the early 1990s was derived from his energetic trading and exportation of hard wood, diamonds, and various agricultural products. At this time the NPFL was France's third-largest supplier of tropical hard woods.[1]

Each of the peace processes that was negotiated in the 1990s set out to restore Liberia as a state and, if successful in that process, would almost certainly have stripped the warlords of their military power, their opportunities for trade and extortion, and their control over a relatively downtrodden civil population. Moreover, as most of them had supervised the commission of atrocities in the course of the war, it was likely they faced the prospect of some form of retribution, if not from the law at any rate from vengeful elements of the population. In these circumstances, unless they were men of great vision and ambitious for the future prosperity and success of the state of Liberia, as opposed to themselves, there was very little incentive for them to encourage a successful peace process. The prospect of national elections meant there would be one winner and a number of absolute losers for whom there could be little honour or protection as members of a parliamentary opposition. In the long history of Liberian politics, the concept of parliamentary opposition was undeveloped and during the Doe regime being identified as "the opposition" amounted to the kiss of death.

In Liberia, the warlords were usually ready to negotiate but not to relinquish their powers, which is what would have shown that they were genuinely interested in a peace settlement. In these circumstances, only enormous outside pressure could bring warlords into a peace process as effective participants. Locally, war exhaustion, desertions, and depleted funds could help to build up this pressure. By 1996 there were signs that the Liberian civil population was increasingly hostile and resistant to the warlords. Later on, the overwhelming vote for Taylor was in reality a vote for the only leader who could deliver peace. Externally, the leaders of neighbouring states were tired of bearing the cost and disruption of the adjacent conflict which, from time to time, came spilling across their borders. Consequently they put pressure on their client factions, threatening to withdraw base facilities, rights of access, and political support. Finally, the combination of war exhaustion and unbearable outside pressures forced the warlords to abandon their lucrative lifestyle as local despots and consider becoming part of a state once again.

The actual removal of power from the warlords into the hands of a higher office at state level was the critical moment in the transfer from conflict to peace. It moved the process on from the rhetoric of peace negotiations into a new chapter of developments. It was nevertheless a moment of great tension for the warlords, all of whom were anxiously watching each other to see if any one was going to renege on the disarmament process and take advantage of the weakness of the others. Moving from warlord to political candidate forced the leaders into an extremely vulnerable position where their relative strengths and weaknesses as faction leaders counted for very little and they would have to survive on their political skills alone. In this situation there is no doubt that each warlord cheated on the peace process and withheld vital elements of their forces to act as an insurance policy against the possibility that their rivals might attempt to re-arm and crush them.

Even in the most propitious circumstances it was unlikely that disarmament could be successful. It was more accurately a useful device to remove surplus and unserviceable weapons from the Liberian hinterlands. In the Abuja II disarmament experience, the first weapons to be handed over were in these categories. Serviceable weapons were simply wrapped in plastic sheeting and hidden for the future. A genuine disarmament process that removed a substantial number of effective weapons from the hands of active faction fighters required more than a bald announcement of the disarmament process and the setting-up of weapon collection sites. In the Zimbabwe-Rhodesia experience, after a prolonged information campaign by local radio, fighters were encamped with their weapons and no attempt was made to disarm them until they were either called up as part of the new Zimbabwean defence forces or demobilized. By the time this demobilization phase was under way the state had already passed into a new chapter of development in law and order in which the AK47 had become more or less superfluous. Liberia took longer to reach this stage and it was the forceful intervention of ECOMOG under its energetic commander General Victor Malu that exerted the local pressure that caused the reluctant faction fighters to hand in the weapons that had been for so long essential to their survival and credibility.

However, the climate for disarmament was undeveloped. The military aspects of the peace process had outpaced the civil arrangements for re-development. When the disarmed youths left the demobilization centres there were no employment schemes to take them off the streets and into gainful employment. The gangs of disarmed fighters loitering in the suburban areas of Monrovia and Tubmanburg threatened the election process and the return of a more civil society. They were the products of enormous social changes and the danger was that they would return to the only lifestyle they knew: extortion from the civil population.

The lessons of the Liberian peace process were reflected in the simultaneously unfolding peace process in Bosnia. Here too the military disarmament programme had run far ahead of the civil development plan, leaving gangs of unemployed disarmed militiamen, particularly in the Serb areas, on the streets of every garrison town. In Liberia, as in Zimbabwe, the presence of a large, uncommitted military force that supported the peace process was a key factor in success – in the case of Zimbabwe it was the Rhodesian security forces of the previous regime; in the case of Liberia it was ECOMOG. ECOMOG had demonstrated in Operation Octopus that in a pitched battle it could defeat even the most powerful factions in Liberia. By 1996 there was no question of the factions resisting ECOMOG; the question instead was whether ECOMOG itself had the commitment to enforce the spirit and letter of the agreed peace process. As it turned out it had, and this was probably crucial in persuading the reluctant warlords to relinquish their power.

External intervention forces

One of the most important lessons of the Liberian crisis is that, where the structures of governance have in effect collapsed, and where the consequences of the failure of that government have begun to affect the safety and population of the neighbouring states, external intervention is always an option to be considered by the affected neighbours. An overwhelming desire for containment has occurred in several instances in the post-Cold War chronology, from Somalia to Albania.

In the case of Liberia, after the failure of its central government to control violence began to have a serious impact on its neighbours, countries in the region decided that some form of intervention was essential to contain the situation. An intervening force is questioned and scrutinized at every level as regards the declared and hidden meanings behind its actions (the American involvement in Somalia is a good example). But few interventions have received such sustained and enduring criticism as the ECOMOG involvement in the Liberian dispute. Here it was widely alleged in the initial stages of the crisis that Nigeria led other countries to interfere because of its selfish desire to protect President Doe.

The reason for suspecting the motives of the intervening force vary. The whole issue of intervention is a controversial subject. The countries and organizations that might want to intervene in a conflict must have an interest in the particular country in which they are intervening, despite the fact that the concept of impartiality was to be one of the important principles of UN peacekeeping at its inception. Although the likelihood of self-interest is prevalent, it is possible for an intervention to be driven by an overall sense of altruism that is tinged with only a degree of national self-interest, such as the wider security implications if the situation got worse. Even so, in the case of regional intervention, the intervening states must be prepared for widespread and wilful misinterpretation of their motives. There is a tendency for people to believe that, when countries commit enormous resources to the resolution of conflicts in other countries, they must have a hidden agenda. Having formed this impression, it becomes natural to misinterpret the actions of intervention forces and to support allegations that the intervention is not altruistic.

The conduct of the forces after they have entered the conflict-torn country is also an issue that has attracted attention, emphasized for example in 1996 by the allegations of brutality by Canadian and European forces in Somalia. In Liberia, too, there have been some serious allegations regarding the conduct of the regional peacekeeping force. ECOMOG has been accused of a whole range of activities: the looting of Liberian resources, the organization of client armed factions, encouraging relationships with Liberian women, and brutality against elements of the Liberian population. Although we found some of these allegations to be true, there were also cases of obvious exaggeration. The lessons of these allegations have a wider applicability.

In the case of ECOMOG it was sometimes hard for local leaders in Liberia to accept the obvious gap between the apparently altruistic mission of the intervening forces and their behaviour on the ground. To argue the case from ECOMOG's position, it is important to establish that its troops had been put in an impossible position. ECOMOG battalions in and around Monrovia found themselves intermittently paid, poorly sheltered, and logistically under-resourced but compelled to remain for indefinite spells in a hostile and uncomfortable situation. It was inevitable that individual elements of ECOMOG, possibly without official sanction, would begin to supplement their meagre lifestyle from local sources. This activity included mild forms of day-to-day extortion. Long stays overseas in these circumstances led to a degree of integration with the local community. However, integration with such a traumatized population meant that, when a warlord attacked or threatened a local community, this also threatened the environment of the local ECOMOG battalion. In this way ECOMOG troops became part of the problem, not just during periods of overt hostility with the factions, but throughout their tenure of duty. ECOMOG's most vociferous critics from the United Nations and the professional northern defence forces were unable to understand that regional forces placed in this very poorly resourced position for extended periods had no option but to behave in a highly partial and exploitative manner in order to survive. The golden rules of peacekeeping, articulated in chapter 1, were a manifestation of a different era of peacekeeping forces. Deployed to the ordered buffer zones of the Arab-Israeli wars, armed forces at the interface were under the strict control of the state and rations would arrive routinely in convoys of expensive white vehicles. ECOMOG, in contrast, was an African solution to an African problem; however desirable it might have been to abide by the rules of traditional peacekeeping, these had become largely irrelevant.

This justification of ECOMOG's behaviour is undermined by very serious allegations that in some cases the physical looting of Liberia's heavy industrial assets and raw materials was organized and condoned at the highest level, particularly by some authorities in Nigeria. If in the longer perspective of history these allegations turn out to be true, the argument that ECOMOG was in Liberia for largely altruistic reasons becomes untenable. However, it could be maintained that, at battalion level, given the conditions of their service, ECOMOG's sub-units and individuals were going to behave as they did, whether or not senior officials were involved at higher levels in serious looting activities in and around Monrovia.

The wider lessons for the international community and the African region in particular are first of all that, given the continuing lack of commitment of northern states to African disasters, regional intervention forces will continue to be a likely prospect for the future. Furthermore, any intervention or peacekeeping force, whether deployed for altruistic or for narrowly selfish reasons, that is under-resourced and deployed for long periods will gradually become reliant on the local economy for its survival and lose its impartiality. In these circumstances, those who argue against the deployment of any form of intervention on the grounds that it only exacerbates the violence and prolongs the crisis have failed to see that, in the final stages of Liberia's peace settlement, ECOMOG provided an essential element in its success – the presence of an uncommitted but powerful force that was going to see the process to its agreed conclusion. Traditional peacekeepers may claim that this is not peacekeeping; but the overwhelming lesson of this experience has been that the principles of traditional peacekeeping are no longer relevant to complex emergencies. It may be that, rather than a powerful and highly organized intervention dominated by northern defence forces, an African solution is the best form of intervention in an African emergency.

In the continuing chronology of interventions for peace, every force has turned out to be different. As suggested at the beginning of this chapter, the Liberian crisis has similarities to many other complex emergencies of this period. The closest comparison so far is to the United Nations Mission in Georgia (UNOMIG), where a CIS or Russian peacekeeping force maintains local security and the modalities of the peace process are monitored by UN observers. Just as, in their rough and ready manner, the Russian peacekeepers have maintained a workable peace between the warring parties, so the West African troops of ECOMOG secured a settlement in Liberia.

The lessons learned by elements of the international response have been important too. In chapters 4 and 5 it was explained how the international community, and in particular the United Nations, had underestimated the necessary scale of the peace process. Liberia has been a peace process on the cheap. In particular, the need for reconciliation has been greatly undervalued, and the resources for this aspect of the peace process were cut and cut again until the rehabilitation and reconciliation phases of the operation were no longer recognizable manifestations of the original plan. There were also important mistakes in the overall coordination of the activities of the international forces and agencies: failures of communication and cooperation between ECOMOG and UNOMIL, between the relief agencies, and between civilian and military officials. These too have been discussed at length in chapters 4 and 5 and there is a sameness about their debate that pervades practically every multinational operation in this period.

What distinguishes the Liberian crisis and the response to it is that it has been essentially an African operation. Liberia witnessed the prototype of an African solution, a sub-regional intervention to contain a conflict that threatened to destabilize a much wider area than Liberia. Although it has been a much criticized and abused solution, now, after the relatively free, peaceful, and conclusive election of Charles Taylor, it must be regarded as an initiative that has achieved a measure of success. In the long-term historical analysis, it is possible that evidence may be uncovered that reveals that ECOMOG was deployed and kept in Liberia for corrupt and selfish reasons. But, after our best efforts and with the information available to us at the time of our research, we have found little substantive evidence to support these allegations. Despite the fact that, on a local scale, corruption and looting were a day-to-day phenomenon in the ECOMOG garrison, there was also a good-hearted aspect to their behaviour that could have been strongly interpreted as a manifestation of a genuinely altruistic purpose in their presence. Meanwhile, the gradual restoration of civil society in Liberia continues and, long after the departure of the last platoon of ECOMOG soldiers, the long-term success of the peace process will still be questioned. At a meeting after his election, Charles Taylor famously remarked that the generation that will replace him and his government is still in its early teenage years. But what kind of society will they create – these children who survived the brutalizing years of Liberia's tragedy?

Note

1. Mark Duffield, "Post-modern Conflict: War Lords, Post-Adjustment States and Private Protection," *Journal of Civil Wars*, April 1998.

Postscript

At the end of his first year in office, President Taylor confessed to all Liberians that his administration had not been able to meet the expectations of the people, especially as regards the challenges of post-war reconstruction. He attributed this failure to the lack of expected assistance from the international community. This won him criticism from some of his opponents, many of whom attributed his failure to lack of foresight and careless management of state affairs.

Perhaps the most important problem Taylor faced during the first year was the management of domestic security. Two of the former armed factions, ULIMO-J and ULIMO-K, were allegedly taking steps to undermine the government. Although the leader of ULIMO-J, Roosevelt Johnson, was invited into the cabinet as a minister, the relationship between him and the President deteriorated to the point where he was removed from the government. He was later accused of plotting a coup and had to be taken out of the country by the American embassy before the crisis degenerated into another violent outburst. The relationship between the government and ULIMO-K remains potentially explosive, but it has been contained without any violent incidents. Taylor's management of domestic security reached its lowest ebb when Sam Dokie, a former Taylor ally who later defected to the opposition, and members of his family were killed by people suspected to be agents of the state. Although the government denied any involvement and promised to investigate the matter, not many Liberians believed the denial.

The creation of a new national army continues to constitute a major controversy. Although it was expected that ECOMOG would assist in the creation of the national army, Taylor later fell out with ECOMOG and the regional peacekeepers were expelled from Liberia. To date, a national army has still not been created and the criticism has been levelled against Taylor that he is trying to use his former guerrillas to form the national army.

By 1998 the main problem confronting Liberia was the crisis in neighbouring Sierra Leone, where Taylor is allegedly supporting the Revolutionary United Front rebels fighting the Kabbah government. The conflict has made the border between the two countries unsafe, and Taylor has persistently alleged that former factions, especially ULIMO-K, have used the opportunity of the war in Sierra Leone to threaten his government in Liberia. Taylor's support for the rebels has also earned him criticism from other countries in the region, especially Nigeria, which in fact issued a subtle threat that it would not take any support for those killing Nigerian soldiers in Sierra Leone lightly. Although the efforts to bring peace to Sierra Leone continue, there are still problems in many parts of the country. It is widely believed that the futures of both Liberia and Sierra Leone are inextricably linked and, until there is an enduring peace in Sierra Leone, Liberia will have to take its neighbour's security situation on board in its security calculations.

Appendices

1
Details of the Bamako Agreement, November 1990

- to cease all hostilities immediately after signing the agreement;
- to refrain from building weapons;
- to confine troops to positions to be determined by ECOMOG in consultation with the parties; and to allow ECOMOG to inspect all ships, vehicles and aircraft to ensure that the agreement is respected by the parties;
- to assist ECOMOG in drawing up a buffer zone to separate opposing forces;
- to release all hostages, and political and war prisoners;
- to cooperate with all humanitarian agencies providing relief to Liberians, and to respect the Red Cross;
- to cooperate fully with the ECOWAS Standing Mediation Committee, ECOWAS Secretariat, and ECOMOG for the maintenance and restoration of peace;
- upon the formation of the future interim government, it shall take measures with the assistance of ECOWAS to begin disarming the warring parties.

2

Details of the Banjul Agreement, December 1990

- to form a future interim government from an All-Liberian Conference in Liberia within the next 60 days;
- to constitute a Technical Committee to work out security arrangements for the hosting of the All-African Conference under ECOWAS supervision;
- to seek assistance from ECOWAS and other friendly nations and organizations to help repatriate and resettle Liberians before the All-Liberian Conference;
- upon the formation of the future Interim Government, it shall take measures with ECOWAS assistance to begin disarming the warring factions;
- to continue the cease-fire, and remain where parties were when the Bamako cease-fire agreement was signed on 28 November 1990; and make all efforts to conclude the modalities within 30 days;
- to consider all seaports and airports as military-free zones immediately.

3
Stipulations of the Lomé Accord, February 1991

- immediate cessation of hostilities of military and para-military nature;
- refraining from importation and acquisition of weapons and war materials;
- confinement of troops to position to be determined by ECOMOG in consultation with parties;
- assisting ECOMOG in drawing up buffer zones;
- release of all hostages, political prisoners, and prisoners of wars;
- cooperation with all humanitarian agencies in their efforts to provide relief and assistance for the people;
- full cooperation with ECOWAS and ECOMOG.

4

The Cotonou Agreement, July 1993

THIS AGREEMENT is made this twenty-fifth day of July one thousand nine hundred and ninety-three –

BETWEEN THE Interim Government of National Unity of Liberia (IGNU) of the first part and the National Patriotic Front of Liberia (NPFL) of the second part and the United Liberation Movement of Liberia for Democracy (ULIMO) of the third part.

PART I

Military issues

SECTION A

Article 1

DECLARATION

1. The Parties to this Agreement hereby agree and declare a cease-fire and the cessation of hostilities – to become effective at the date and time and on the conditions stipulated in article 2 and section C below.

2. The parties further declare that all parties or groups within and without the perimeter of Liberia shall refrain from act(s) or activity(ies) that may violate or facilitate the violation of the cease-fire.

Article 2
EFFECTIVE DATE

The Parties also agree that the cease-fire stated herein-above and the cessation of hostilities shall take effect seven days from the date of signing of this Agreement, commencing at 12 midnight.

SECTION B

Article 3

SUPERVISORY AND MONITORING AUTHORITY

1. The ECOMOG and the United Nations Observer Mission shall supervise and monitor the implementation of this Agreement. The Parties hereby expressly recognize the neutrality and authority of the Economic Community of West African States (ECOWAS) Military Observer Group (ECOMOG) and the United Nations Observer Mission in respect of the foregoing. Accordingly, the ECOMOG and United Nations observers shall enjoy complete freedom of movement throughout Liberia.

2. By "ECOMOG Peace-Keeping Force" is meant an expanded ECOMOG which includes the forces of ECOWAS Member States and African troops from outside the West African region.

3. The Parties agree further that in order to monitor and ensure against any violation of the cease-fire between the period of the effective date of the cease-fire and the arrival of ECOMOG and full contingent of the United Nations Observer Mission, a Joint Cease-fire Monitoring Committee is hereby established, which shall have the authority to monitor, investigate and report all cease-fire violations. The Committee shall comprise an equal number of representatives from each of the parties hereto, ECOMOG and an advance team of the United Nations Observer Mission. Each group of the Joint Cease-fire Monitoring Committee shall be chaired by the United Nations observer in the group. It shall freely travel throughout the country. The committee shall automatically be dissolved and deemed to be dissolved upon the arrival and deployment of ECOMOG and the full contingent of the United Nations Observer Mission.

SECTION C

Article 4

TERMS AND CONDITIONS

1. Prohibitions upon the Parties:

   The Parties agree not to:

   (a) Import any weapons and war-like materials by any means into Liberia;

   (b) Use the period of the cease-fire to engage in any military build-up whether in manpower or armaments; or

   (c) Engage in any other activity that would violate or result in the violation of the cease-fire.

2. Adherence to stipulations on military embargo

The Parties recognize and accept that the military embargo imposed on and upon all warring parties by ECOWAS and the United Nations Security Council shall remain in full force and effect.

3. Creation of buffer zones

ECOMOG shall create zones or otherwise seal the borders, whichever is militarily feasible, of Liberia–Guinea, Liberia–Sierra Leone and Liberia–Cote D'Ivoire to prevent cross-border attacks, infiltration or importation of arms. There shall be deployed United Nations observers in all of such zones to monitor, verify and report on any and all of the foregoing and the implementation thereof.

4. Monitoring and supervision of entry points

All points of entry including sea ports, airfields and roads shall be monitored and supervised by ECOMOG. There shall be deployed United Nations observers to monitor, verify and report on the implementation of the foregoing activities.

5. Position of warring parties at declaration of cease-fire

The warring parties shall remain and maintain their positions held as at the effective date of this cease-fire, until the commencement of encampment.

SECTION D

Article 5

ACTS OF VIOLATION

1. The Parties hereto hereby agree to honour every and all provisions of this Agreement, and stipulate that any party committing any acts of violations shall be held liable for such violations.

2. The following acts shall constitute violation of the cease-fire:

(a) Importation of arms and ammunition, incendiary devices and other war-related items;

(b) Changing or improvement of existing positions or fortification or alteration of existing positions;

(c) Attack (whether with conventional or unconventional weapons) against the position of any warring faction by another, or firing at an individual of a warring faction established to have been carried out at the instance of the authority of the warring party to which he/she belongs;

(d) The systematic use of conventional or unconventional weapons (i.e. knives, cutlasses, bows and arrows, etc);

(e) Recruitment and training of combatants and/or groups or persons after the effective date of this Agreement;

(f) Any proven use of communication devices, facilities or propaganda designed to incite or having the effect of inciting hostilities between any of the warring parties;

(g) Planting of mines and incendiary devices subsequent to the effective date of the cease-fire; refusal to disclose the existence of or places where such devices or mines have been planted; and deliberate failure to co-operate or furnish maps (where available) where such devices have been planted;

(h) obstruction of the implementation of any of the provisions of the Agreement by any party or its authorized agent;

(i) Harassments or attacks upon ECOMOG, the United Nations Observer Mission or the Joint Cease-fire Monitoring Committee;

(j) Obstructions of the activities of ECOMOG, United Nations observers and the Joint Cease-fire Monitoring Committee.

SECTION E

Article 6

DISARMAMENT

Disarmament being the ultimate objective of the cease-fire, the Parties hereto agree and express their intent and willingness to disarm to and under the supervision of ECOMOG, monitored and verified by the United Nations Observer Mission. In conformity therewith, the parties agree that:

1. All weapons and warlike materials collected shall be stored by ECOMOG in armouries designated by ECOMOG, monitored and verified by United Nations observers.

2. All weapons and warlike materials in the possession of the parties shall be given to ECOMOG, monitored by United Nations observers, upon appropriate recording and inventory, and placed in designated armouries.

3. Said armouries shall be secured by ECOMOG, monitored and verified by United Nations observers, upon proper documentation or inventory of all weapons and warlike materials received.

4. Each of the warring factions shall ensure that its combatants report all weapons and warlike materials to ECOMOG, monitored and verified by United Nations observers, upon proper inventory. Such weapons and warlike materials, upon inventory, shall be taken to the designated armouries by ECOMOG, under the monitoring and verification of United Nations observers.

5. All non-combatants who are in possession of weapons and warlike materials shall also report and surrender same to ECOMOG, monitored and verified by United Nations observers. Such weapons and warlike materials shall be returned to the owners after due registration, licensing and certification by the governing authority after the elections.

6. ECOMOG shall have the authority to disarm any combatant or non-combatant in possession of weapons and warlike materials. The United Nations observers shall monitor all such activities.

7. For the sole purpose of maintaining the cease-fire, ECOMOG shall conduct any search to recover lost or hidden weapons, observed and monitored by the United Nations observers.

SECTION F

Article 7

ENCAMPMENT

1. Purpose

(a) The Parties agree and fully commit themselves to the encampment of their combatants in encampment centres established by ECOMOG, monitored and verified by United Nations observers, the purpose of which shall be, in addition to the disarmament and demobilization, to serve as a transit point for the further education, training and rehabilitation of said combatants; and

(b) Consistent with the above, the parties agree to submit to ECOMOG and the United Nations observers, a complete listing of their combatants and weapons and warlike materials and their locations to the nearest encampment centres.

2. Commencement of encampment

The Parties agree that encampment shall commence immediately upon the deployment of ECOMOG and the United Nations Observer Mission. Copies of the schedule of encampment shall be furnished to all the parties hereto.

3. Identification and security of encampment sites

In consultation with the Parties, ECOMOG and the United Nations Observer Mission shall identify locations for encampment. Security of encampment sites shall be provided by ECOMOG, monitored and verified by United Nations observers.

SECTION G

Article 8

PEACE ENFORCEMENT POWERS

1. It is also agreed upon that ECOMOG shall have the right to self-defence where it has been physically attacked by any warring faction hereto.

2. There shall be established, upon deployment of ECOMOG and the full contingent of the United Nations Observer Mission, a Violation Committee consisting of one person from each of the parties hereto and ECOMOG and the United Nations Observer Mission, chaired by a member of the United Nations Observer Mission.

3. All violations of the cease-fire shall be reported to the United Nations Observer Mission/observers who shall, immediately upon receipt of the information of violation, commence an investigation and make findings thereof. In the event the violations can be cured by the United Nations observers, they shall pursue such a course. However, should such a course not be possible, the United Nations observers shall submit their findings to the Violations Committee. The Violations Committee shall invite the violating party/(ies) for the purpose of having such party/(ies) take corrective measures to cure the violations within such time-frame as may be stipulated by the committee. Should the violating party not take the required corrective measures, ECOMOG shall be informed thereof and shall thereupon resort to the use of its peace-enforcement powers against the violator.

SECTION H

Article 9

DEMOBILIZATION

1. The parties hereby agree that any warring faction or factions that may have non-Liberian fighters or mercenaries shall repatriate such persons, or when found, upon evidence, shall be expelled by the Government of the Republic of Liberia.

2. Further, the Parties hereby call upon the United Nations, other international organizations and countries, to programme and finance the process of demobilization, retraining, rehabilitation and re-absorption of all former combatants to normal social and community life.

3. It is agreed by the Parties hereto that each party shall immediately commence a community information or educational programme, explaining to the pubic by means of communication devices or any form of media, the essence and purpose of the cease-fire, encampment, disarmament and demobilization. Such programme shall include other social institutions.

SECTION I

Article 10

PRISONERS-OF-WAR

The Parties hereby agree that upon signing of this Agreement all prisoners-of-war and detainees shall be immediately released to the Red Cross authority in an area where such prisoners or detainees are detained, for onward transmission to encampment sites or the authority of the prisoner-or-war or detainee. Common criminals are not covered by this provision.

SECTION J

Article 11

SUBMISSION BY PARTIES TO AUTHORITY OF TRANSITIONAL GOVERNMENT

Consistent with the provisions of paragraph 5 of article 14 of this Agreement, all Parties agree to submit themselves to the authority of the Transitional Government.

SECTION K

Article 12

SCHEDULE OF IMPLEMENTATION

Schedules of implementation of this Agreement, including a schedule for disarmament, encampment and demobilization of combatants, shall be drawn by ECOMOG and the United Nations observers. This schedule of implementation shall be given to each of the warring parties prior to implementation. The Parties undertake that they will create no obstacles to the full implementation of any of the foregoing activities.

PART II

Political Issues

SECTION A

Article 13

REVIEW AND REAFFIRMATION OF THE YAMOUSSOUKRO ACCORDS

The Parties to this Agreement reaffirm that the Yamoussoukro Accords provide the best framework for peace in Liberia, noting the links between the ECOWAS peace plan and the Yamoussoukro Accords.

SECTION B

Article 14

STRUCTURE OF GOVERNMENT

1. The Parties observe that Liberia is a unitary State and as such agree to form a single transitional Government, styled THE LIBERIA NATIONAL TRANSITIONAL GOVERNMENT. The authority of the transitional Government shall extend throughout the territorial limits of the Republic of Liberia.

2. The mandate of the transitional Government is to provide essential government services during the transitional period and to also hold and supervise general and presidential elections in accordance with the ECOWAS peace plan. The Transitional Legislative Assembly or the Council of State shall have power to enact or cause to be enacted any rule(s), regulations(s), or law, or take any action(s) which may facilitate the holding of free and fair democratic elections.

3. Formal installation of the Council of State shall take place in Monrovia, the capital city of the Republic of Liberia, and the Council of State shall also be permanently headquartered there.

4. The Parties further agree that the aforesaid transitional Government shall be selected in accordance with the below listed provisions and installed in approximately thirty (30) days of the date of signature of this Agreement, concomitant with the commencement of the disarmament process. Upon the installation of the transitional Government, both IGNU and NPRAG [National Patriotic Reconstruction Assembly Government] shall cease to exist and shall be deemed dissolved.

5. The Parties further agree that the transitional Government shall operate as closely as practicable under the Constitution and laws of Liberia.

6. The Parties further agree, warrant and promise that from the date of signature of this Agreement, no loans shall be negotiated or contracted in the name of or on behalf of the Liberian Government except to ensure the carrying out of the operations and activities of governmental and other public services. All financial transactions entered into by the transitional Government shall be formally submitted to the Transitional Legislative Assembly for ratification.

7. The Parties also agree that the transitional Government shall have three branches: Legislative, executive, and judicial.

EXECUTIVE

(i) The Parties further agree that, during the transitional period, the executive powers of the Republic shall be vested in a five (5) member Council of State which is hereby established. Each of the parties shall appoint one (1) member to the Council, whilst the remaining two (2) shall be selected in accordance with the following procedures:

Each of the Parties shall nominate three (3) eminent Liberians who together shall select two (2) of their number to be additional members of the Council.

(ii) Each Party shall submit the name of its appointee to the Council and also the names of its three (3) nominees in accordance with the provisions of the preceding paragraph to the office of the current Chairman of ECOWAS within a period of seven (7) days from the date of signature of this Agreement. Copies of the list of these names shall also be forwarded to each of the Parties.

(iii) The Parties shall, not later than three (3) days from submission of the aforesaid names, jointly and mutually determine the time and venue for the selection of the two (2) additional members of the Council. This entire selection process shall not exceed ten (10) days after the determination of the time and place of the meeting. If at the appointed place and time, any of the nominees fail to appear, the nominating party shall forfeit its right to renominate any other person(s), and the selection process shall proceed.

(iv) Proof of the selection of the two additional Council members shall be made by a written statement signed by all the nominees (excluding the two nominees selected) who participated in the selection process confirming same. The statement shall be forwarded to the current Chairman of ECOWAS with copy of each of the Parties.

(v) The Council shall select from amongst its members a Chairman and two (2) Vice-Chairmen.

(vi) The Council shall conduct and be responsible for the day-to-day operation of Government. All decisions shall be made by consensus of all the members.

(vii) The Council shall also devise and implement appropriate procedural rules in respect of its operation.

(viii) The Parties shall, in consultation with each other, determine the allocation of cabinet posts.

JUDICIAL

8. The parties further agree that, for purposes of continuity, there shall be no change in the existing structure of the Supreme Court. ULIMO shall have the right to nominate the fifth member of the court to fill the vacancy which currently exists. The nominee by ULIMO to the Supreme Court shall meet the established criteria and successfully undergo a screening by his or her peers in the Court.

LEGISLATURE

9. The Parties agree that the Transitional Legislative Assembly shall be a unicameral body composed of thirty-five (35) members. Both IGNU

and NPFL shall each be entitled to thirteen (13) members, and ULIMO nine (9) members. The Parties agree that ULIMO shall have the right to nominate the Speaker from one of its members in the Assembly.

SECTION C

Article 15

ELECTIONS MODALITIES

1. The Parties agree that, in order to enhance the inclusive nature of the transitional Government, ULIMO shall have the right to nominate two members to the Elections Commission, thus expanding the existing Elections Commission to seven (7) members. For the purpose of continuity the present structure shall remain the same.

2. Supreme Court: The Supreme Court shall adjudicate all matters arising out of the elections during the transition, in accordance with the constitution and laws of the country.

3. Voters registration: Voters registration shall commence as soon as possible having due regard for the need to expedite repatriation.

4. Observers and monitors: The transitional Government and the Elections Commission will work out the modalities for the participation of observers and monitors in the electoral process.

5. Financing: Financing will be sought from the national and international communities.

6. The Parties agree that the elections to be conducted shall conform to the several United Nations and internationally accepted codes of conduct and the Elections Commission shall accordingly be guided thereby.

SECTION D

Article 16

TENURE, AND MANDATE OF THE TRANSITIONAL GOVERNMENT

1. The transitional Government shall be installed approximately one month after the signing of this Agreement, concomitant with the commencement of the disarmament process.

2. The transitional Government shall have a life span of approximately six (6) months commencing from the date of its installation.

3. General and presidential elections shall take place approximately seven (7) months from the signature of this Agreement.

4. Holders of positions of leadership within the transitional Government (i.e. members of the Council of State, Supreme Court Justices, members of the Elections Commission, Cabinet Ministers, members of the Transitional Legislative Assembly, Managing Directors or Heads of Public Corporations and Autonomous Agencies) shall be ineligible to contest the election provided for in paragraph 3 of this article.

SECTION E

Article 17

HUMANITARIAN ASSISTANCE

The Parties agree that every effort should be made to deliver humanitarian assistance to all Liberians, particularly children, who are malnourished and suffering from related diseases. Convoys of humanitarian assistance should travel to all areas of Liberia through the most direct routes, under inspection to ensure compliance with the sanctions and embargo provisions of this Agreement.

SECTION F

Article 18

REPATRIATION OF REFUGEES

1. The Parties hereby commit themselves immediately and permanently to bring to an end any further external or internal displacement of Liberians and to create the conditions that will allow all refugees and displaced persons to respectively voluntarily repatriate and return to Liberia to their places of origin or habitual residence under conditions of safety and dignity.

2. The Parties further call upon Liberian refugees and displaced persons to return to Liberia and to their places of origin or habitual residence and declare that they shall not be jeopardized in any ethnic, political, religious, regional or geographical considerations.

3. The Parties also call upon the relevant organizations of the United Nations system, particularly the Office of the United Nations High Commissioner for Refugees and the United Nations Development Programme, other intergovernmental and non governmental organizations, to implement programmes for the voluntary repatriation, return and reintegration of the Liberian refugees and internally displaced persons.

4. The Parties proclaim that they shall, jointly or individually, cooperate in all necessary ways with themselves and with the above-mentioned organizations in order to facilitate the repatriation, return and reintegration of the refugees and displaced persons. Amongst others, they agree to:

(a) Establish all necessary mechanisms or arrangements, such as joint repatriation committees, which would facilitate contacts, communications and work with the relevant organizations for purposes of implementing the repatriation, return and reintegration operation and to enable effective decision-making and implementation of the relevant activities;

(b) Facilitate access by the Office of the United Nations High Commissioner for Refugees and displaced persons who have returned so as to deliver the necessary humanitarian assistance and programmes and monitor their situation;

(c) Guarantee and provide security to the Office of the United Nations High Commissioner for Refugees and the other relevant organizations, their staff, vehicles, equipment and resources necessary to carry out their work; and

(d) Provide all other necessary facilities and support that will be necessary to facilitate the implementation of the return, voluntary repatriation and reintegration of refugees and displaced persons.

SECTION G

Article 19

GENERAL AMNESTY

The Parties hereby agree that upon the execution of this Agreement there shall be a general amnesty granted to all persons and parties involved in the Liberian civil conflict in the course of actual military engagements. Accordingly, acts committed by the Parties or by their forces while in actual combat or on authority of any of the Parties in the course of actual combat are hereby granted amnesty. Similarly, the Parties agree that business transactions legally carried out by any of the Parties hereto with private business institutions in accordance with the laws of Liberia shall in like manner be covered by the amnesty herein granted.

5

The UNOMIL Mandate, September 1993

Para. 2 Decides to establish UNOMIL under its authority and under the direction of the Secretary-General through his Special Representative for a period of seven months, subject to the proviso that it will continue beyond 16 December 1993 only upon a review by the council based on a report from the Secretary-General on whether or not substantive progress has been made towards the implementation of the Peace Agreement and other measures aimed at establishing a lasting peace;

Para. 3 Decides that UNOMIL shall comprise military observers as well as medical, engineering, communications, transportation and electoral components, in the numbers indicated in the Secretary-General's report, together with minimal staff necessary to support it, and shall have the following mandate:

(a) To receive and investigate all reports on alleged incidents of violations of the cease-fire agreement and, if the violation cannot be corrected, to report its finding to the violations committee established pursuant to the Peace Agreement and to the Secretary-General;

(b) To monitor compliance with other elements of the Peace Agreement, including at points on Liberia's borders with Sierra Leone and other neighbouring countries, and to verify its impartial application, and in particular to assist in the monitoring of compliance with the embargo on delivery of arms and military equipment to Liberia and the cantonment, disarmament and demobilization of combatants;

(c) To observe and verify the election process, including the legislative and presidential elections to be held in accordance with the provisions of the Peace Agreement;

(d) To assist, as appropriate, in the coordination of humanitarian assistance activities in the field in conjunction with the existing United Nations humanitarian relief operation;

(e) To develop a plan and assess financial requirements for the demobilization of combatants;

(f) To report on any major violations of international humanitarian law to the Secretary-General;

(g) To train ECOMOG engineers in mine clearance and, in cooperation with ECOMOG, coordinate the identification of mines and assist in the clearance of mines and unexploded bombs;

(h) Without participation in enforcement operations, to coordinate with ECOMOG in the discharge of ECOMOG's separate responsibilities both formally, through the Violations Committee, and informally.

Source: UN Doc. S/RES/866, 22 September 1993, section 12.

6

The Akosombo Agreement, September 1994

This agreement, which supplements and amends the Cotonou Agreement, is made and entered into this 12th day of September AD 1994 by and between the National Patriotic Front of Liberia (NPFL) represented by and through its leader Charles G. Taylor (hereinafter referred to as THE PARTY OF THE FIRST PART), the United Liberation Movement of Liberia for Democracy (ULIMO) represented by and through its leader Lt. Gen. Alhaji G. V. Kromah (hereinafter referred to as THE PARTY OF THE SECOND PART), and the armed forces of Liberia represented by and through its Chief of Staff Hezekiah Bowen (hereinafter referred to as THE PARTY OF THE THIRD PART) hereby:

WITNESSETH:

PREAMBLE

NPFL, ULIMO and AFL reaffirm their acceptance of the Cotonou Agreement as the framework for peace in Liberia. However, having realized the slow pace in the full implementation of the Cotonou Agreement, resulting from the failure of disarmament and the inability of the Liberia National Transitional Government (LNTG) to achieve the objective of its mandate within a six-month period as set forth under Section B Article 14 (2) of the said Cotonou Agreement: and

Having noted with grave concern the protracted human suffering and the undue hardships to which the people of Liberia (inside and outside the country) have been overly subjected as a result of the senseless Liberian civil crisis: and

Having realized the urgent need to bring this ugly civil crisis to an immediate and lasting end:

Do hereby agree to the following:

Part I

MILITARY ISSUES

DECLARATION

SECTION A

ARTICLE 1

Count 1 is amended to read as follows:

The parties to this agreement hereby agree and declare a ceasefire and the cessation of hostilities effective as of the signing of this amendment.

SECTION B

ARTICLE 3

SUPERVISORY AND MONITORING AUTHORITY

Count 1 is amended to read: That the LNTG, ECOMOG and UNOMIL in collaboration shall supervise and monitor the implementation of this Agreement.

The parties hereby expressly recognize the neutrality and authority of ECOMOG and UNOMIL in respect of the foregoing.

Accordingly, the LNTG shall ensure that ECOMOG and UNOMIL shall enjoy complete freedom of movement throughout Liberia.

SECTION C

ARTICLE 4

TERMS AND CONDITIONS

Count 4 is amended to read: The LNTG, in collaboration with ECOMOG and UNOMIL, shall ensure that all points of entry including sea ports, airfields and roads shall be monitored and supervised.

Count 5 is amended to read: The warring parties shall undertake to discharge and move to designated assembly points within the time frame in the schedule to be attached to this document.

Count 6 That the LNTG shall enter into a Status of Forces Agreement with ECOWAS within 30 days from the signing of this agreement.

Count 7 That the existing Status of Mission Agreement already executed with United Nations (UNOMIL) is herein incorporated by reference and is applicable.

SECTION D

ARTICLE 5

ACTS OF VIOLATION

Count 2 is amended to read: The following acts shall constitute violations of the Agreement:

Sub-Section (b): Any change or improvement of existing positions aimed at acquiring territory.

Sub-Section (c): Any deliberate discharge (whether with conventional or unconventional weapons) against the position of any warring party by another, or firing at any individual or property or any seizure or abduction of individuals and properties.

Sub-Section (f): While the right to communication shall not be abridged, any proven use of communication devices, facilities or propaganda designed to incite or having the effect of inciting hostilities between any of the warring parties.

Sub-Section (h): Obstruction of the implementation of any of the provisions of the Agreement by any party and/or individual.

Sub-Section (i): Harassment, intimidations, or attacks upon any official of the LNTG, relief organizations, ECOMOG, UNOMIL, Ceasefire Violations Committee as well as individuals.

Sub-Section (j): Obstruction of the activities of the LNTG, ECOMOG, UNOMIL and the Ceasefire Violations Committee.

Sub-Section (k): The facilitation or creation of new or splinter armed groups. To this end, any individual or group of individuals suspected of creating or assisting to create any new armed splinter group or facilitating existing splinter group(s) (directly or indirectly) shall:

1. Not be recognized under the Cotonou Agreement.

2. Shall be disarmed and disbanded by ECOMOG in collaboration with LNTG verified by UNOMIL.

3. Thereafter be prosecuted under the laws of Liberia.

SECTION E

ARTICLE 6

DISARMAMENT

The introductory paragraph is hereby amended to read: The ultimate objective of disarmament under the Cotonou Agreement being primarily to create a conducive security environment for absolute peace in order to have free and fair elections in the country, NPFL, ULIMO and AFL hereby agree to disarm to ECOMOG with the cooperation of the LNTG and monitored and verified by UNOMIL in accordance with the schedule to be attached to this Agreement. The parties further mandate the LNTG to begin the formation of appropriate national security structures to facilitate the disarmament process. Accordingly appropriate measures shall be undertaken to enable the AFL to assume its character as a national army. Until such measures are completed the AFL like all other parties and warring groups shall be completely disarmed in accordance with the Cotonou Agreement. In order to ensure a secure environment for the proper functioning of the unified government in Monrovia the LNTG in collaboration with ECOMOG shall ensure that no group or individuals bear arms in the perimeter of the capital. However, the personal security of the leaders of the warring parties shall be reflected in the Status of Forces Agreement.

Count 4 is amended to read: Each of the warring parties shall ensure that its combatants report all weapons and warlike materials to ECOMOG which would be inventoried by ECOMOG, monitored and verified by LNTG and UNOMIL. Upon proper inventory, such weapons and warlike materials shall be taken by ECOMOG to the designated armouries, monitored and verified by UNOMIL and LNTG.

Count 5 is amended to read: All non-combatants who are in possession of weapons and warlike materials shall also report and surrender same to ECOMOG, monitored and verified by LNTG and UNOMIL. Such weapons and warlike materials shall be returned to the owners after due registration, licensing and certification by the governing authority after elections.

Count 7 is amended to read: For the sole purpose of maintaining the ceasefire, ECOMOG shall conduct any search to recover lost or hidden weapons, observed and monitored by UNOMIL and LNTG.

SECTION F

ARTICLE 7

ENCAMPMENT

Count 1 is amended to read: The parties agree and fully commit themselves to the encampment of their combatants, and maintenance of command and control in encampment centres, established by ECOMOG, UNOMIL and LNTG in collaboration with the parties. The encampment centres shall, in addition to disarmament and demobilization, serve as transit points for further education, training and rehabilitation of said combatants.

SECTION G

ARTICLE 8

PEACE ENFORCEMENT POWERS

The following amendments are hereby made to wit:

That in the event any party, new armed group or splinter group and/or individuals refuse to desist from acts in violation of the Agreement, the LNTG, in collaboration with ECOMOG, shall have the power to use the necessary forces available to compel compliance.

All violations of the ceasefire shall be reported to UNOMIL who shall, on immediate receipt of the information of violation, commence an investigation and make findings thereof. In the event the violation can be cured by the party, UNOMIL shall pursue such course. However, should such a course not be possible, UNOMIL shall submit their findings to the Ceasefire Violations Committee. The Violations Committee shall invite the violating Party(ies) for the purpose of having such party(ies) take corrective measures to cure violations within such time frame as may be stipulated by the committee. Should the violating party not take the required corrective measures, and the use of peace enforcement powers are recommended against the violator – the LNTG in collaboration with ECOMOG shall thereupon take the necessary action.

SECTION H

ARTICLE 9

DEMOBILISATION

Count 2 is amended to read: Further, the parties hereby call upon the LNTG, UN, OAU, ECOWAS and other international organizations and countries, to design a programme which recognises the peculiarities of the parties and finance the process of demobilization, retraining, rehabilitation and reintegration of all former combatants to normal social and community life.

Count 3 is amended to read: It is agreed that the LNTG, in collaboration with the parties, shall immediately commence a community information or educational programme, explaining to the public by means of communication devices or any form of media, the essence and purpose of ceasefire, encampment, disarmament and demobilisation. Such programme shall include other social institutions.

Count 4 Internal security arrangements including police, customs and immigration will be put in place immediately. Planning for restructuring and training of the AFL will be the responsibility of the LNTG, with the assistance of ECOWAS, United Nations and friendly Governments.

SECTION K

ARTICLE 12

SCHEDULE OF IMPLEMENTATION

This article is amended to read: The attached schedule of implementation to be attached to this agreement, including disarmament, encampment and demobilization of combatants, preparation of a status of forces Agreement, restricting of AFL and dissolution of the parties drawn up by ECOMOG and UNOMIL in collaboration with the parties, shall be given to each of the parties prior to implementation. The parties undertake that they will create no obstacles to the full implementation of any of the foregoing activities.

PART II

POLITICAL ISSUES

SECTION A

Section B Article 14 (7) is hereby amended to read thus:

EXECUTIVE

(i) The parties further agree that during the transitional period leading up to inauguration of an elected government, the executive powers of the republic shall be vested in a five member Council of State which is hereby established. Each of the parties (AFL, NPFL and ULIMO) shall appoint one member to the council and the remaining two, representing unarmed Liberians, shall be chosen among prominent Liberians, one appointed by the Liberian National Conference recently convened in Monrovia and the other by NPFL and ULIMO. The designation of Chairman and two

Vice-Chairmen shall be determined through a process of elections to be carried out within 7 days of the signing of this Agreement. The new Council of State will be inducted under the auspices of the Chairman of ECOWAS or his representative within 14 days of the signing of this Agreement.

(ii) The Council of State shall conduct and be responsible for the day to day operations of Government. All decisions shall be made on the basis of a simple majority.

(iii) The council shall also devise and implement appropriate rules of procedure in respect of its operations, to be signed by all members on the occasion of their induction into office.

(iv) The parties hereby agree that the allocation of Ministries, Public Corporations and Autonomous Agencies as agreed by the parties in Cotonou in November 1993 shall be maintained, taking into account existing factions in respect of existing vacancies. All boards of Public Corporations shall be constituted in accordance with the Acts creating said Corporations.

(v) In the case where the executive post is allocated to one party the two deputy posts shall be allocated to the two other parties. In the case where there are more than two deputy posts in a given Ministry, Public Corporation or Autonomous Agency, the Council of State shall appoint qualified Liberian citizens to occupy the third and or remaining deputy posts.

(vi) The Council of State shall also exercise its executive prerogative power to appoint qualified citizens in all other subordinate presidential appointed posts as may be provided by law in consultation with parties.

Each of the parties shall have the right to review the status of its appointees in the LNTG through the Council of State and any change in appointment by the Council of State should follow as closely as possible the constitution's procedures. Once appointments have been made to the Council of State changes can only be effected for cause and then consistent with existing laws.

LEGISLATURE
SECTION B
ARTICLE 14

Count 9 is amended to read:

(i) That the parties agree that the Transitional Legislative Assembly shall be a unicameral body composed of 48 members. The TLA is expanded by 13 eminent citizens selected by the Ministry of Internal Affairs from each of the 13 counties, and appointed by the Council of State.

(ii) The parties further agree that the TLA shall give consideration to providing appropriate benefits for the heads of warring parties.

Article 16 (1) is hereby amended to read:

(2) Is hereby amended to read: That the transitional government shall have a life span of approximately 16 months commencing from the date of installation of the five member Council of State.

(3) Is hereby amended to read: That General and Presidential Elections shall take place on October 10, 1995, and the newly elected Government shall be installed on the first Monday of 1996.

SECTION H

ARTICLE 20

The parties agree that all provisions of the Cotonou Agreement not amended here are herein incorporated by reference and the same are hereby applicable and remain in full force and effect except for the below listed provisions:

(1) Part I, Section A Art. 2

(2) Part I, Section B Art. 3, Count 3

(3) Section D Art. 5 (d)

(4) Part II, Section A Art. 13

(5) Part II, Section B Art. 14,4,6,7 i, ii, iii, iv

DONE AT AKOSOMBO, REPUBLIC OF GHANA

THIS 12 DAY OF SEPTEMBER 1994

CHARLES G. TAYLOR

LEADER

NATIONAL PATRIOTIC FRONT OF LIBERIA

(NPFL)

LT. GEN. ALHAJI G. V. KROMAH

NATIONAL CHAIRMAN

UNITED LIBERATION MOVEMENT OF
LIBERIA FOR DEMOCRACY (ULIMO)

LT. GEN. J. HEZEKIAH BOWEN
CHIEF OF STAFF
ARMED FORCES OF LIBERIA (AFL)

WITNESSED BY

HIS EXCELLENCY FLT. LT. J. J. RAWLINGS
PRESIDENT OF THE REPUBLIC OF GHANA AND
CURRENT CHAIRMAN OF ECOWAS

AMBASSADOR TREVOR GORDON-SOMERS
SPECIAL REPRESENTATIVE OF THE UNITED NATIONS
SECRETARY GENERAL IN LIBERIA

7
Accra Clarification of the Akosombo Agreement, December 1994

This agreement on the clarification of the Akosombo Agreement made this Twenty-First Day of December One Thousand Nine Hundred and Ninety-Four is intended to clarify and expand pertinent provisions of the said Akosombo Agreement.

Part I Military Issues

Section A, Article 1

Ceasefire

The Parties to this Agreement hereby declare a ceasefire and the cessation of hostilities effective as of 23.59 hours on the 28th day of December 1994.

Section C, Article 4

Terms and Conditions (Safe Havens and Buffer Zones)

Consistent with Section C Article 4 count 5 of the Akosombo Agreement, the parties agree to facilitate the establishment of Safe Havens and Buffer Zones throughout Liberia in accordance with a plan to be drawn up by the LNTG in collaboration with UNOMIL and ECOMOG in consultation with the parties. In this connection, the deployment of ECOMOG and UNOMIL, the establishment of Buffer Zones, Safe Havens and other measures necessary to restore normalcy throughout the territory of Liberia, shall be undertaken in accordance with the Cotonou and Akosombo Agreements.

In keeping with Section C Article 4 count 6, the LNTG shall enter into a Status of Forces Agreement with ECOWAS within seven (7) days as of the seating of the Council of State established under this Agreement.

Section H, Article 9

Demobilization

Consistent with Section H Article 9 count 4 of the Akosombo Agreement it is agreed by the parties that in the reorganization of the Armed Forces of Liberia, the Police, Immigration and other Security Agencies, the combatant and non-combatants who satisfy conditions for recruitment shall be considered for inclusion. In this connection, the Council of State established under the Akosombo Agreement clarified by this agreement shall establish appropriate committees which will be charged with determining the criteria for recruitment, taking advantage of the relevant expertise of ECOMOG and UNOMIL.

Section K, Article 12

Schedule of Implementation

The parties hereby agree to abide by the schedule of implementation hereto attached and incorporated herein by reference.

Part II Political Issues

Section A

Executive

Consistent with Part II Section A (i) of the Akosombo Agreement the provisions for the function and structure of the Five-Member Council of State provided for in the Cotonou and Akosombo Agreements are hereby reconfirmed.

The procedure for the appointment of the relevant officials of government as enshrined in the Akosombo Agreement is hereby reaffirmed. Such officials shall be appointed based on merit.

The parties agree that a five-member Council of State shall be established.

The first four members of the new Council of State shall be appointed as follows:

NPFL	1
ULIMO	1
AFL/COALITION	1
LNC	1

The fifth member of the Council of State shall be a traditional chief selected by the NPFL and ULIMO in the person of Honourable Tamba Taylor in accordance with Part II Section A (i) of the Akosombo Agreement and agreed by the parties.

Consistent with Part II Section A (i) of the Akosombo Agreement, induction of the Council of State shall take place in the City of Monrovia under the auspices of the Chairman of ECOWAS or his designee within fourteen (14) days as of the ceasefire date.

Section H, Article 20

Consistent with Section 20 of the Akosombo Agreement, the parties reaffirm the acceptance of the ECOWAS Peace Plan including the Cotonou and Akosombo Agreements as the best framework for peace in Liberia.

All Provisions of the Akosombo Agreement not herein clarified remain in full force and effect.

Done at Accra, Republic of Ghana, this 21st Day of December 1994

Charles G. TAYLOR, Leader of the National Patriotic Front of Liberia (NPFL)

Ltg. Alhaji G. V. KROMAH, National Chairman of the United Liberation Movement of Liberia for Democracy (ULIMO)

Ltg. J. Hezekiah BOWEN, Chief of Staff, Armed Forces of Liberia (AFL)

Attested to:

His EXCELLENCY Flt. Lt. Jerry John RAWLINGS, President of the Republic of Ghana and current Chairman of ECOWAS.

8

Accra Acceptance and Accession Agreement, December 1994

This ACCEPTANCE and ACCESSION undertaking made and entered into this 21st day of December A.D. 1994 by Lofa Defence Force (LDF), represented by Mr. Francois Massaquoi; the Liberian Peace Council (LPC), represented by Dr. G. E. Saigbe Boley, Sr; the Central Revolutionary Council (CRC-NPFL), represented by J. Thomas Woewiyu; ULIMO, represented by Major General Roosevelt Johnson; the Liberian National Conference (LNC), represented by the counsellor J. D. Bayogar Junius, all of them hereinafter collectively referred to as the NON-SIGNATORIES to the Akosombo Agreement, hereby:

WITNESSETH:

WHEREAS, an agreement, referred to as the "Akosombo Agreement" was made and entered into on the 12th day of September, by and between the National Patriotic Front of Liberia (NPFL), the Armed Forces of Liberia (AFL), and the United Liberation Movement (ULIMO), in an effort to establish a cease fire, facilitate disarmament, encampment, demobilization, and to pave the way for a free and fair election; and

WHEREAS, the NON-SIGNATORIES TO THE AKOSOMBO AGREEMENT did not participate in the discussions leading to the Akosombo Agreement; and

WHEREAS, a need arose for further discussions between the signatories to Akosombo for clarification and expansion of the provisions therein with the view of facilitating the acceptance and the implementation of the Agreement, in which said discussions the NON-SIGNATORIES fully participated; and

WHEREAS, after intense discussions and negotiations between the parties to the Akosombo Agreement and the NON-SIGNATORIES thereto, the NON-SIGNATORIES have agreed to accept the terms and conditions of the Akosombo Agreement with the clarifications thereto as set forth and contained in the agreement on the clarification of the said Akosombo Agreement.

Now THEREFORE, THE NON-SIGNATORIES TO THE AKOSOMBO AGREEMENT, in consideration of their participation in the discussions on the clarifications of the Akosombo Agreement, and upon and accepted by them, agree as follows to wit:

1. That the Lofa Defence Force (LDF), the Liberian Peace Council (LPC), and the Central Revolutionary Council (CRC-NPFL), in their individual capacities; the LNC, and ULIMO agree to accept, and to accede to, and by this document hereby accept, and accede to the Akosombo Agreement and agreement on clarification of the aforesaid Akosombo Agreement.

2. That the non-signatories commit themselves individually and collectively to the terms and conditions of the Akosombo Agreement and the agreement on clarification of the said agreement, undertake to fully implement and discharge all the tasks and the responsibilities, and to abide by all the terms and conditions as set forth and contained under the said Akosombo Agreement, and the agreement on clarification of the said Akosombo Agreement, as if they were signatories thereto and/or specifically named therein.

IN WITNESS THEREOF, THE PARTIES HERETO
Have hereunto set their hands and affixed their signatories this
21st day of December A.D. 1994 in the City of Accra.

ULIMO
Represented by and through its Chairman
Major General Roosevelt Johnson

Lofa Defence Force (LDF)
Represented by and through its Leader
Francois Massaquoi

Liberia Peace Council (LPC)
Represented by and through its Chairman
Dr. G. E. Saigbe Boley, Sr.

The Central Revolutionary Council (CRC-NPFL)
Represented by and through its Chairman
Jucontee Thomas Woewiyu

Liberia National Conference (LNC)
Represented by and through its Chairman
Counsellor J. D. Bayogar Junius

Attested to:

His Excellency FLT. LT. JERRY JOHN RAWLINGS
PRESIDENT OF THE REPUBLIC OF GHANA AND
CURRENT CHAIRMAN OF ECOWAS

9

Abuja Agreement, August 1995

This Agreement amends and supplements the COTONOU Accord, the AKOSOMBO Agreement and its Accra Clarification.

SECTION A

ARTICLE I

CEASE-FIRE

The parties to this agreement hereby declare cease-fire and the cessation of hostilities effective at 12 o'clock midnight August 26th, 1995

SECTION K

ARTICLE 12

SCHEDULE OF IMPLEMENTATION

The parties hereby agree to abide by the schedule of implementation attached to the agreement on the Clarification of the AKOSOMBO Agreement with such modifications in terms of dates as are required by virtue of the delay in the implementation of the said agreement.

PART II
POLITICAL ISSUES
SECTION A

EXECUTIVE

The Parties agree that during the transitional period leading to the inauguration of an elected government the executive powers of the Republic of Liberia shall be vested in a six-member Council of State to be composed as follows:

a) NPFL   Mr. Charles Ghankay Taylor

b) ULIMO   LTG. Alhaji G. V. Kromah

c) COALITION   Dr. George E. S. Boley Sr.

d) LNC   Oscar Jaryee Quiah

e)   Chief Tamba Taylor

f)   Mr. Wilton Sankawulo

The Chairman of the Council shall be Mr. Wilton Sankawulo. All other members of the Council shall be Vice-Chairmen of equal status. In case of permanent incapacitation a new Chairman shall be appointed within the ECOWAS framework.

The Parties hereby agree that the allocation of ministries, public corporations and Autonomous Agencies agreed by the parties in COTONOU, Benin, on November 3–5, 1993 shall be maintained. The parties, however, agree that the allocations for the erstwhile IGNU shall revert to LPC/COALITION. LTG Hezekiah Bowen, Francois Massaquoi, Thomas Woewiyu, Laveli Supuwood and Samuel Dokie shall be given ministerial or other senior Government positions.

ULIMO-J shall occupy the following positions:

MINISTRIES

1 – MINISTER OF STATE FOR PRESIDENTIAL AFFAIRS

2 – MINISTER OF TRANSPORT

3 – MINISTER OF RURAL DEVELOPMENT

4 – MINISTER OF STATE WITHOUT PORTFOLIO

PUBLIC CORPORATION/AUTONOMOUS AGENCIES

1 – NATIONAL BANK
2 – CORPORATIVE DEVELOPMENT AGENCIES (CDA)
3 – AGRICULTURAL INDUSTRIAL TRAINING BOARD (AIIB)
4 – FORESTRY DEVELOPMENT AUTHORITY (FDA)

DEPUTY MINISTRIES

1 – MINISTRY OF POST & TELECOMMUNICATION
2 – MINISTRY OF JUSTICE
3 – MINISTRY OF EDUCATION
4 – MINISTRY OF INFORMATION

DEPUTY MANAGING DIRECTORS/DEPUTY DIRECTORS GENERAL

1 – NICOL – NATIONAL INSURANCE CORP. OF LIBERIA
2 – N.H.A – NATIONAL HOUSING AUTHORITY
3 – LWSC – LIBERIA WATER SEWAGE CORP.
4 – NHSB – NATIONAL HOUSING AND SAVINGS BANK
5 – FS – FIRE SERVICE
6 – GA – GENERAL AUDITING
7 – IPA – INSTITUTE OF PUBLIC ADMINISTRATION
8 – NFAA – NAT~~ ~~ FOOD ASSISTANCE AGENCY

SECTION C

ARTICLE 15

ELECTION MODALITIES

The operations of the Elections Commission shall be monitored by ECOWAS, OAU and the UN.

SECTION D

ARTICLE 16

TENURE AND MANDATE OF THE TRANSITIONAL GOVERNMENT

The Transitional Government hereby established shall be installed within 14 days after the signing of this agreement.

The Transitional Government shall have a life span of approximately twelve (12) months commencing from the date of its installation.

Holders of positions within the Transitional Government as defined by the COTONOU Accord who wish to contest the election provided for under the Schedule of Implementation shall vacate office 3 months before the date of elections. They shall be replaced by their nominees or by persons nominated by the parties represented in the Council of State.

The Chairman of the Council of State shall be ineligible to contest the first Presidential and Parliamentary elections to be held pursuant to this agreement.

SECTION G

ARTICLE 8

PEACE ENFORCEMENT POWERS

Enforcement of violations of the cease-fire shall be in accordance with the terms of the COTONOU Accord.

All provisions of the COTONOU and AKOSOMBO Agreements as clarified by the Accra Agreement not therein amended shall remain in full force and effect.

DONE AT ABUJA, FEDERAL REPUBLIC OF NIGERIA, 19TH DAY OF AUGUST, 1995

CHARLES GHANKAY TAYLOR
LEADER
NATIONAL PATRIOTIC FRONT OF LIBERIA (NPFL)

LTG. ALHAJI G. V. KROMAH
NATIONAL CHAIRMAN
UNITED LIBERATION MOVEMENT OF LIBERIA
FOR DEMOCRACY (ULIMO)

DR. G. E. SAIGBE BOLEY SR.
LEADER
LIBERIA PEACE COUNCIL (LPC)

LTG. J. HEZEKIAH BOWEN
ARMED FORCES OF LIBERIA

MAJOR-GENERAL ROOSEVELT JOHNSON
UNITED LIBERATION MOVEMENT OF LIBERIA
FOR DEMOCRACY (ULIMO-J)

FRANCOIS MASSAQUOI
LOFA DEFENCE FORCE (LDF)

JUCONTEE THOMAS WOEWIYU
NATIONAL PATRIOTIC FRONT OF LIBERIA
CENTRAL REVOLUTIONARY COUNCIL (NPFL-CRC)

CHEA CHEAPOO
LIBERIA NATIONAL CONFERENCE (LNC)

WITNESSED BY

DR. OBED ASAMOAH
FOR AND ON BEHALF OF HIS EXCELLENCY
FLT-LT. JERRY JOHN RAWLINGS
PRESIDENT OF THE REPUBLIC OF GHANA AND
CHAIRMAN OF ECOWAS

CHIEF TOM IKIMI
FOR AND ON BEHALF OF HIS EXCELLENCY
GENERAL SANI ABACHA, HEAD OF STATE,
COMMANDER-IN-CHIEF OF THE NIGERIAN ARMED FORCES

HIS EXCELLENCY PRESIDENT CANAAN BANANA
O.A.U. EMINENT PERSON IN LIBERIA

HIS EXCELLENCY ANTHONY B. NYAKYI
U.N. SECRETARY-GENERAL'S SPECIAL
REPRESENTATIVE TO LIBERIA

10
Final Communiqué of ECOWAS Meeting on Liberia, Abuja, August 1996

1 Heads of State and Government of the Committee of Nine on Liberia held their fourth meeting at the ECOWAS Executive Secretariat in Abuja on 17 August 1996 under the Chairmanship of His Excellency, General Sani Abacha, Head of State, Commander-in-Chief of the armed forces of the Federal Republic of Nigeria and current Chairman of the ECOWAS Authority. Heads of State and Government considered ways to put the Liberian peace process back on course, in conformity with the Abuja Accord.

2 The following Heads of State and Government or their duly accredited representatives were present at meeting:
His Excellency Matthieu KEREKOU, President of the Republic of Benin Head of Government.

His Excellency Blaise COMPAORE, President of Burkina Faso Head of Government.

His Excellency Jerry John RAWLINGS, President of the Republic of Ghana.

His Excellency General Sani ABACHA, Head of State, Commander-in-Chief of the Armed Forces of the Federal Republic of Nigeria.

His Excellency Captain Edward SINGHATAY, vice-president and Minister of Defence of The Gambia Representing the President of the Republic of The Gambia.

Mr. Barry Moussa BARQUE, Minister of State, Minister of Foreign Affairs and Co-operation of the Togolese Republic Representing the President of the Togolese Republic.

Mr. Amara ESSY, Minister of Foreign Affairs Representing the President of the Republic of Côte d'Ivoire.

His Excellency Lamine CAMARA, Minister of Foreign Affairs of the Republic of Guinea representing the President of the Republic of Guinea.

Mr. Massokhna KANE, Minister of Africa Economic Integration of the Republic of Senegal Representing the President of the Republic of Senegal.

3   The following guests were also present at the session:
His Excellency Professor Wilton SANKAWULO, President of the Council of State of the Liberia National Transitional Government.

His Excellency Alpha Cumar KONARE, President and Head of State of the Republic of Mali.

His Excellency Ibrahim MAINASSARA BARE, President of the Republic of Nigeria.

His Excellency Alhaji Ahmad Tejan RABBAH, President of the Republic of Sierra Leone.

4   The following were invited as observers:

   – OAU Eminent Persons in Liberia

   – Special Representative of the Secretary General of the United Nations in Liberia

5   The following persons also attended the meeting in an advisory capacity:

   – Mr Edouard Benjamin, ECOWAS Executive Secretary

   – Major-General Victor S. Malu, ECOMOG Field Commander

6   The fourth meeting of the Heads of State and Government of the Committee of Nine was preceded by a meeting of Chiefs of Staff of the Armed Forces of ECOWAS Member States and a meeting of Ministers of Foreign Affairs of the Committee of Nine on Liberia.

7   Heads of State and Government reviewed the situation in Liberia as presented in the report of the thirteenth meeting of Chiefs of Staff of the Armed Forces of ECOWAS Member States and the report of the

eighth meeting of Ministers of Foreign Affairs of the Committee of Nine to bring the Liberian peace process back on course and focused attention on the following issues:

- Assessment of the implementing of the Accra Mechanism;
- Extension of the Abuja Peace Agreement of August 1995 and review of its schedule of implementation;
- Measures to ensure compliance with the Peace Plan by the Liberian parties;
- Performance of the Council of State;
- Status of Monrovia;
- Elections in Liberia;
- Strengthening of ECOMOG;
- Restructuring the Armed Forces, Police and other security agents;
- Return of arms seized from ECOMOG and property looted from the UN and other agencies;
- Humanitarian assistance to Liberia.

ASSESSMENT OF THE IMPLEMENTATION OF THE ACCRA MECHANISM

Heads of State and Government noted the non-observance of several important obligations inherent in the mechanism put in place by the seventh meeting of Ministers of Foreign Affairs of the Committee of Nine with the aim of relaunching the peace process.

EXTENSION OF THE ABUJA AGREEMENT OF 19 AUGUST 1995 AND REVIEW OF ITS IMPLEMENTATION SCHEDULE

Heads of State and Government reaffirmed that the Abuja Agreement which was designed to usher in peace and lead to the organization of free and democratic elections on 20th August 1996 remained the most appropriate legal framework for finding a peaceful settlement to the Liberian crisis. They therefore decided that it should be retained in its entirety. However, given that very little progress had been made in its application, it had not been possible to adhere to its implementation schedule.

SCHEDULE OF IMPLEMENTATION

Consequently, Heads of State and Government reaffirmed that the Abuja Agreement remained the best and last framework for finding durable peace in Liberia and should thus be retained in its entirety. It was therefore approved that the validity of the Abuja Agreement was extended for another nine months from 21 August 1996 to 15 June 1997, the following programme of implementation shall be undertaken before the holding of free, fair and democratic elections on or about 30 May 1997.

August 20–31, 1996   Cease-fire, disengagement of factions from check points and present combat positions.

September 1, 1996 – 30 November, 1996   Delivery of logistic supplies by the international/donor community to ECOMOG.

August 20, 1996 – January 31, 1997   Verification of cease-fire and disengagement by ECOMOG, UNOMIL, and LNTG

October 3–10, 1996   Assessment meeting in Liberia by Chairman's Special Envoy with ECOMOG, UNOMIL, Representatives of donor community and LNTG

October 12, 1996 – January 31, 1997   Recce Mission by ECOMOG and UNOMIL of arms collection centres

November 4 – November 8, 1996   Committee of Nine meeting (Ministerial) in Monrovia

November 7, 1996 – January 31, 1997   Deployment of ECOMOG to agreed safe havens by Committee of Nine

November 22, 1996 – January 31, 1997   Disarmament, demobilisation and repatriation

January 6–13, 1997   Verification visit to Liberia by Chairman's Special Envoy with ECOMOG, UNOMIL, Representatives of donor community and LNTG

January 20 – April 15, 1997   Preparation for elections

March 10–15, 1997   Committee of Nine meeting, Monrovia

April 17–24, 1997   Assessment visit to Liberia by Chairman's Special Envoy with ECOMOG, UNOMIL, Representatives of donor community and LNTG

May 30, 1997   Election Day

The new schedule of implementation of the Abuja Agreement also provides for the dissolution of all factions by 31 January, 1997, registration by 28 February, 1997 of the members of the Council of State and public office holders who wish to run for election. The new government is expected to be sworn in on 13 June 1997.

Heads of State and Government adopted a mechanism designed to ensure strict compliance with the peace plan by all Liberian parties.

MEASURES TO ENSURE COMPLIANCE WITH THE PEACE PLAN

Heads of State and Government deplored the lack of sincerity and commitment shown by the Liberian factions to the peace process. They therefore adopted a decision envisaging measures that might be invoked against any persons found guilty of acts capable of obstructing the peace plan concluded by the signatories to the Abuja Agreement. Such measures which would be invoked against a defaulting party would include:

- travel and residence restrictions;
- freezing of business activities and assets in Member States;
- exclusion from participation in the electoral process;
- restrictions on the use of the airspace and territorial waters of Member States;
- expulsion of members of the families of the Liberian leaders and their associates from the territories of Member States;
- request for the UN Security Council to impose Visa restrictions;
- restrictions on imports from Liberia;
- invoke the OAU 1996 Summit Resolution which calls for the establishment of a war crimes tribunal to try all human rights offences against Liberians.

Heads of State and Government reaffirmed the need for Member States to observe the arms embargo declared against the warring factions and therefore adopted a decision designed to ensure strict compliance therewith. They urged Member States, particularly countries bordering Liberia, to adopt all measures to stop the flow of arms from their territories into that country and noted with appreciation the measures taken by the Republic of Cote d'Ivoire in this connection. They recognised the right of ECOMOG to carry out a search on anyone including members of the Liberia National Transitional Government and any other government official on the territory of Liberia.

ECOMOG was directed to ensure that only airports under its control were operational. Heads of State and Government decided to set up a committee that may prescribe sanctions to be taken by Member States against persons who obstruct implementation of their peace plan. Heads of State and Government reaffirmed their resolve not to recognise any government which comes to power by force of arms.

PERFORMANCE OF THE COUNCIL OF STATE

Heads of State and Government were concerned about the performance of the Council of State and felt that a change in the leadership of the Council would improve upon its effectiveness and cohesiveness.

Heads of State and Government, therefore, agree to the appointment, by the signatories to the Abuja Agreement, of Mrs. Ruth Perry, a former Senator of the Republic of Liberia, as the new Chairman of the Council of State. The Heads of State expressed their appreciation to the out-going Chairman, Professor Wilton SANKAWULO, for his services rendered under rather difficult circumstances.

They also stressed that, in future, any Council member found wanting would be replaced.

Heads of State and Government adopted a code of conduct for observance by members of the Council of State and other public office holders in implementing the Abuja Agreement and these would be used as a yardstick for assessing the performance, individually and collectively.

STATUS OF MONROVIA

Heads of State and Government expressed satisfaction at the measures taken by ECOMOG to restore relative calm to Monrovia. They however expressed concern at recent incidents of harassment, abduction and assassination of civilian members of rival factions or other ethnic groups. They strongly condemned the growing tendency to partition the city of Monrovia along factional lines and mandated ECOMOG to intensify its efforts to restore Monrovia and environs to its original safe havens status.

ELECTIONS IN LIBERIA

Heads of State and Government noted that, because of the failure of successive peace plans, it had been impossible to organise free, fair and democratic elections. They directed that the process should be set in motion for the holding of elections in Liberia on or about 30 May 1997. To this end, they recommended that modalities for the organisation of elections be formulated, taking into account the electoral laws of Liberia.

They appealed to the United Nations, donors and non-governmental organisations for support and ensuring that the elections are successfully organised.

STRENGTHENING OF ECOMOG

Heads of State and Government took note of the information that successful implementation of the peace plan would require deployment of

18,000 troops to Liberia. They commended the efforts of those Member States of ECOWAS which had promised to contribute troops once adequate logistics support was provided.

Heads of State and Government expressed gratitude to the Government of the United States which has embarked on its second assistance package involving provision of logistics and communications equipment.

RESTRUCTURING THE ARMED FORCES, POLICE AND OTHER SECURITY FORCES

Heads of State and Government expressed grave concern over the fact that security agencies have deep affiliations with the factions and condemned the control wielded over the police by fighters and non-qualified personnel.

They endorsed the proposal to restructure the armed forces, the police and other security forces to reflect geographical and ethnical balance. They noted the offer by the British Government to sponsor the **"Train the Trainers" Programme**. ECOWAS should look into the possibility of obtaining the required assistance from countries within the region.

RETURN OF ARMS SEIZED FROM ECOMOG AND PROPERTY LOOTED FROM THE UN AND OTHER AGENCIES

Heads of State and Government strongly condemned the seizure of ECOMOG arms and ammunition by fighters belonging to the armed factions. They also condemned the looting of vehicles and other assets from the United Nations and non-governmental agencies. Heads of State and Government directed the Liberian faction leaders to return the arms and ammunition seized from ECOMOG and to release to the UN and other organizations the vehicles and other property looted from them. They called on the authorities of countries bordering Liberia to assist in identifying, confiscating and returning such property on their territory to their rightful owners.

HUMANITARIAN ASSISTANCE TO LIBERIA

Heads of State and Government firmly condemned the crimes, atrocities and other acts by the Liberian fighters which violate the rules of armed warfare. They issued a fresh warning to the factions to desist from such acts which are offensive to the international community. Heads of State and Government directed the faction leaders and their fighters to undertake to abide by the terms of the Geneva Convention of 12 August 1994 and the annexed Protocols as well as the United Nations Conventions on the rights of the child. They called on the faction leaders to guarantee the safety of relief personnel in Liberia, to enable them to resume their operations.

Heads of State and Government expressed gratitude to the OAU and to the United Nations, for their constant support in the quest for peace in Liberia.

At the end of their deliberation, Heads of State and Government expressed their sincere gratitude and deep appreciation to His Excellency, General Sani ABACHA and to the Government and the people of Nigeria for the warm, brotherly hospitality extended to them during their stay in Abuja.

DONE AT ABUJA, THIS 17TH DAY OF AUGUST, 1996
HEADS OF STATE AND GOVERNMENT
OF THE COMMITTEE OF NINE

Bibliography

UNPUBLISHED MATERIAL

Balogun, M. A., "ECOMOG Operations," lecture at National War College, Lagos, Nigeria, 15 February 1994.

Biambo, F. I., "Nigeria Navy in Its Peacekeeping Roles," paper presented during the Navy Week Seminar '92, at the NNS Quorra, May 1992.

Bundu, A., "The Role, Experience and Lessons of Security Co-operation within ECOWAS: The Lessons in Liberia," paper presented at a High-Level Workshop on Conflict Resolution, Crisis Prevention and Management & Confidence-Building, Organized by UN Department for Disarmament Affairs, Yaounde, Cameroon, 17–21 June 1991.

———— "The ECOMOG Operation in Liberia: A Political and Diplomatic Perspective," text of lecture delivered at the National War College, Lagos, Nigeria, 5 October 1993.

Iweze, C., "The International and Multinational Dimension of ECOMOG Joint Operation," lecture delivered at the National War College, Lagos, Nigeria, 15 February 1994.

Olurin, A., text of a lecture on military operations in Liberia, delivered at the National War College, Lagos, Nigeria, 2–5 October 1993.

OFFICIAL DOCUMENTS

ECOMOG, "Situation Paper Re Encampment and Disarmament Exercise," ECOMOG Headquarters, 6 December 1991.

────── "An Update on the Liberian Crisis from the Nigerian Contingent," DHQ/20/18/OPS, 11 May 1994.
────── "Current Situation on the Liberian Crisis," June 1994.
ECOWAS, Decision *A/DEC.1/8/90* on the Cease-fire and the Establishment of an ECOWAS Cease-fire Monitoring Group for Liberia, 6–7 August 1990.
────── "Final Communiqué of the First Session of the ECOWAS Standing Mediation Committee," Banjul, The Gambia, 6–7 August 1990.
────── "Final Communiqué of First Extra-Ordinary Session of the Authority of Heads of States and Governments," Bamako, 27–28 November 1990.
────── "Regulations for the ECOWAS Cease-fire Monitoring Group (ECOMOG) in Liberia," ECW/HSG/SMC/1/6/Rev.1, 13 August 1990.
────── "ECOMOG Field Commander's Report to the Ninth Meeting of Chiefs of Staff of ECOMOG Contributing Nations," Tunis, June 1994.
"Statement of Intent and Commitment by Parties to the Liberian Conflict," 26 July 1994.
Whitaker, C. S., "A New Era of Peacekeeping: The African Stake," paper for a conference of Commission on Regional Conflict Resolution of the project: Africa–Soviet–U.S. Co-operation, October 1991.

PUBLISHED MATERIAL

OFFICIAL DOCUMENTS

Abuja Agreement, signed 19 August 1995, ECOWAS, 1995.
Accra Acceptance and Accession Agreement, signed 21 December 1994, ECOWAS, 1994.
Akosombo Agreement, signed 12 September 1994, ECOWAS, 1994.
Babangida, I. B., *The Imperative Features of Nigerian Foreign Policy and the Crisis in Liberia*, Impromptu Press Briefing, Lagos, 31 October 1990.
Boutros-Ghali, Boutros, *An Agenda for Peace: Preventive Diplomacy, Peacemaking and Peace-keeping*, New York: United Nations, 1992
────── *Supplement to An Agenda for Peace*, January 1995.
Cotonou Agreement, signed 25 July 1993, ECOWAS, 1993.
ECOWAS, *Protocol on Non Aggression*, 1977.
────── *Protocol on Mutual Assistance on Defence*, 1981.
────── *Final Communiqué of the Seventeenth Session of the Authority of Heads of State and Government*, Abuja, 5–7 August 1994.
────── *Final Report of the Fifth Meeting of Foreign Ministers of the Committee of Nine on Liberia*, Abuja, 15–16 May 1995.
────── *Final Communiqué of the Third Meeting of Heads of State and Government of the Committee of Nine*, Abuja, 17–21 May 1995.
────── *Report of the Meeting between Foreign Ministers of the Committee of Nine and the Liberian Parties*, Abuja, 19 May 1995.
────── *Positions of the Warring Factions on Unresolved Issues Relating to the Liberian Crisis*, Abuja, 19 May 1995.

────── *Final Report of the Consultative Meeting on the Liberian Peace Process*, Sixth Meeting of the Ministers of Foreign Affairs of the Committee of Nine on Liberia, Abuja, 16–19 August 1995.
────── *Final Communiqué of the ECOWAS Meeting on Liberia*, Fourth Meeting of the Heads of State and Government of the Committee of Nine, Abuja, 17 August 1996.
Mezzolama, F., *Investigation of the Relationship between Humanitarian Assistance and Peacekeeping Operations*, Internal Report of the UN Joint Inspection Unit, JIU/REP/95/6, Geneva, 1995.
Official Journal of ECOWAS, Vol. 17, June 1990.
────── Vol. 18, December 1990.
────── Vol. 19, July 1991.
────── Vol. 20, November 1991.
────── Vol. 21 (Special Supplement), 1992.
UN Doc. A/44/301, *Comprehensive Review of the Whole Question of Peacekeeping Operations in All Their Aspects*, Report of the Special Committee on Peacekeeping Operations, 9 June 1989.
UN Doc. A/48/403, *Improving the Capacity of the United Nations for Peacekeeping: Report of the Secretary General*, 14 March 1994.
UN Doc. S/22133, 22 January 1991.
UN Doc. S/25402, *Report of the Secretary-General on the Question of Liberia*, 12 March 1993.
UN Doc. S/1994/463, *Third Progress Report of the Secretary-General on the United Nations Observer Mission in Liberia*, 18 April 1994.
UN Doc. S/1995/158, *Ninth Progress Report of the Secretary-General on the United Nations Observer Mission in Liberia*, 1995.
UN Doc. S/1995/881, *Thirteenth Progress Report of the Secretary-General on the United Nations Observer Mission in Liberia*, 23 October 1995.
UN Doc. S/RES/788, 19 November 1992.
UN Doc. S/RES/813, 26 March 1993.
UN Doc. S/RES/856, 10 August 1993.
UN Doc. S/RES/866, 22 September 1993.

ARTICLES

Abdul Raheem, T., "Western NGOs in Africa: Bodyguards of the Advancing Recolonization," *NGO Monitor*, Vol. 1, No. 1, October–December 1996.
Africa Watch, "Liberia: A Human Rights Disaster," 1990.
────── "Liberia: The Cycle of Abuse," 1991.
────── "Waging War to Keep Peace: The ECOMOG Intervention and Human Rights," 1993.
Alao, A., "ECOMOG in Liberia. The Anaemic Existence of a Mission," *Jane's Intelligence Review*, Vol. 5, No. 9, 1993.
────── "Peacekeeping in Sub-Saharan Africa," *Brassey's Defence Yearbook*, 1993.

Amnesty International, "Liberia: A New Peace Agreement – An Opportunity to Introduce Human Rights Protection," September 1995.

Anderson, J., Address at Peacekeeping Symposium – Peacekeeping: Norms, Policy and Process, Centre for International and Strategic Studies, York University, 9–14 May 1993.

Armon, Jeremy, "The Disarmament Exercise in Liberia," Paper presented at the Foreign and Commonwealth Office Discussion on Liberia, 1997.

Avebury, E., "Liberia: The Role of the United Nations," *Africa World Review*, November 1993 – April 1994.

Berdal, M. R., "Whither UN Peacekeeping?: An Analysis of the Changing Military Requirements of UN Peacekeeping with Proposals for its Enhancement," *Adelphi Paper* 281, IISS, 1993.

Berkeley, B., "Liberia: Between Repression and Slaughter," *The Atlantic Monthly*, December 1992.

Burkhalter, H., and Omaar, R., "Failures of State," *Africa Report*, November–December 1990.

Clarke, W., and Herbst, J., "Somalia and the Future of Humanitarian Intervention," *Foreign Affairs*, Vol. 75, No. 2, March/April 1996.

Conteh-Morgan, E., and Kadivar, S., "Ethno-political Violence in the Liberian Civil War," *Journal of Conflict Studies*, Vol. 15, No. 1, 1995.

Diamond, L., "Ethnicity and Ethnic Conflict," *Journal of Modern African Studies*, Vol. 25, No. 1, 1987.

Dobbie, C., "A Concept for Post-Cold War Peacekeeping," *Survival*, Vol. 36, No. 3, Autumn 1994.

Duke, S., "The United Nations in Intra-state Conflict," *International Peacekeeping*, Vol. 1, No. 4, Winter 1994.

Eban, A., "The UN Idea Revisited," *Foreign Affairs*, Vol. 74, No. 5, September/October 1995.

Fetherston, A. B., "Putting the Peace Back into Peacekeeping: Theory Must Inform Practice," *International Peacekeeping*, Vol. 1, No. 1, Spring 1994.

Goulding, M., "The Evolution of United Nations Peacekeeping," *International Affairs*, Vol. 69, No. 3, 1993.

Gow, J., and Dandeker, C., "Peace-support Operations: The Problem of Legitimation," *The World Today*, Vol. 51, Nos. 8–9, August–September 1995.

Hagglund, G., "Peacekeeping in a Modern War Zone," *Survival*, Vol. 32, May–June 1990.

Holst, J. J., "Enhancing Peacekeeping Operations," *Survival*, Vol. 32, May–June 1990.

Howe, J., "The United States and United Nations in Somalia," *The Washington Quarterly*, Summer 1995.

Huband, M., "Doe's Last Stand," *Africa Report*, July–August 1990.

James, A., "Internal Peacekeeping: A Dead End for the UN?," *Security Dialogue*, Vol. 24, No. 4, 1993.

Kufuor, K. O., "Developments in the Resolution of the Liberian Conflict," *American University Journal of International Law and Policy*, Vol. 15, 1993.

Mackinlay, J., "Powerful Peacekeepers," *Survival*, Vol. 32, May–June 1990.

——— "Improving Multifunctional Forces," *Survival*, Autumn 1994.

Musah, B., "An Operational Overview of Ghanbatt 7," *EXODUS II*, Vol. 7, February–September 1993.

Nwokedi, E., "Regional Integration and Regional Security: ECOMOG, Nigeria and the Liberian Crisis," *Travaux et Documents*, No. 35, Centre d'Etude d'Afrique Noire, Domaine Universitaire, France, 1992.

Ofuatey-Kodjoe, W., "The ECOWAS Intervention in Liberia: Regional Organization and the Resolution of Internal Conflicts," *The Ralph Bunche Institute on the United Nations Occasional Paper Series*, No. XVII, 1994.

———— "Regional Organizations and the Resolution of Internal Conflicts: The ECOWAS Intervention in Liberia," *International Peacekeeping*, Vol. 1, No. 3, 1994.

Olaiya, A., "ECOMOG Mission & Mandate," *The Peacemaker*, Vol. 1, No. 1, September 1991 – March 1992.

Olonisakin, 'F., "UN Cooperation with Regional Organizations in Peacekeeping: ECOMOG and UNOMIL in Liberia," *International Peacekeeping*, Vol. 3, No. 3, 1996.

———— "African Home Made Peacekeeping Initiatives," *Armed Forces and Society*, Vol. 23, No. 3, 1997.

Olurin, A. I., "Peacekeeping in Africa: The Liberian Experience," *The Peacemaker*, Vol. 2, No. 1, September 1992 – September 1993.

Omede, A., "Nigeria's Military Role in Liberia," *African Journal of International Affairs and Development*, Vol. 1, No. 1, 1995.

Reno, W., "Foreign Firms and the Financing of Charles Taylor's NPFL," *Liberian Studies Journal*, Vol. 18, No. 2, 1993.

———— "Reinvention of an African Patrimonial State: Charles Taylor's Liberia," *Third World Quarterly*, Vol. 16, No. 1, 1995.

Rikhye, I. J., "The Future of Peacekeeping," Occasional Paper No. 2, International Peace Academy, 1989.

———— "The United Nations of the 1990s and International Peacekeeping Operations," *Southampton Papers in International Policy*, No. 3, 1992.

Riley, S. P., "Intervention in Liberia: Too Little, Too Partisan," *The World Today*, Vol. 49, No. 3, 1993.

Ruggie, J. G., "Wandering in the Void: Charting the U.N.'s New Strategic Role," *Foreign Affairs*, November/December 1993.

Sesay, A., "The Limits of Peace-keeping by Regional Organization: The OAU Peace-keeping Force in Chad," *Conflict Quarterly*, Vol. 11, 1991.

———— "Collective Security or Collective Disaster: Regional Peacekeeping in West Africa," *Security Dialogue*, Vol. 26, No. 2, 1995.

———— "Civil War and Collective Intervention in Liberia," *Review of African Political Economy*, Vol. 23, No. 67, 1996.

———— "Politics and Society in Post War Liberia," *Journal of Modern African Studies*, Vol. 34, No. 3, 1996.

Sesay, A., and Alao, A., "One Step Forward, Two Steps Backward: Liberia in 1994," *The World in Conflict* 1994/95, London, Jane's Information Group, 1995.

Yeboah, A., "The Rebel's Tactics," *EXODUS II*, Vol. 7, February – September 1993.

BOOKS AND CHAPTERS IN BOOKS

Abi-Saab, G., *United Nations Operation in the CONGO: 1960–1964*, Oxford, Oxford University Press, 1978.

—— "United Nations Peacekeeping Old and New: An Overview of the Issues," in Daniel Warner (ed.), *New Dimensions of Peacekeeping*, Dordrecht, Martinus Nijhoff Publishers, 1995.

Adibe, C., *Disarmament and Conflict Resolution in Liberia*, Geneva, UNIDIR, 1996.

Adisa, J., "The Politics of Regional Military Cooperation: The Case of ECOMOG," in M. A. Vogt (ed.), *The Liberian Crisis and ECOMOG: A Bold Attempt at Regional Peacekeeping*, Lagos, Gabumo Publishing Press, 1992.

Akabogu, C., "ECOWAS Takes the Initiative," in M. A. Vogt (ed.), *The Liberian Crisis and ECOMOG: A Bold Attempt at Regional Peacekeeping*, Lagos, Gabumo Publishing Press, 1992.

Andrews, H. G., *Cry, Liberia, Cry*, New York, Vantage Press Inc., 1993.

Armon, J., and Carl, A., "The Liberian Peace Process 1990–1996," in *Accord: An International Review of Peace Initiatives*, London, Conciliation Resources, 1996.

Berhanykun, A., "OAU–UN Relations in a Changing World," in Yassin El-Ayouty (ed.), *The Organization of African Unity after Thirty Years*, Westport, Conn., Praeger, 1994.

Beyan, A. J., *The American Colonization Society and the Creation of the Liberian State: A Historical Perspective, 1822–1990*, Larnham, University Press of America, 1991.

Boley, S. G. E., *Liberia: The Rise and Fall of the First Republic*, London, Macmillan, 1984.

Brehum, L., *Liberia: The War of Horror*, Accra, Adwinsa Publication, 1991.

Cassal, C., *Liberia: History of the First African Republic*, New York, Fountainhead, 1979.

Cervenka, Zdenek, *The Organization of African Unity and its Charter*, London, C. Hurst, 1969.

Charters, D. A. (ed.), *Peacekeeping and the Challenge of Civil Conflict Resolution*, New Brunswick, Center for Conflict Studies, 1994.

Clapham, C., *Liberia and Sierra-Leone: An Essay in Comparative Politics*, Cambridge, Cambridge University Press, 1978.

Clower, Robert, Dalton, George, Harwitz, Mitchell, and Walters, A. A., *Growth Without Development*, Evanston, Ill., Northwestern University Press, 1966.

Cox, A. M., *Prospects for Peacekeeping*, Washington D.C., Brookings Institution, 1968.

Daniels, A., *Monrovia Mon Armour*, London, John Murray, 1992.

Diehl, P. F., *International Peacekeeping*, Baltimore, Md., Johns Hopkins University Press, 1993.

Dixon, W. N., *Great Lessons of the Liberian Civil War*, Monrovia, People International, 1992.

Dunn, E., and Tarr, S. B., *Liberia: A National Polity in Transition*, Metuchen, N.J., Scarecrow Press, 1988.

Durch, W., "Structural Issues and the Future of UN Peace Operations," in Don Daniel and Bradd Hayes (eds.), *Beyond Traditional Peacekeeping*, New York, St. Martins Press, 1995.
Enoanyi, B. F., *The Trouble with Us: Reflections of a Liberian Journalist*, Monrovia, Monitor Books, 1990.
―――― *Behold Uncle Sam's Step Child*, Sacramento, San Mar Publishers, 1991.
Evans, G., *Cooperating for Peace: The Global Agenda for the 1990s and Beyond*, New South Wales, Allen & Unwin, 1993.
Goetze, B. A., "The Future of Peacekeeping: A Military View," in Alex Morrison (ed.), *Peacekeeping, Peacemaking, or War: International Security Enforcement*, Ontario, Canadian Institute of Strategic Studies, 1994.
Gordenker, L., and Weiss, T. G., "The Use of Soldiers and Peacekeepers in Coping with Disasters," in Leon Gordenker and Thomas G. Weiss (eds.), *Soldiers, Peacekeepers and Disasters*, London, Macmillan, 1991.
Gow, J., "Strategic Peacekeeping: UNPROFOR and International Diplomatic Assertion," in Espen Barth Eider (ed.), *Peacekeeping in Europe*, Oslo, Norwegian Institute of International Affairs, 1995.
Guannu, J. S., *An Introduction to Liberian Government: The First Republic and the People's Redemption Council*, New York, Exposition Press, 1982.
―――― *Liberian History up to 1847*, New York, Exposition Press, 1983.
Harbottle, M., and Egge, B., *The Thin Blue Line: International Peacekeeping and Its Future*, New Haven, Conn., Yale University Press, 1974.
Higgins, R., "A General Assessment of United Nations Peacekeeping," in A. Cassese (ed.), *United Nations Peacekeeping: Legal Essays*, Alphen Aan Den Rijn, Sijhoff & Noordhooff, 1978.
Horn, C. von, *Soldiering for Peace*, London, Cassell, 1966.
International Peace Academy, *Peacekeeper's Handbook*, New York, IPA, 1978.
Iweze, C. Y., "Nigeria in Liberia: The Military Operations of ECOMOG," in M. A. Vogt and A. E. Ekoko (eds.), *Nigeria in International Peacekeeping 1960–1992*, London, Malthouse, 1993.
James, A., *The Politics of Peacekeeping*, London, Chatto & Windus, 1969.
―――― *Peacekeeping in International Politics*, London, International Institute for Strategic Studies, 1990.
―――― "The History of Peacekeeping: An Analytical Perspective," in Centre for International and Strategic Studies, *Peacekeeping: Norms, Policy and Process*, Ontario, York University, 1993.
Johnson, P., *The Gun That Liberates Should Not Rule*, Lagos, Pax Cornwell Publishers, 1991.
Jonah, J. O. C., "The OAU: Peacekeeping and Conflict Resolution," in Yassin El-Ayouty (ed.), *The Organization of African Unity after Thirty Years*, Westport, Conn., Praeger, 1994.
Keller, E. J., "United States Foreign Policy on the Horn of Africa: Policymaking with Blinders on," in Gerald J. Bender, James S. Coleman, and Richard L. Sklar (eds.), *African Crisis Areas and US Foreign Policy*, Berkeley, University of California Press, 1985.

Kupolati, R., "The Nigerian Contingent in the Organization of African Unity Peace-keeping Operation in Chad," in M. A. Vogt and A. E. Ekoko (eds.), *Nigeria in International Peacekeeping 1960–1992*, London, Malthouse, 1993.

Liebenow, G., *Liberia: The Evolution of Privilege*, Evanston, Ill., Northwestern University Press, 1966.

―――― *Liberia: The Quest for Democracy*, Bloomington, Indiana University Press, 1987.

Mackinlay, J., *The Peacekeepers: An Assessment of Peacekeeping Operations at the Arab-Israeli Interface*, London, Unwin Hyman, 1989.

―――― "The Role of Military Forces in a Humanitarian Crisis," in Leon Gordenker and Thomas G. Weiss (eds.), *Soldiers, Peacekeepers and Disasters*, London, Macmillan, 1991.

―――― (ed.), *Guide to Peace Support Operations*, Thomas Watson Institute for International Studies, Brown University, Providence, 1996.

Marks, E., "UN Peacekeeping in a Post-Cold War World," in Edward Marks and William Lewis, *Triage for Failing States*, Washington D.C., Institute for National Strategic Studies, National Defense University, 1994.

Morrison, A. (ed.), *The Changing Face of Peacekeeping*, Toronto, Canadian Institute of Strategic Studies, 1995.

Pogany, I., *The Arab League and Peacekeeping in Lebanon*, Aldershot, Gower, 1987.

Quinn, D. J., "Peace Support Operations: Definitions and Implications," in Dennis J. Quinn (ed.), *Peace Support Operations and the U.S. Military*, Washington D.C., National Defense University Press, 1994.

Ratner, S. R., *The New Peacekeeping: Building Peace in Lands of Conflict after the Cold War*, London, Macmillan, 1995.

Rikhye, Indar Jit, *The Theory and Practice of Peacekeeping*, London, Hurst & Co., 1984.

Rikhye, Indar Jit, and Skjelbaek, Kjell (eds.), *The United Nations and Peacekeeping: Results, Limitations and Prospects: The Lessons of Forty Years of Experience*, London, Macmillan, 1990.

Ruiz, H., *Uprooted Liberians: Casualties of a Brutal War*, Washington D.C., US Committee for Refugees, 1992.

Sawyer, A., *The Emergence of Autocracy in Liberia: The Tragedy and Challenge*, San Francisco: Institute of Contemporary Studies, 1992.

Segal, D. R. (ed.), *Peacekeepers and Their Wives: American Participation in the Multinational Force and Observers*, Westport and London, Greenwood Press, 1993.

Shick, T., *Behold, The Promised Land: A History of Afro-American Settler Society in Nineteenth Century Liberia*, Baltimore, Md., Johns Hopkins University Press, 1980.

Simma, B., *The Charter of the UN: A Commentary*, Oxford, Oxford University Press, 1994.

Smith, H., "The Challenge of Peacekeeping," in Hugh Smith (ed.), *Peacekeeping Challenges for the Future*, Canberra, Australian Defence Studies Centre, 1993.

Thakur, R., "From Great Power Collective Security to Middle-Power Peacekeeping," in Hugh Smith (ed.), *Australia and Peacekeeping*, Canberra, Australian Defence Studies Centre, 1990.

Umodem, G. E., "Brief History of Liberia," in M. A. Vogt (ed.), *The Liberian Crisis and ECOMOG*, Lagos, Gabumo Publishing Press, 1992.

United Nations, *The Blue Helmets: A Review of United Nations Peacekeeping*, New York, UN Department of Public Information, 1990.

US Lawyers Committee for Human Rights, *A Report on Liberia*, New York, 1986.

Vogt, M. A., "The Problems and Challenges of Peacekeeping," in M. A. Vogt (ed.), *The Liberian Crisis and ECOMOG: A Bold Attempt at Regional Peacekeeping*, Lagos, Gabumo Publishing Press, 1992.

Waldheim, K., *In the Eye of the Storm*, London, Weidenfeld & Nicolson, 1985.

Weiss, T., "UN Military Operations after the Cold War: Some Conceptual Problems," in Centre for International and Strategic Studies, *Peacekeeping: Norms, Policy and Process*, Ontario, York University, 1993.

Wippman, D., "Enforcing the Peace: ECOWAS and the Liberian Civil War," in L. F. Damrosch (ed.), *Enforcing Restraint: Collective Intervention in Internal Conflicts*, New York, Council of Foreign Relations Press, 1993.

Wreh, T., *The Love of Liberty... The Rule of President William V. S. Tubman in Liberia 1944–1971*, London, C. Hurst, and Monrovia, Wreh News Agency, 1976.

Zartman, I. W., "Conflict Reduction: Prevention, Management and Resolution," in Francis M. Deng and I. William Zartman (eds.), *Conflict Resolution in Africa*, Washington D.C., Brookings Institution, 1991.

—— (ed.), *Collapsed States: The Disintegration and Restoration of Legitimate Authority*, Boulder, Colo., Lynne Rienner Publishers, 1995.

About the authors

Abiodun Alao was trained at the universities of Ibadan and Ife (both in Nigeria), and at King's College London, where he obtained, respectively, a BA degree in History, an MA in International Relations, and a PhD in War Studies. He has held teaching and research positions in universities in Western and Southern Africa, as well as in London at the Department of War Studies and the Centre for Defence Studies at King's College London. He is currently at the African Security Unit at the Centre for Defence Studies. His work on the Liberian peace process has concentrated on the peace agreements.

John Mackinlay began his career as an army officer serving in Malaya, Brunei, Nepal, North Borneo, and Northern Ireland. His academic interest in international forces began as a staff officer in the Sinai, and in 1985, as a Defence Fellow at Churchill College, Cambridge, he travelled extensively through the Arab-Israeli war-zones including Beirut and South Lebanon to research his Assessment of Peacekeeping Operations at the Arab-Israeli Interface, which he completed as a PhD at King's College London in 1990. His interest in the Liberian peace process has focused on the organization of the factions and the transition of power during the peace process.

'Funmi Olonisakin attended the University of Ife, Nigeria, where she obtained a BSc in Political Science, and King's College London, where she obtained an MA and PhD in War Studies. She is currently a MacArthur Foundation Research Associate with the Department of War Studies and a Research Associate at the Centre for Defence Studies at King's College London. She has worked as a Research Associate at the University of Pretoria. Her interest in the Liberian peace process has been in the role of regional peacekeeping in the effort to achieve stability during implementation of the peace agreements.

Index

Abacha, General Sani 104, 166, 167, 174
Abuja I xii–xiii, 77, 162–6
  coordinated peace process 79–84
  failure 88
  gaps between planning and
    implementation 84–7
  planning for peace process 79
  supplements and amendments 78
Abuja II 90–2, 169–71
  disarmament and demobilization
    process 96–100
  implementation 92–6
Accra Acceptance and Accession
    Agreement 73, 159–61
Accra Clarification of the Akosombo
    Agreement 73–4, 156–8
"Agenda for Peace", UN 10
aid 18, 25
  see also humanitarian aid
airports 50, 130
Akashi, Mr 55
Akosombo Agreement 72–3, 147–55
  Accra clarification 73–4, 156–8
Albania 121
All-African Conference 130
Alliance of Political Parties 105, 106
All Liberia Coalition Party (ALCOP) 104,
    105, 106

All-Liberian Conference 130
American Colonization Society (ACS)
    13–14
Americo-Liberians 12, 14–15, 16, 18, 23–4
amnesty, Cotonou Agreement 144
Andrews, Henry 106
Angola 54, 59, 74n.8
Arab League 9
Armed Forces of Liberia (AFL)
  Abuja I 82, 84, 85
  Abuja II 99, 173
  Accra Acceptance and Accession
    Agreement 159
  Akosombo Agreement 73, 147, 150, 152
    Accra clarification 74, 157, 158
  Banjul Agreement 31
  civil war 20–1, 22, 23
  Cotonou Agreement 45, 61
  Doe regime 19
  Lomé Accord 38n.6
  rebuilding 107–9, 126
Armon, Jeremy 99–100
arms
  Bamako Agreement 129
  Cotonou Agreement 49, 134, 135
  Lomé Accord 131
  see also disarmament
Asamoah, Dr. Obed 166

185

INDEX

Babangida, General Ibrahim 34
Bakut, Ishaya 35, 36
Bamako Agreement 31, 129
Banana, Canaan 50n.1, 166
Banjul Agreement 30, 31, 130
Barque, Barry Moussa 168
Benjamin, Edouard 168
Boley, G. E. Saigbe, Sr 73
   Abuja I 78, 163, 166
   Accra Acceptance and Accession
      Agreement 159, 160
   elections (1997) 104
Bosnia 7, 69, 120
Boutros-Ghali, Boutros 10
Bowel, Lt. Gen. J. Hezekiah
   Abuja I 163, 166
   Akosombo Agreement 147, 155
      Accra clarification 74, 158
Buchanan 22
buffer zones 42, 129, 131, 134, 156–7
Burkina Faso 34, 93

Camara, Lamine 168
Cambodia 54, 58, 59, 74n.8
cantonment *see* encampment
cash-for-guns benefit 82
cease-fire
   Abuja Agreement 162, 165
   Akosombo Agreement 148
   Banjul Agreement 30, 130
   Cotonou Agreement 42–3, 132–3, 134
   Lomé Accord 31–2
Cease-fire Violations Committee 137, 138, 146, 149, 151
Central Revolutionary Council
   (CRC-SPFL) 73
   Accra Acceptance and Accession
      Agreement 159, 160, 161
   Akosombo Agreement, Accra
      Clarification 74
cessation of hostilities 129, 131, 132–3, 148
Chad 9
Cheapoo, Chea 166
children
   social reconstruction 111, 112
   soldiers 21, 45–6, 81–2, 87, 95, 118
      "School for Gun" programme 113
Christie concession 17
Church 15
Cold War 7, 8–9, 14
Committee of Five 32, 34–5

Committee of Nine 35, 38n.10, 91, 92
community information programme 138, 152
Compaore, Blaise 34, 167
complex emergencies 5–6, 7
Congo 4
corruption 18
Côte d'Ivoire
   Abuja II 171
   Committee of Five 35
   Cotonou Agreement 134
   ECOMOG 34, 94
Cotonou Agreement xii–xiii, 41–4, 132–44
   aftermath of failure 72–4
   lessons from 68–72
   obstacles to success 44–50
   reasons for failure 52–3
      disarmament 58–61
      ECOMOG 61–4
      fundamental flaws 53–8
      UN coordination 64–8
Council of State (COS)
   Abuja I 78, 88, 163, 165
   Abuja II 92, 172
   Akosombo Agreement 152, 153
      Accra clarification 74, 157–8
   Cotonou Agreement 42, 140–1
coups 18, 19
Cyprus 4

Dayton Implementation Force 7
decree 88A 19
demobilization
   Abuja I 78, 79–80, 81–2, 85–7
   Abuja II 94–100
   Akosombo Agreement 151–2
      Accra clarification 157
   armed forces, new 109
   Cotonou Agreement 138
Demobilization and Reintegration
   Office 84
democratic feudalism 12
Dennis, Arthur 56–7
diamonds 110
disarmament
   Abuja I 78, 79–81, 82, 85–7
   Abuja II 94–100
   Akosombo Agreement 150
   Angola 59, 74n.8
   Bamako Agreement 129
   Banjul Agreement 130
   Cambodia 54, 58, 59, 74n.8

Cotonou Agreement 43, 52, 58–61,
 70–1, 136
 Mozambique 54
 peace process implementation 119–20
 Yamoussoukro Accords 32
 Zimbabwe 53, 74n.8, 120
Disarmament Committee 84
Dixon, W. Nah 18
Doe, Master Sergeant Samuel Kanyon
 18–20, 23, 24
 civil war 20, 21, 22–3
 Côte d'Ivoire's attitude to 34
 ECOMOG 30, 121
 Interim Government of National
  Unity 31
 kidnap and death 35
 NDPL 104
 Nigeria's attitude 34
 parliamentary opposition, lack of 119
 US support 20, 25
Dokie, Samuel 125, 163
Dominican Republic 9
Dongoyaro, Major General Joshua 35, 36

Eckhard, Fred 107
ECOMOG
 Abuja I 80–1, 85, 86
  coordination 83, 84
  failure 88
 Abuja II 92–3, 95, 170–3
  disarmament and demobilization
   process 98, 99, 100
 Akosombo Agreement 148, 149, 150,
  151
  Accra clarification 156, 157
 armed forces, new 109
 attitude to NPFL 103
 Bamako Agreement 31, 129
 civil wars 28
 Cotonou Agreement 42, 43–4, 133–7
  disarmament 60
  lessons 69, 71, 72
  obstacles to success 45
  reasons for failure 55–7, 58, 61–4
  UN coordination 65
 criticisms 121–2, 124
 deployment 66
 elections (1997) 107
 expulsion from Liberia 126
 kidnap of soldiers by NPFL 33, 88
 lessons 123
 locus of power 116

Lomé Accord 32, 131
 mandate 29–30
 NGOs 112
 operational development 33–7
 Operation Octopus 33
 peace process implementation 120
 reporting relationship with UNOMIL 56
 UNOMIL 32, 146
 Yamoussoukro Accords 33, 42
Economic Community of West African
 States see ECOWAS
economic reconstruction 110, 111–12
ECOWAS 28–9, 33–4
 1990 meeting 31
 Abuja I 163, 164
 Abuja II 167–74
 Akosombo Agreement 149, 151, 152,
  153
  Accra clarification 158
 Bamako Agreement 129
 Banjul Agreement 31, 130
 Cotonou Agreement 133, 134, 139, 140,
  141
  aftermath 72
 elections (1997) 104, 106
 intervention in Liberia 28
 Lomé Accord 131
 Military Observer Group see ECOMOG
 social reconstruction 113
education 17
educational programme 138, 152
elections
 1984 19
 1997 103–7
 Abuja I 164
 Abuja II 172
 Cotonou Agreement 43, 57, 67–8, 142
 voting rights 15
Elections Commission 103–4
 Abuja I 78, 164
 Cotonou Agreement 57, 68, 142
encampment
 Abuja I 80, 81, 86–7
 Abuja II 94
 Akosombo Agreement 151
 Cambodia 54
 Cotonou Agreement 137
 Lomé Accord 32
 Yamoussoukro Accords 32
 Zimbabwe 53
Enoanyi, Bill Frank 26
Essy, Amara 168

ethnic composition of Liberia 14–17
ethnic divisions 18–19, 20, 21
European Union (EU) 113
executive
   Abuja I 163–4
   Akosombo Agreement 152–3
      Accra clarification 157–8
   Cotonou Agreement 140–1
exports 24, 110
external debt 18
Eyadema, Gnassingbe 31

feudalism, democratic 12
Firestone 17, 25, 50
Food and Agriculture Organization (FAO) 83, 111
food programmes 66, 98
food supplements 48
foreign investment 17, 49–50
foreign scholarship programme 17
France 29
Free Democratic Party 105
freedom of speech and expression 19

Gambia 35
Gbarnga 22, 59, 116
Geneva Convention 173
Georgia 123
Ghana 35, 62, 93, 94
Gio people 20, 21
Golan 4
Gordon-Somers, Trevor 43, 54–6, 155
Great Britain 92, 109, 173
Guinea 134
Guinea-Bissau 35
Gulf War 7, 25, 63

hostages 129, 131
hostilities, cessation of 129, 131, 132–3, 148
Houphouët-Boigny, President 32, 34
humanitarian aid 7
   Abuja I 83
   Abuja II 173–4
   Bamako Agreement 129
   Cotonou Agreement 48, 68, 70, 143, 144
   Lomé Accord 131
   UNOMIL Mandate 146
Humanitarian Assistance Coordination Office (HACO) 83–4, 95
Humanitarian Assistance Unit 83–4
Humanitarian Coordinator 83–4

Ikimi, Tom 166
incendiary devices 135, 146
income distribution 17
Independent National Patriotic Front of Liberia (INPFL) 22, 23, 31, 38n.6, 41
indigenous Liberians 14–17, 23–4
inflation 18
information programme 138, 152
Inienger, John 35, 36
Interim Government of National Unity (IGNU)
   Abuja Agreement 163
   concessions 37, 42
   Cotonou Agreement 41, 44, 132, 140, 141–2
   creation 31, 35
   ECOMOG 36, 42
iron ore 49, 50, 110

Johnson, Prince Yomie 22, 23, 30, 41
Johnson, Major General Roosevelt 73, 125
   Abuja Agreement 88, 166
   Accra Acceptance and Accession Agreement 159, 160
Johnson-Sirleaf, Ellen 105, 106–7
Joint Cease-fire Monitoring Committee 43, 133, 135
Jonah, Dr James 50n.1
judiciary 141
Junius, J. D. Bayogar 159, 161

Kabbah government 126
Kane, Massokhna 168
Karpeh, General 32
Kerekou, Matthieu 167
Konare, Alpha Cumar 168
Krahn people 19, 21
Kromah, Lt. General Alhaji G. V. 73
   Abuja I 78, 88, 163, 165
   Abuja II 100
   Akosombo Agreement 147, 154
      Accra clarification 74, 158
   Cotonou Agreement 41, 44
   elections (1997) 104, 106
   Movement for the Redemption of Muslims 32
Kupolati, Rufus 35, 36

land mines and incendiary devices 135, 146
land ownership 15–16

League of Nations 16
Lebanon 9
legislature 141–2, 153–4
Liberia Mining Company 17
Liberia National Transitional Government (LNTG)
 Abuja I 78, 79, 81, 82, 87, 163–5
 Abuja II 170, 171
 Akosombo Agreement 72, 147–54
  Accra clarification 156–7
 Cotonou Agreement 139–43
  disarmament 60
  obstacles to success 45
  reasons for failure 54, 57
  UN coordination 66–7
 elections (1997) 104
Liberian National Conference (LNC) 73
 Abuja I 163
 Abuja II 94
 Accra Acceptance and Accession Agreement 159, 160, 161
 Akosombo Agreement, Accra clarification 74, 158
Liberian National Union 105
Liberian Peace Council (LPC) 73
 Abuja I 84, 85, 163
 Abuja II 96, 99, 100
 Accra Acceptance and Accession Agreement 159, 160
 Akosombo Agreement, Accra clarification 74
 armed forces, new 108–9
 Cotonou Agreement 45, 63, 71
Liberian People's Party 19, 105, 106
Liberian Refugees Repatriation and Resettlement Commission (LRRRC) 84
Liberian United Defence Force 32
Libya 25
locus of power 116–18
Lofa Defence Force (LDF) 73
 Abuja I 84, 85
 Abuja II 99
 Accra Acceptance and Accession Agreement 159, 160
 Akosombo Agreement, Accra clarification 74
Lomé Accord 31–2, 131
looting 47, 50, 88, 92, 122

Mainassara Bare, Ibrahim 168
Mali 94
Malu, Major-General Victor S. 35, 36, 120, 168
Mandingo people 21
Mano people 20, 21
Masonic Temple 15
Massaquoi, Francois 159, 160, 163, 166
Masuku, Lookout 108
Matthews, Bacus 106
mercenaries 138
Micro-project Programme of Reintegration and Resettlement 113
Milam, William 36
military embargo 42, 134, 146, 171
Military Staff Committee, UN 3
mining 17, 110
Monroe, James 14
Monrovia 14, 116, 172
Monrovia-Roberts air terminal 50
moral decline 111
Mountain, Ross 54
Movement for Justice in Africa (MOJA) 17, 18
Movement for the Redemption of Muslims 32
Mozambique 54, 104
Mugabe, Robert 108

National Democratic Party of Liberia (NDPL) 19, 104, 105
National Disarmament and Demobilization Commission (NDDC) 84, 94–5, 112
National Patriotic Front of Liberia (NPFL) 20–3, 102–3
 Abuja I 84, 85
 Abuja II 96, 98, 99
 Accra Acceptance and Accession Agreement 159
 Akosombo Agreement 147, 150, 152
  Accra clarification 74, 158
 Banjul Agreement 31
 Compaore's support 34
 Cotonou Agreement 41, 42, 43–4, 132, 142
  disarmament 59, 61
  ECOMOG 63, 64
  obstacles to success 45, 47, 48, 49
 Doe's resignation, demand for 31
 ECOMOG 30, 33, 36, 37
  Cotonou Agreement 63, 64
  elections (1997) 104–5
 IGNU, rival government to 35
 invasion of Sierra Leone 32

National Democratic Party of Liberia
    (NDPL) (cont.)
  Lomé Accord   38n.6
  Operation Octopus   33
  split   73
  Yamoussoukro Accords   41–2
National Patriotic Party (NPP)   104–5, 106
National Patriotic Reconstruction Assembly
    Government (NPRAG)   140
National Readjustment Commission
    (NRC)   82, 84
National Reformation Party   105
National Volunteer Programme   113–14
natural resources   17, 24
newspapers   19
Nigeria
  ECOMOG   30, 34, 35–6, 121
    Cotonou Agreement   42, 62, 63, 64, 71
  francophone opposition to   29
  Liberian elections (1997)   104, 106
  looting allegations   122
  relations with Liberia   34
  soldiers in Sierra Leone   126
Nimba   20
Nkomo, Joshua   108
non-governmental organizations (NGOs)
    6, 81, 111, 112–14
North Atlantic Treaty Organization
    (NATO)   8
Nyakyi, Anthony B.   166

oil crisis   18
Olurin, Olatunji   35, 36
Omega navigation stations   25
Opande, Major General Daniel   43
"open door policy", Tubman   17
Operation Octopus   33, 36, 41, 111, 120
Operation Thunderbolt   61
Organization of African Unity (OAU)   9,
    42, 151, 164, 174
Organization of American States (OAS)   9

Patriotic Front, Zimbabwe   54, 74n.8
People's Alliance Party   18
People's Democratic Party of Liberia   105
Perry, Ruth   92, 172
police   173
political prisoners   19, 129, 131
ports   50, 130
prisoners of war   129, 131, 138
Progressive Alliance of Liberia   17
Progressive People's Party   105

promissory notes   95
prostitution   111

Quanoo, General Arnold   35
Quiah, Oscar Jaryee   78, 163
Quiwonkpa coup   19–20

Rabbah, Alhaji Ahmad Tejan   168
rail lines   50
Rawlings, Flt. Lt. Jerry John
  Abuja I   166
  Abuja II   167
  Accra Acceptance and Accession
      Agreement   161
  Akosombo Agreement   72, 155
  Accra clarification   74, 158
reconciliation   60, 79
reconstruction   110–12
records, historical   xii
Red Cross   129, 138
Reformation Alliance Party   105
refugees   20, 48
  repatriation   43, 48, 52, 143–4
regional peacekeepers   7–10
Restore Hope intervention   7
revenge   60
Rhodesia see Zimbabwe
rice   18
Robertsfield airport   25
rubber   49, 110
Rwanda   69

safe havens   156–7, 172
Sankawulo, Wilton   78, 163, 168, 172
Sankoh, Foday   32
Sawyer, Amos   35, 36, 41, 42
"School for Gun" programme   113
seaports   50, 130
security forces   173
  see also Armed Forces of Liberia
Senegal   35
Sesay, Amadu   15, 16
Shagaya, John   35, 36
Sierra Leone   32, 126, 134, 145
Singhatay, Captain Edward   167
slaves   12, 13–14, 16
Smith, Ian   108
Soames, Lord   55
social reconstruction   110–12
Soglo, President   50n.1
Somalia   7, 69, 121
South Africa   104

Special Emergency Life Food (SELF) 114
Standing Mediation Committee (SMC),
 ECOWAS 28, 31, 35, 38n.10
Standing Operating Procedures (SOPs) 57
Status of Forces Agreement 149, 150
Status of Million Agreement 149
subsistence farming 24
Suez 4
Supreme Court 141, 142
Supuwood, Laveli 163
Susukuu 113
Symbolic Arab Security Force 9
Syria 9

Tanzania 42, 62
Taylor, Charles Ghankay 21, 102-3
 Abuja I 78, 88, 163
 Abuja II 100
 Akosombo Agreement 147, 154
  Accra clarification 74, 158
 armed forces 107
 attitude to Nigeria 34
 civil war 20, 22-4
 Cotonou Agreement 41, 42, 47, 59, 61
 ECOMOG 30, 36, 37, 42
 election (1997) 103-4, 105-7
  first year in office 125-6
 future 114, 124
 IGNU, rival government to 35
 locus of control 116
 on Malu 36
 peace process implementation 118, 119
Taylor, Tamba 78, 158, 163, 165
timber 110
Tipoteh, Togba-Nah 106, 113
Togo 35
Tolbert, William 17, 18, 24, 34
Tongogara, Josiah 108
traditional peacekeeping 3-4, 5, 7
"Train the Trainers" Programme 92, 173
transitional government see Liberia
 National Transitional Government
Transitional Legislative Assembly (TLA)
 141, 153-4
True Whig Party 15, 16
Tubman, William 16-17

Uganda 42, 62
ULIMO 32
 Abuja I 163
 Abuja II 99

Accra Acceptance and Accession
 Agreement 159, 160
Akosombo Agreement 147, 150, 152
Cotonou Agreement 41, 132, 141, 142
 disarmament 61
 obstacles to success 45
split 73
 see also ULIMO-J; ULIMO-K
Yamoussoukro Accords 41-2
ULIMO-J 73, 125
 Abuja I 84, 85, 163
 Abuja II 96-7, 98, 99, 100
 Akasombo Agreement, Accra
  clarification 74
 armed forces, new 108-9
ULIMO-K 73, 125
 Abuja I 84, 85
 Abuja II 96, 98
 Akosombo Agreement, Accra
  clarification 74
 Sierra Leone 126
Union of Liberian Associations in the
 Americas 17
United Liberation Movement of Liberia for
 Democracy see ULIMO
United Nations
 Abuja I 164
 Abuja II 92, 172, 173, 174
 Akosombo Agreement 151, 152
 Charter 3, 8, 9, 10
 Children's Fund (UNICEF) 81-2, 83,
  95, 111
 Conventions on the rights of the
  child 173
 Cotonou Agreement 64-8, 138
  lessons 69-70
 Development Programme 81-2, 83, 111,
  143
 Educational, Scientific and Cultural
  Organization (UNESCO) 83
 elections (1997) 106, 107
 High Commissioner for Refugees
  (UNHCR) 83, 111, 143, 144
 Humanitarian Assistance Co-ordination
  Office (UN-HACO) 111, 112
 Mission in Georgia (UNOMIG) 123
 Observer Mission in Liberia see
  UNOMIL
 regional peacekeepers 8, 9, 10
 Secretariat 7, 8
 Security Council
  Cotonou Agreement 134

Security Council (cont.)
   regional peacekeeping   8, 9
   traditional peacekeeping   3–4, 5, 7
Special Coordinating Office for
   Liberia   54
traditional peacekeepers   3–4, 5, 7
United People's Party   105, 106
United Progressive Party   19
United States of America
   Abuja II   173
   civil war   23, 25–6
   Doe regime, implicit support for   20, 25
   Dominican Republic peacekeeping
     effort   9
   ECOMOG troops, airlift   93–4
   Gulf War   63
   historical connection to Liberia   12, 13–14
   Liberian elections (1997)   107
   Liberia's importance to   24–5
   regional peacekeeping   7, 8
   slaves   12, 13–14
Unity Party   105, 106, 107
UNOMIL
   Abuja I   80, 81, 83, 86
   Abuja II   92, 93, 94, 95, 170
   Akosombo Agreement   148, 150, 151, 152
     Accra clarification   156, 157, 158
   civil war   28
   Cotonou Agreement   42, 43–4, 133–9
     lessons   69–70, 72

   obstacles to success   45, 47
   reasons for failure   55–6, 57
   UN coordination   65
   Mandate   145–6
   organization   55
   relocation   112
   reporting relationship with
     ECOMOG   56, 58
   social and economic reconstruction   112

Violations Committee   137, 138, 146, 149, 151
Voice of America   25

Walker, Delvin   74n.9
Walls, General Peter   108
war, prisoners of   129, 131, 138
Wippman, David   14
Woewiyu, J. Thomas   74, 159, 161, 163, 166
World Food Programme   83, 95, 111
World Health Organization   83, 95
Wotorson, Cletus   106

Yamoussoukro Accords   32–3, 41–2, 139
Yekepa   22
Yugoslavia, former   69

Zimbabwe   103, 108, 109
   disarmament   53, 74n.8, 120
   Independence Agreement   53–4, 55, 74n.8